THE EUROPEAN PEOPLE'S PARTY

Also by Thomas Jansen

ABRÜSTUNG UND DEUTSCHLAND-FRAGE
(Disarmament and the German Question)

EUROPA: Bilanz und Perspektive
(Europe: Results and Perspectives), *co-editor with Werner Weidenfeld*

EUROPA: Von der Gemeinschaft zur Union – Strukturen, Schritte, Schwierigkeiten
(Europe: From Community to Union – Structures, Progress, Obstacles)

LA DÉMOCRATIE CHRÉTIENNE: Force Internationale
(Christian Democracy: An International Force), *co-editor with Hughes Portelli*

PERSÖNLICHKEITEN DER EUROPÄISCHEN INTEGRATION:
Vierzehn Biographische Essays
(Personalities in European Integration), *co-editor with Dieter Mahncke*

The European People's Party

Origins and Development

Thomas Jansen
former Secretary General
of the European People's Party

Foreword by Jacques Santer
President of the European Commission

First published in Great Britain 1998 by
MACMILLAN PRESS LTD
Houndmills, Basingstoke, Hampshire RG21 6XS and London
Companies and representatives throughout the world

A catalogue record for this book is available from the British Library.

ISBN 0–333–72057–1

First published in the United States of America 1998 by
ST. MARTIN'S PRESS, INC.,
Scholarly and Reference Division,
175 Fifth Avenue, New York, N.Y. 10010

ISBN 0–312–21062–0

Library of Congress Cataloging-in-Publication Data
Jansen, Thomas.
The European People's Party : origins and development / Thomas
Jansen ; foreword by Jacques Santer.
p.   cm.
Includes bibliographical references and index.
ISBN 0–312–21062–0
1. European People's Party—History.   2. Christian democratic
parties—European Union countries—History.   I. Title.
JN50.J36 1998
324.24'05—dc21   97–18338
                                                                    CIP

© Thomas Jansen 1998
Foreword © Jacques Santer 1998

Originally published in German as *Die Entstehung einer Europäischen Partei:
Vorgeschichte, Gründung und Entwicklung der EVP*, Europa Union Verlag, Bonn, 1996

Translated into English by Barbara Steen with the help of the Robert Schuman Foundation,
Luxemburg.

This book is printed on paper suitable for recycling and made from fully managed and
sustained forest sources.

10   9   8   7   6   5   4   3   2   1
07   06   05   04   03   02   01   00   99   98

Printed and bound in Great Britain by
Antony Rowe Ltd, Chippenham, Wiltshire

Political parties at European level are important as a factor for integration within the Union. They contribute to forming a European awareness and to expressing the political will of the citizens of the Union.

Article 138A (European Parties), Treaty of Maastricht

Contents

Foreword

The subject-matter of this book is crucial to the future of the European Union and its political system. Transnational political parties are a phenomenon which has, at best, been dealt with very inadequately, in academic and political literature. Indeed, Thomas Jansen's book is the first monograph on the birth and development of a European party.

Political parties are the link between the citizen and political institutions. They are the means by which citizens are able to participate in the decision-making process and the generation of the political will to act. This holds good at every political level – municipal, regional and national – and is also true of politics at European Union level.

Here, however, party structures have not reached full maturity. It is difficult for parties to secure public participation in the same way. The reasons for this are clearly set out in this book. Not least among them are deficiencies in the institutional structure of the Union. The Maastricht Treaty has happily launched a far-reaching public debate about this right. The problem was being debated in the context of the Intergovernmental Conference (1996/7), which led to the Treaty of Amsterdam. Extensive reforms have been decided on. They must be implemented if the institutions are to be made both reliably transparent and efficient.

The difficulties which attended ratifying the Maastricht treaty clearly demonstrated the need for radical reforms of the Union's political-institutional system. Public opinion resisted. It found the whole process unfamiliar. It felt excluded. And it also became evident that, if we were to deal with the tasks facing us – for example, the introduction of a Single European Currency, and enlargement to include several new Member States – this would have to be based on a Union-wide consensus on the part of the citizens, and on vital, active European parties.

In his opening passage the author usefully sets out the context, both in terms of political science and of history, of the birth of European political parties. He thus affords the reader an insight into the gradual formation of a European party system, at the same time affording an overview of the European party-political landscape. And he persuasively argues that the making of the European People's Party is a model example.

For more than a decade – from 1983 to 1994 – Thomas Jansen, the author of this book, was intimately involved in the process he describes. Having come to the end of this chapter in his career, he is now turning his attention to an academic study of the subject. In his search for objectivity he has largely succeeded in putting aside his own practical and political involvement. But his account is amply informed by direct experience. It makes for a particularly pleasing and unusual book. Many political events cannot be verified from archives. We only know about them when somebody who was actually there makes the effort to describe them.

I myself am involved in many different ways with the proceedings and phenomena described and analysed here. As Secretary General and President of the Christian-Social Party of Luxembourg, in the 1970s I was personally involved with the birth and construction of the EPP. As Prime Minister of my country after 1983, I took part in fairly regular EPP Conferences of party and government leaders. These involved the debate and decision-making behind several of the party's key political directions. From 1987 to 1990 I was directly responsible for the development of the EPP.

I look back on this period with pleasure and satisfaction, with its many interesting meetings, and the close and loyal co-operation – infused with a certain pioneering spirit – with colleagues from the various parties and countries. It was agreeable to recall those days through Thomas Jansen's book. And I am pleased that the author has given such an accurate and truthful account of the complex process of building European parties in general, and the development of the EPP in particular.

Other authors will, I hope, be inspired by this work to give their own accounts of the birth and development of the European parties. Political scientists and historians will find a broad, still largely unexplored, area meriting their keenest attention. The same holds good for the parallel efforts to develop European structures in terms of exchanging information and ideas, cooperation, and consensus-building among the trade unions and industrial and employers' associations, as well as in social and cultural organisations. All such examples of a common will to build the Union, demonstrated by common action at European level, prove to me that the integration process is much further advanced than public opinion has yet realised. And it is that developing common European will which is, in the end, the foundation stone of our institutions.

JACQUES SANTER
President of the European Commission

Part I
The Evolution of a European Party System

1 The Emergence of European Parties

One of the conditions of democracy is public political debate and deci-sion-making. Democracy also means that citizens should be able, if they wish, to get personally involved. It is fundamental that people should see the community in which they live as their business, and feel comfortable with that fact. The same goes for the European Union, whose success depends on the participation and consent of its citizens. Like the competi-tion for power in its institutions, the debate about its structure must be carried out under public scrutiny, and the transmission belt in both cases is the party-political.system. As with all the different social forces in play at different levels in the Union, rival political parties must, if they are to be effective, organise themselves – as integration proceeds – so that they can properly represent the will and interests of their chosen constituency in the Union.

None of this was lost on politicians in countries which were involved from the beginning in the process of European unification. The major political parties began at an early stage to co-operate with like-minded sister parties in the various Community countries. From the late 1940s and through the 1950s, European 'party families' began to form. They reached agreement among themselves, and increasingly they also acted in concert. One fruit of this developing integration came in the mid-1970s. As the first direct elections to the European Parliament approached in 1979[1] the first formal party federations established themselves.[2]

THE EUROPEAN PARTY CONFEDERATIONS

Confronted by the challenge of the European elections, the Liberals, like the Social Democrats and the Christian Democrats, saw the need to put in place pan-European organisations. Members of the European Parliament were notable enthusiasts. As early as 1952 they had formed parliamentary groups in the Parliamentary Assembly of the European Coal and Steel Community (ECSC), and again in the European Parliament in 1958 fol-lowing the foundation of the European Economic Community (EEC), and the European Atomic Community (EAC). They felt a stronger and stronger need to be able to rely on 'European parties'. With the approach of direct elections, the national parties had an interest in running a co-ordinated European election campaign. The national parties also hoped to benefit from the publicity which might possibly accrue from belonging to a supranational organisation. The opportunities afforded by this kind of confederation in Community politics were obvious, even at this early stage.[3]

The timing, and the reason, for founding confederations of parties (or party-like structures) demonstrate what has often been observed: parties essentially innovate because they are forced into it by elections. It is another proof of the great importance of elections to the democratic process. And the commitment to the first direct elections to the European Parliament shown by traditional parties from all Member States demonstrated something else: they saw the electoral process itself, and the elected Parliament, as essential elements in the construction of a politically united Europe.

The concentrated work done on their political programmes by the party confederations in the run-up to the first European elections[4] was followed up, and intensified, in the subsequent five-yearly EP elections. European Parliament deputies co-operating in the various groups have increasingly come to rely on jointly-developed programmes. All are either individually or personally connected to the party federations. Only a few years after the first European elections, it could be observed that

> the coming together of political programmes at the level of party elites is undeniable.... The European Communities have placed Euro-socialists and Social Democrats, Left-wing Liberals and National Liberals, Christian Democrats and Conservatives, with all their differences, in a closer communicative relationship with each other than could be achieved earlier, because of the diffusion of ideologies.[5]

This 'coming together' process had an observable effect on how national parties and/or their leaders saw those parties, and how they projected that identity outwards. In 1977, for instance, with all their MEPs sitting together in the CD Group in the European Parliament, the three traditional 'Christian' parties in the Netherlands found the process being accelerated by their co-operation at EP level. The Catholic People's Party, the Christian-Humanistic Union, and the Anti-Revolutionary Party felt impelled to join forces. A year earlier, all three had been co-founders of the EPP. The fusion produced the Christian Democratic Appell (CDA). At the same time, new alliances were gradually formed. However, it was not until the political-ideological sea-change of 1989 that these were formalised. The British and Scandinavian Conservative parties felt increasingly drawn to the EPP, which is inspired by Christian Democracy; they eventually joined too. The Italian Communists found their way into the European Social-Democratic Party (ESP). The Reformists and Radicals sought an alliance with the European Liberal and Democratic Reform Party (ELDR).

If they were to arrive at common views and positions, more and more national party leaders recognised that they needed to discuss general political issues with partners beyond their own national borders. Those issues could not be dealt with in the context of the respective European Parliament groups – the agenda of the European Council; the fundamental direction of foreign and security policy; socio-political developments and their implications for their party programmes; how to organise transnational co-operation itself.

More or less systematic co-operation between like-minded parties brought in its train progressively more elaborate organisational and communications structures. Soon enough this led to the expectation (fully justified, as became clear a few years later) that completing the European Community's political system could involve the rise of a transnational party system. And this would be a key element in shaping the integration process, as well as for the future constitutional order of the European Community:

> In the context of a political infrastructure at European level, effective European parties can be a counterweight to the bureaucratised and inter-governmental character of the EC's political debate and decision-making process, and help to remove both the democratic deficit and the lack of legitimacy. Party formations at European level could progressively undertake tasks such as the organisation of elections, and the articulation and bringing together of social interests. Or, if at least the pre-conditions for fulfilling these functions were put in place, then this would be a first step in the direction of realising a power system at European level based on party democracy.[6]

It was logical, in this context, that a clause was included in the Maastricht Treaty which ascribed a special role in the integration process to 'political parties at European level'. Ahead of a proper European Union, today's party confederations really are on the threshold of being 'European Parties'.[7]

In autumn 1992 the federation of Social-Democratic parties in the European Community, established in 1974, adopted a new constitution to become the ESP, the European Social-Democratic Party. As early as 1976, when it was founded, the European People's Party signalled its ambition to become a European party. In November 1990 it adopted a new constitution which clearly underlined this intention. The European Liberal and Democratic Federation, established in 1976, became the European Liberal and Democratic Reform Party (ELDR). In summer 1993 the European Greens also banded together, though as a pan-European association. But it too foresaw establishing a party at Union level.[8]

Little attention has been given to this development, either by academia or in political writing in general. It is symptomatic that in a recently-published handbook[9] about parties in the Federal Republic of Germany, the transnational dimension of the subject is not mentioned – despite the fact that the following observation is made:

> The 'national development' of parties and party systems in Europe is increasingly determined by transnational procedures. National navel-gazing is becoming obsolete. This also applies to the study of specific party systems and their parties.[10]

To focus more public attention on them seems appropriate, given the special role the EU political system will assign to European parties.

THE FUNCTION AND ROLE OF PARTIES

Political parties in democratic systems of government are associations of citizens. Operating under communally agreed rules and procedures, they agree on a programme which reflects the expectations, ideas, and interests of a segment of the population, large or small. This is in the hope of securing as much support as possible, so that they can form a government which will translate their programme into practice.

The point of forming parties, and their function, is to work together to fight elections and participate in the other processes (set out in the constitution) by which a government is put in place. So they are concerned with winning, using, and holding on to power. Alternatively, parties are about securing influence on those who hold power. They are at the same time concerned with gaining control over the bureaucrats who are experts in the exercise of power.

Political parties are established and develop as products of the constitutional order, within which they struggle for power and influence. So their function is above all determined by the construction and shaping of communal institutions in which they are active, as well as by the rules of the particular political system. They exploit such possibilities as the system offers. But they are always attempting to expand these possibilities, or to create new ones in which they can be effective.

Party organisation naturally follows whatever is the established national political order, and evolves according to constitutional change. By the same token, political parties also play a part in moulding the constitution. Ideas rooted in party programmes, in ideology, or established political models, are relevant alongside parties' straightforward interest in optimising the conditions for their exercise of influence, and their chances of gaining and holding on to power by designing or changing the constitution to suit their interests. The constitutional order is based on a general consensus demanding the assent of all the competing parties. So it is normally more stable and resistant, and therefore a more powerful matrix, than the attempts by individual parties to gain advantage through changing the structures and rules.

If political parties in democratic systems help to shape the constitutional order, they are themselves shaped by the existing constitution, or by tradition, which obviously has a powerful impact on the way the parties develop their specific models or conceptions of what they want. In other words, if it is to become effective, even a party which preaches centralism will have, in a federal structure, to develop a decentralised organisation.

The *raison d'être*, the very viability of a political party, springs from its capacity to develop and argue for a project, one which either shapes communal life or solves common problems – a project supported by a significant portion of the population. The significance of individual parties depends on the extent of that popular consensus. That in turn depends on the project's credibility: how far is it susceptible to being translated into reality? But practicability is not just a matter of logic, nor of how attractive the proposed measures are. A party has to be capable of putting a project into practice. This means it must be able to secure enough power in the political system in which it operates.

So political parties concentrate their attention, their efforts, and their resources, on bringing the centres of power either partially or wholly under their control. In parliamentary democracies with a federal, i.e. decentralised structure, parties have to be active at the various levels of the political system. This holds good in cities and parishes, in districts and provinces, in the Länder or regions, as at the centre of the federation itself.

So the form which parties' involvement takes is, so to speak, 'stepped' – it will be shaped by the facilities to exert power which becomes available through the occupation of positions at different political levels. A balanced federal system is one which distributes power (that is, the competences and the instruments needed to exercise them) equally at all levels. Similarly, the parties organise themselves and their actions so that they can be equally present at all levels, and can take their proper part in the battle for the division of power.

THE EUROPEANISATION OF THE PARTY SYSTEM

Such a theory of the function and role of parties also explains the rise of transnational party confederations, and their transformation into European parties. It implies describing these organisations as 'parties'. Also other interpretations by modern political science and sociology agree on such a description.[11]

In any event, the description 'European parties' cannot be denied to party confederations by declaring that an essential element – individual membership – is missing.[12] The individual members of the European parties are necessarily identical to those individual organisations at national, regional, and local level which support them. In a federal nation state, too, it is only possible to become an individual member of a federal party (in Germany, for instance, the CDU or the SPD) by joining a local or district branch. Membership of the regional (Land) or federal (Bund) association automatically follows from this.

European parties are not – or not yet – felt to be as effective as national parties. That is a consequence of the fact that the basis of power in the Union is not in the European Parliament, but rather – as before – in national governments, which for their part draw their legitimacy from national parliaments, and also procure their power from them.

What this means is that in a transnational, European context, the possibilities for parties to influence constitutional and legal developments remain far more limited than in the nation state. National governments, with their authority in the European Council to determine constitutions and make laws, have so far largely succeeded in withholding both influence and control over these matters from the European Parliament. In this they have exploited the fact that European affairs are still under the thumb of the foreign ministries, and that European politics is therefore treated as foreign policy. Beyond that, inter-governmental methods of procedure and negotiation also largely exclude national parliaments.

As long as this remains the case, the possibilities for the parties to help in building the European Union and its politics remain minimal. Because of their limited influence on national government's European policies, they can only get their ideas across through the political groups in the European Parliament.

So the way political party structures develop, and the way in which parties deploy their resources, is defined by constitutional developments. Their efforts to build up their own community and transnational structures, and to evolve their own capacity to act at European level, have been contained within the limits of what has been demanded of them by the progress of integration and its institutionalisation.

In other words, the development of European parties is not possible in one fell swoop. It is obviously not yet realistic to imagine that a party confederation – such as the European People's Party – organises supra-nationally in accordance to its own political programme.

But looking back on the Europeanisation process affecting political parties in the EU over the past decades, one thing is evident. Individual parties or party formations themselves helped determine both the rhythm and the effects of a process they themselves put in train. That is especially true of the degree to which parties go along with the process: it is the measure of their influence. Another example is the role of political groups in the European Parliament, which articulate a common political will – more or less powerfully. The same goes for the programmes of the parties or party formations which help determine the parties' capability of contributing to forge a supranational consensus while remaining in step with national moods and social currents and forces.

The impact of European co-operation on leaders of national parties should not be underestimated. The gradual evolution of a European political culture, and of the consciousness that goes with it, demonstrably tends to 'europeanise' the party system and advances the case for integration within the European Union.

THE FEDERAL PERSPECTIVE

There can be no doubt that the evolution of a European party structure is highly significant to the further development of European union, and to a functioning transnational political system. Article 138A of the Maastricht Treaty gives constitutional expression to this, and provides an important foundation for future efforts.

National political parties must be present at the European level as well if they are to promote their interests, have influence, and play their part in shaping the process of progressive integration towards European union. The EU's essential elements are all federal in character. The alliances of parties, previously organised to operate purely at national level, become European parties, and become active as such. They cannot, nor do they wish to, follow a particular national model. Unlike national parties, they do not naturally conform to the same unified pattern at all levels. But they respect the existing, tried and tested, structure of their member parties, which is their foundation and on which they rely. The process is one of federative parties seeking to organise, and to translate into political reality at European level, their members' joint plan of action. The European People's Party statutes, for instance, express this in the following way: member parties retain 'their name, identity, and freedom of action in the context of their national responsibilities'. (Article 2)

> The creation of European parties will not…make national parties redundant. Rather, Europe extends the function of parties in the EU Member States, and in countries which will potentially join…. The reality of the common institutions, on the basis of which parties formulate their tasks, is changing…. The doors of the constitutional state are wide open. European politics has become an everyday routine, which also applied to political parties. We are in the middle of the process of Europeanisation of party democracy.[13]

It is hard to predict which organisational model the European parties will follow from now on. That will be largely dependent on the constitutional development of the European Union. But it can be assumed on past experience that future decisions about party structure will – if they owe anything to established models – base themselves on a federal constitution. The main examples are in Germany and Austria, where autonomous parties operating at 'Land' level ally themselves to federal parties in the national context.

It is also evident, after examining the function and role of parties in different political systems, that little is to be gained from borrowing from the party systems in other continent-wide federations of states (for instance: United States of America, Canada, Australia, India, Brazil). Their federalism – quite unlike that of the European Union – is based on centralising and egalitarian conceptions. And parties in such federations have developed out of a *status quo* of relatively mature constitutional arrangements. European parties, by contrast, are evolving 'on the hoof' – as the constitutional arrangements take shape.

AN INITIATIVE BY EUROPEAN PARTY LEADERS

On July 1 1991, a joint letter was sent to the presidents of the European Council, the Council of Ministers, the European Parliament, and the EC Commission, by the chairmen of the Federation of European Liberals, Democrats, and Reformers (ELDR), the European People's Party (EPP), and the Union of Socialist Parties of the European Community (USP). It called for a clause about the role of 'European Parties' in shaping political consensus and political will to be written into the Treaty on European Union.[14] The initiative for this letter came from the President of the EPP, Belgian prime minister Wilfried Martens. It proved easy enough for him to convince both his two colleagues and compatriots, the Liberal Willy De Clercq and the Socialist Guy Spitaels, of the significance of his proposal. This was intended, as the letter said,

> explicitly to acknowledge the role of European parties in the process of integration and of democratising the European Union's political system.

The chairmen of the three European parties (or party confederations) proposed the following clause in the Treaty:

> European Parties are essential to integration within the Union. They are integral to building consensus and expressing the political will of the citizens of the Union. European parties are the federative associations of national parties with a presence in the majority of EU Member States, sharing the same aims and political direction, and forming a single group in the European Parliament. They must give a public account of where their funding comes from.

The first part of this formulation, which is inspired by the text of Clause 21 of the German constitution, makes clear that the role accorded to the parties in the context of the Community (or the European Union) is essentially the same as parties in the national context. This is solid federal thinking. In a federal state, parties and cross-party alliances essentially share the same function, and work along the same lines at their respective levels. But, of course there will always be different ways of operating, depending on the competencies to be taken into account at different political levels.

It was in this spirit that the European party chairmen felt, that their proposal would render it possible 'to establish a European legislative system in the medium term... which would give European parties a context for their work.'

Apart from their parliamentary groups, which operate on the basis of a statute sanctioned by the European Parliament, not one of the legal preconditions for the activities of existing party confederations (or European Parties) and their executive bodies is in place.

European party confederations therefore have no legal existence either, and so cannot directly employ anyone, nor sign contracts, nor for example give receipts for donations. This means that their secretariats, in order to fulfill certain tasks, have in law and in practice to pretend to be acting in the name of either their group in the European Parliament, or of particular national member parties.[15] This is not a sound state of affairs, and severely detrimental to the flexibility and capacity to react, which is demanded of European parties by the increasing momentum and politicisation of integration.

WHAT IS A EUROPEAN PARTY?

European parties are described as 'federal alliances of national parties' in the second part of the draft Article for inclusion in the Treaty on political union. This in practice refers to the associations representing the three classical party families – the Liberals, Social Democrats, and the Christian Democrats. Their members are committed to permanent co-operation, based on agreed statutes, and a programme agreed by the appropriate bodies designed to put their common policies into practice. The aim of this co-operation within the federation is to create and maintain 'a unity of action of the members at European level'. The EPP's rules of association further demand of member parties that:

> they argue the EPP's agreed positions in the European Community at national level. They further retain their names, identities, and freedom of action in the context of their national responsibilities.

So one can assume that, as Europe develops, future groupings of parties planning to operate or organise themselves at European level will opt for a federative structure. It seems quite impossible, as is argued above, for any European Party to survive in the long term, or be at all effective, unless it has independent member associations, especially in the Union's Member States.

The attempt by the Italian Radical Marco Panella to found a 'transnational' Federalist Party, a few years ago, was based on a false conception of federalism. It remained stuck, as most people predicted, in propagandist babble. The idea was that of a single European party to which every European could simply belong irrespective of his or her nationality, or national party membership. What federalism doesn't mean, as Panella must have come to realise, is a voluntaristically created unit which will simply steamroller out of the way any particularities. Rather, federalism is a process whereby several independent elements join together, and together create a unified whole – but without losing their individual identities.

The other elements of the definition set out in the draft Article seemed important to its authors in order to set sensible legal parameters to party competencies. A European party would hardly merit the name if it could not rely on national organisations in a number of member states 'with the same direction and aims', and which would be unable to unite the representatives of the various member parties in a single parliamentary group.

THE MAASTRICHT TREATY: ARTICLE 138A

The reactions of the presidents to the letter they received from the three party leaders varied. Jacques Delors, with whom Wilfried Martens discussed the matter, did consider the initiative positive and encouraged it – in a personal capacity. Its political importance was immediately clear to him. But he did not want to have the Commission involved, since it was a matter for parties and their groups. So at institutional level it was above all a matter for the European Parliament. This position was also confirmed by other members of the Commission who were approached on the matter.

The president of the European Parliament, Enrique Baron Crespo, supported the party leaders' initiative, and himself took his own initiatives. Following a meeting on 2 October 1991 to discuss how to proceed, he referred to the connection between the development of parties and the voting system and suggested as follows: that 82 deputies on European lists drawn up by the party confederations should be elected in addition to those elected on the basis of national voting systems. Voters would then have two votes, one for a national and another for a European list. The advantage of such a solution would above all consist in creating 'a purely European element' in the composition of Parliament, and give the European federations of parties a new and significant role. Moreover, the election of 82 extra deputies on European lists would improve the numerical relationship of voters to those they elected – under this arrangement, the only effective factor in the distribution of mandates would be the number of votes secured. Another effect of this would be fairer representation for countries with big electorates, which were under-represented as things stood. The whole idea promised a number of positive effects, one of them being greater commitment by member states and their political forces to the European elections. It would also accelerate the process whereby political forces were coming together at a Community level, and strengthen party confederations.[16]

The reaction both of Prime Minister Ruud Lubbers, President of the European Council, and of foreign minister Hans van den Broek, president of the EC Council of Ministers, was reticent to a degree. Their attitude was affected by severe disagreements in the Intergovernmental Conference preparing the Maastricht Treaty. In any event, the Dutch Presidency did not take up the suggestion. The draft Treaty on European Union which lay before the European Council on 9/10 December 1991 contained no reference to European parties.

On 6 December the eve of the meeting of the European Council, an EPP conference of party and government leaders took place in The Hague. On the basis of a report by Ruud Lubbers there was a detailed discussion about the aims of the Maastricht Treaty, and on how far preparations had got.

Wilfried Martens, who was in the chair, ensured that he had the explicit backing of government leaders taking part in the meeting by having a list – one he had himself drawn up – of several points discussed individually: these were the 'essentials' for the EPP.[18] Among them was the question of the draft clause on European parties. Martens got the green light, and the support of everyone for his *démarche* – he now intended to insist on the inclusion of the clause during the Maastricht Conference.

In the European Council to discuss Maastricht, Martens met no resistance to his proposal. Only the Portuguese Prime Minister, Cavaco Silva, asked for clarification. The European Council then agreed without further intervention. But the wording of the clause remained open. This was to be left to the conference of diplomats entrusted with editing the decisions and agreed texts of the Maastricht 'summit'.

Article 138A of the Treaty on European Union, finally signed on 7 February 1992 by 12 foreign and finance ministers, read as follows:

Political parties at European level are important as factors for integration within the Union. They contribute to forming a European awareness and to expressing the political will of the citizens of the Union.

It is worth noting that the definition contained in the party leaders' proposal was not taken up. Specifying any specific model as the norm was thus avoided.[19]

THE EUROPEAN PARTIES' COMMON RESPONSIBILITY

The successful initiative by the three party leaders did not fall out of the sky. It matured thanks to joint efforts over a fairly long time. In 1989, the secretaries-general of the three party federations had begun meeting from time to time to talk about common problems, and to exchange experiences. These conversations produced the idea of bringing their party presidents together to put in train joint discussions on 'the development and role of European parties or party federations in the Community's political system', and on 'relations with the groups in the European Parliament'.[20]

The first meeting of Wilfried Martens, Guy Spitaels, and Willy De Clercq took place on 18 September 1990. They agreed on a further meeting, and a joint press conference – on a day just before the European Council was to meet in Rome on 12 December 1990 to convene the Intergovernmental Conference on the Treaty on European Union (in other words, the further development of the 'Community's political system'). The chairmen explicitly wanted to make a joint statement on these matters, in order to put their demands about the role of parties firmly on the agenda.

The communiqué released on 12 December in connection with their second meeting declared that:

> Since their foundation in the mid-70s, both the European People's Party and the Union of Social-Democratic Parties in the European Community, and the European Liberals and Democrats, have all in their own way made major contributions to European integration. Despite their political rivalry, and their opposed positions on numerous questions, both as regards content and method, all three European parties or federations of parties stress their common responsibility for the proper functioning of democracy and for the success of the European Union. To that end, they are working closely with their different political groups in the European Parliament. These groups play a major part in the continuing efforts to create a transnational consensus inside the different political families.
>
> They take it as read that, without parties to express the political will of the citizens, there is no democracy! This holds good at all levels of

political representation, and logically for the European Community as
well, and above all for the European Union.

The federal and democratic union which is the goal of Social
Democrats, Liberal, and Christian Democrats, must be a vital community, one in which the citizens feel at home. So the European parties or
transnational federations of parties have an indispensable role which
only they can fulfill. It is a role which is essential if a broad consensus is
to be created, and if the effectiveness of the European institutions themselves is to be guaranteed.[21]

Further meetings between the party presidents and secretaries-general
during 1991 served to prepare the July 1 initiative and to spread the word
about it; the follow-up was also discussed on these occasions.

Article 138A of the Maastricht Treaty articulates the recognition that,
if the further unification of Europe is to be successful, and a transnational government system is to be effective, then the further development of European party structures is highly significant. At the same
time, this constitutional recognition of the role and function of the
parties serves as an important constitutional basis for future efforts. The
existence of 'political parties at European level' is recognised. Parties
are accorded the task of advancing the process of integration, of building
a European consciousness, and expressing 'the will of the citizens of the
Union'. It is a matter of 'a framework of rules which allow for a number
of concrete possibilities'.[22]

So, in the course of 1992, following the signing of the Maastricht
Treaty, several meetings of the three party leaders took place. Also present
were the chairmen of the political groups and the President of the
European Parliament. Everything turned on the question of what was now
to be done, and who was to do what, to breathe life into Article 138A.
Two sets of problems loomed large: inextricably bound up with each
other, but perhaps needing to be dealt with separately. These were completing the picture with a 'law on parties' or a 'statute on parties', and the
eventual possibility created by the new treaty situation of financing
European parties with Community funds.

It soon became clear to those taking part that, until there was legal cer-
tainty, but also for reasons of political culture and morality, the financial
question could not be posed until a number of conditions had been met.
There had to be in place unambiguous, legally binding rules about the
organisation, activity, and behaviour (including conduct of public
finances) of European parties. But even apart from the question of

financing the parties, rules of this kind are urgently needed, above all because of political integration.

ESSENTIAL ELEMENTS OF A STATUTE FOR EUROPEAN PARTIES

Such a 'European parties statute' would have to define what is meant by the concepts of 'European parties' or by 'political parties at European level'. Exactly what are their tasks? What rules apply to their structure, working methods, and finances? This statute would have to define the essentials clearly enough for an independent, inter-institutional authority, or the European Court, to be able to identify a 'political party at European level' under Article 138A. The main elements of such a statute[23] are roughly these:

Definition Political parties at European level (European parties) are federative associations of national or regional parties. Member parties (as national or regional sections) must be functional in most (or in several) member states of the European Union, and be recognised as parties by the various different laws applying to political parties (or equivalent regulations) or to elections. Their deputies belong, if there are enough of them, to the same group in the European Parliament.

Tasks Under the subsidiarity principle, European parties only undertake those tasks which could not be better tackled by member parties, or could not be tackled by them acting on their own. These specific tasks are, *inter alia*, developing a European consciousness; assisting the building of consensus and of political will among the citizens of the Union; evolving a programme to shape the Union and its institutions; creating a connection between the citizens of the Union and their institutions; informing the public about fundamental and topical problems in European politics, and about the consequences of possible solutions; encouraging the Union's citizens to take an active part in political life; active political education; the co-ordination of member parties' European election campaigns; assisting with the selection of candidates in elections to the European Parliament; exercising influence (in accordance with its political programme) on the Commission and the Council, as well as – through their parliamentary groups – on decisions made in the European Parliament and the Committee of the Regions.

Constitution   A European party must have a written constitution agreed in a democratic process. It will fulfill certain minimum pre-conditions. It must in any event provide for: a regular 'Congress' (assembly of delegates) meeting every two or three years at which decisions are made about the programme and about policy; democratically legitimate decision-making bodies meeting periodically which also control the executive; accountable management. Also the constitution must regulate, or set out ground-rules on, the following points: name and headquarters; composition and competencies of party organs; rights and duties of member parties, of its structures, and of individual members; conditions for acquiring (and losing) membership; rules of procedure and deadlines for calling meetings of party bodies; financial arrangements.

Financing   European parties should have public (Community) funds at their disposal in order to fulfill their legally-defined tasks. The contribution must not be allowed to exceed the amount of own resources set out in the annual budget or accounts. These own resources can consist of: contributions from national or regional member parties and parliamentary groups; contributions of individual members; gifts from supporters. The European parties must give a public account of where their financial resources come from supporters. The European parties must give a public account of where their financial resources come from.

2 The 1994 European Elections – Transforming the Party Landscape

The course of the campaign for the European elections, which took place from 9 to 12 June 1994, once again showed how hard national party leaders in all Member States find it to resist the temptation to exploit such occasions for immediate, domestic purposes. The programmes developed by European party bodies and made available to the campaigning member parties were, it is true, faithfully represented. But little or no attempt was made to 'sell' them. European policy altogether was only rarely an issue at all. So this time again there was little opportunity for the European parties to present themselves. Lacking their own resources or instruments, they scarcely have any profile of their own. The 1994 elections demonstrated that once again.

The results confirmed the dominant position of parties organised at European level, above all the European Social Democratic Party (ESP) and the EPP. The three parliamentary groups able to rely on European parties, apart from the ESP and EPP, the European Liberal and Democratic Reform Party (ELDR), together won over 398 seats; the other seven groups could only muster 169. It showed the increasing trend for power to be concentrated in the hands of traditional forces. However there was also a certain fragmentation to left and right of the groups holding the centre ground.

The parliamentary groups of the two big parties, EPP and ESP again command a two-thirds majority, necessary if parliament is to be respected by the Council of Ministers in legislative matters. Neither of the two groups could manage that kind of majority in tandem with other possible partners, so parliament was only workable if they combined forces. The responsibility this placed on them persuaded the leaders of both groups and parties to renew a co-operation which was mutually beneficial. The arrangement was the same as in the preceding parliamentary term, when it had mostly worked well. The arrangement included agreement about who would be President of the parliament. The German EPP politician Egon Klepsch was succeeded by the German ESP politician Klaus Haensch, demonstrating that even in the case of the most sensitive personnel decisions, national political criteria – at European level – take second place to party political considerations.

19

THE EUROPEAN SOCIAL DEMOCRATIC PARTY

Although the ESP did not quite achieve its expected election triumph, at around 200 deputies it was once more the largest single group in parliament. In France and Spain, in particular, they sustained losses. The results in France were especially painful because the reason was the success of a group of Socialist dissidents led by Bernard Tapie. The setback could only partly be made up by gains by the post-Communist leftist party (PDS) in Italy.

At the ESP's Congress in Barcelona in March 1995, the chairman of the German ESP, Rudolf Scharping, was elected President. He succeeded the Belgian Willy Claes, who became Nato Secretary General in the summer of 1994. At the same congress, the German Axel Hanisch, who had been Secretary General since 1989, was replaced by Frenchman Jean Pierre Vallin. In his account to the Barcelona congress, Hanisch felt able to declare that:

> Founding the European Social Democratic Party was no mere change of name. It signified a definitive step from a 'loose association' to a real 'European party'. In this connection, the resulting changes to the statutes, and in particular the introduction of majority voting on all matters decided in this way by the Council of Ministers, are of key importance.[1]

In the same spirit, the new President's first speech confirmed the ESP's ambition to be, or become, 'a genuine party'. He said that the debate inside the ESP following the change to the statutes would continue. It could be taken as read that there would soon be a rigorous examination both of the rule limiting majority voting to areas 'in which the Council of Ministers also decides by majority', and of the rule which allowed parties outside the European Union to be members of the ESP.[2]

> After this period of relative inactivity it is now important to return to the issue of Article 138A of the Maastricht Treaty, which was agreed in close collaboration with the other political families, and is a recognition of the significance of European parties for deeper integration. The necessary preparations have been largely completed in the ESP and in the Socialist group. What is now needed is the political will to anchor European parties in the institutions, and to set about making EU citizens aware of them in a deliberate and well-organised way.[3]

Departing Secretary General Hanisch's recommendation certainly reflects the line supported by the vast majority of the ESP, as well as of the mainstream convictions of the EPP and the ELDR.

As early as 1990, the congress held by the 'association' in Berlin had decided to accept sister parties not in the European Community as 'associated parties'. At the same time, given that Austria had applied to join, the Austrian Socialist Party (SPÖ) had been accepted as a full member. Later, sister parties in Sweden, Finland, and Norway followed; by the time the European Union enlarged in January 1995 the ESP had member parties in all member states. Since then, the ESP parliamentary group has had 221 members.

On account of its great tradition, and its deep roots in the political and social life of the member states, the ESP is a natural leader in further developing the political system. That leading position also comes, evidently, from the fact that it is the largest parliamentary force in the European Union. But the ESP finds it more difficult than the EPP to define itself clearly. Most of its members, voters, and deputies are more heterogeneous. So building a consensus is more complicated, which explains why it has in general been more reticent than the EPP about becoming a European party.

THE EUROPEAN PEOPLE'S PARTY

The EPP's showing at the 1994 European elections was what the party had expected, and even somewhat better. The losses in Italy were foreseen: the Partito Popolare – successor party to the collapsed Democrazia Cristiana – achieved only about 10 per cent of the vote, and nine seats. The DC had 27. In Great Britain, the Conservative Party was at a low ebb and achieved only 18 seats – it had previously had 32. But almost everywhere else EPP member parties were fairly successful. The British and Italian losses were made up by substantial gains in Germany and Spain. Altogether, the full members of the EPP achieved 125 seats. To that were added the 18 British and three Danish Conservatives; the Portuguese Fransisco Lucas Pires joined the EPP Group: he had formerly been in the Centro Democratico Social (CDS), and had now been elected on the list of the liberal Partido Socialdemocratico (PSD); seven French Liberals elected on the common UDF/RPR list led by the Christian Democrat Dominique Baudis joined the group, too.

Given the imminent enlargement of the EU, the EPP had some time earlier moved to bring in conservative parties in the Nordic countries to ensure it was properly represented in countries without a deeply-rooted Christian Democratic movement. Eventually, in March 1995, not only were the Austrian Volkspartei and the Swedish Kristdemokratiska

Samhällspartiet taken on board, but also the Swedish Moderaterna and Kansallinen Kokoomus from Finland; Hoyre in Norway was accorded associated party status.

THE EUROPEAN LIBERAL DEMOCRATIC REFORM PARTY

The European election amply confirmed the ELDR's leading position as the third largest group. More deputies were elected from the Netherlands, Belgium, Denmark, and Great Britain, though the Liberals suffered severe losses in a few other countries. In Germany the FDP failed to get past the 5 per cent barrier. In France the Parti Républicain defected to the EPP. Since the French had dominated the ELDR Group for a long time, this was peculiarly painful; however, it had been signalled some time before by the group's former chairman Valéry Giscard d'Estaing's crossing over to the EPP. The disappearance of the Spanish Centro Democratico Social was also a serious loss; the liberal-democratic movement had invested considerable hopes in this party, as it had in its founder and leader, former Prime Minister Adolfo Suarez.

To make up for these losses, the ELDR now looked to the states which were about to join the European Union. Which parties from these new member states could be integrated without endangering its liberal-democratic identity? Both the liberal people's parties in Sweden and Finland joined, as well as the centre parties traditionally committed to defending agricultural interests; so did the Liberal Forum from Austria. The group grew to 52.

The ELDR, in contrast to its two main rivals, suffered from the problem that the few leading political figures in its member parties were hardly prepared to engage in ELDR work: the Portuguese government leader, Anibal Cavaco Silva, for instance, or German foreign minister Klaus Kinkel had government responsibilities. The fact that it proved impossible to organise a meeting of political leaders to coincide with the European Council meeting in Essen (December 1994) was loudly bemoaned as a fiasco by Secretary General Christian Ehlers.[4]

WHO'S WITH WHOM?

The French Liberals' (Parti Républicain) defection to the EPP camp at the expense of the ELDR marked another stage in the movement begun by the decampment to the EPP of Valéry Giscard d'Estaing and several of his friends. This time Giscard's manoeuvre was on a larger scale. He had agreed with Jacques Chirac that everyone should join the EPP Group who had been elected on the common government list of the RPR and UDF, consisting of the liberal-inclined Républicains and the Christian Democrats, who already belonged to the EPP. The EPP conference of EPP party and government leaders in December 1993 had, on the recommendation of Pierre Méhaignerie, chairman of the Centre des Démocrates Sociaux (CDS) signalled its agreement to this. While the Républicains held to this agreement, following the election the Gaullists wanted nothing more to do with it – and reconstituted their own group, the Rassemblement des Démocrates Européens (RDE). The Irish Fianna Fail deputies once more joined the RDE, as did the three deputies belonging to the Portuguese CDS, a party expelled from the EPP in the spring of 1993.

Two further groups of deputies who had been assumed to be candidates for the EPP stayed outside: the eight Portuguese PSD deputies who remained with the Liberal group, and Forza Europa (FE) formed by the 26 deputies elected on the list of Forza Italia. The latter included a number of former Democrazia Cristiana members who had come together again in the Centro Cristiano Democratico (CCD). Following the collapse of the Italian Democrazia Cristiana – the second most important element in the EPP after the German parties – Prime Minister Silvio Berlusconi having succeeded in winning over a large part of the Christian Democrat-inclined electorate, offered his group to be the new Italian partner. But for both internal Italian, and wider 'European' reasons, the offer was not acceptable. The Italians had to establish their own one-nation group, and await developments.

Apart from this Italian Group there was one other new group composed only of one nationality, that of the dissident French Socialists mentioned above. Another group of French dissidents, led by the UDF politician Philippe de Villiers, established a further group; de Villiers had declined to support Dominique Baudis's joint RPR/UDF list because of his Euroscepticism. Opponents of the Maastricht Treaty from various countries joined this group.

The more opaque picture to the right of the EPP, and left of the ESP, was essentially the result of domestic politics. Two conclusions can be drawn from this. One is that European politics after Maastricht, meaning the debate about the future shape of the Union and the role of the nation state, has profoundly affected domestic politics, including the composition of parties and coalitions. Second, that the anti-European groups forming in various European countries do not look like playing any special part at Union level. They are wrapped up in national issues, and are incapable of uniting their forces because of their fixation with the domestic politics of their countries.

Only the transnational organisations emerging from classical political families – the Christian Democrat-oriented European People's Party, the European Socialist Party, and the European Liberal Democratic and Reform Party – fulfil, both in theory and political practice, the essential requirements of European parties. Above all, either through full members or through associated or allied members, they are represented in all or most Union countries.

Other party groups with ambitions to form a European party do not, for the moment, exist. However the European Greens, who organise themselves on a pan-European basis, are keeping this option open. They will be able to exercise it once they have resolved their internal contradictions and the incoherent elements of their European policy.

Any other groups which might qualify as potential European parties lack the necessary cohesion in terms of political programme or culture. Alternatively, for either political or ideological reasons, they have no interest in closer cohesion. But apart from all this, none of the other groups in the European Parliament would at the moment be in a position to draw in representatives from a majority of member states. As for the extreme nationalist and xenophobic right-wingers, they have many differences with each other, and cannot even find enough partners to establish a parliamentary group. The Socialist dissidents will most probably return to the bosom of their family. And attempts to establish a coalition based on representatives of regionalist parties have in the past proved unrealistic. This will no doubt prove to be the case again in the future. They have too little in common, and it is unlikely they will be able to form a party at European level.

ALLIANCES OF POLITICAL FORCES

The relative success of Euro-sceptic, nationalist forces in the 1994 European elections can be seen as a symptom of crisis. It resulted from two different shocks, one being the push towards integration in recent years, the other the drastic change in political topography following the events of 1989. If this analysis is correct – and there is no lack of supporting evidence – then the following developments seem probable. First is the further Europeanisation of the party system, which is likely to go in two directions. The two big camps, the Social Democrats and the

Christian-Democrats, will continue to exercise a magnetic attraction on those politically close to them. Moderate forces, tending towards the centre from the Left, will gradually come into the EPS, and moderate forces tending towards the centre from the right will be drawn into the EPP. This corresponds to the needs of European politics, which require a wide supranational consensus. And this can only be organised by parties or parliamentary groups with adequate social and cultural roots.

In the end, this is also what political parties – of whatever political colour – need. If they want to achieve anything on a European level they have to belong to a multi-national group, one which is as supranational as possible; it also has to be large enough to be politically effective. But this also corresponds to the politics of the end of the age of ideology, which has advanced the cause of essentially non-ideological people's parties. The centre of gravity of parties is no longer the ideology of its leading elites, but the economic and social, or political and cultural, interests of those who support them in elections. Right versus Left, conservative versus progressive, liberal versus Socialist: all these antitheses are losing their ideological exactness. They are increasingly seen as different cultural-political goods in the market of possibilities. From this perspective, certain other differences crumble away: the different shades of opinion and direction between those on the cultural 'Left' (Socialist versus communist), or 'Right' (Liberal versus other 'bourgeois' forces).

All of this explains why the Social Democrats could not avoid accepting post-Communists and others from a left-wing tradition, just as the EPP has admitted conservative, liberal, and other 'bourgeois' forces. It is therefore probable that during the European Parliament's current legislature (1994 to 1999), further changes will occur in the groups. These will result from the efforts of the two largest groups to consolidate their areas of influence and their composition. Gradually those elements which belong together in this new situation will come together. That is all the more likely in view of the fundamental changes in the EU's political system which are expected in the coming years as a result of the Intergovernmental Conference as well as a consequence of the realisation of both the Monetary Union and the Enlargement.

The first sign of movement towards this developing fusion was that the 'Gaullist' group decided to go together with Forza Europa in the summer of 1995; the resulting Union pour l'Europe (UPE) has 56 deputies, and pushed the ELDR Group out of third place; however this drove three Italian FE deputies belonging to the DC successor party CCD to join the EPP, following the CCD's recognition by the EPP as a full member. And in December 1996 the Portuguese PSD left the ELDR and joined the EPP.

As a result, the eight European parliamentarians belonging to this party became members of the EPP group.

THE EXAMPLE OF THE EUROPEAN PEOPLE'S PARTY

There is one clear justification for taking the EPP as a subject to illustrate the emergence, working methods, and development, of confederations of European parties. This is that, in a much more consistent way than any of its rivals, the 'Federation of Christian Democratic Parties of the European Community' (as it was defined in the first article of association of 8 July 1976) always strove to transform itself into a real party. This is evident in its ambitious choice of name, as in the article of association, both of which envisage the goal of supranational opinion-forming, decision-making, and action.

This meant that the EPP's development was more dynamic than that of other party groups. Their spokesmen fully acknowledge this in that they point to the EPP as a model to justify their own efforts to national member parties.[5]

The reason why the EPP was able, in some sense, to pioneer the route to a European party is above all to be found in traditional Christian Democratic thought, and the political programmes that evolved from it. Efforts to achieve European unity by establishing a whole new federative set of relationships between states have always been a constant of Christian Democratic policy.[6] The EPP has developed this traditional European federalist consensus further, and given it deeper roots. It has led to a considerable degree of cohesion which has united Christian Democrats from the different countries of the Community. This is not only in terms of political programmes, but increasingly in practical and strategic questions: in European policy, international relations, and economic and social policy.

This tendency is encouraged by a solid consensus based on the Christian vision of man about political methods and goals. European Christian Democrats, irrespective of their national and cultural origins, more or less consciously renounce all ideology. Normally speaking, they act in a pragmatic way through following the teachings of Christianity, or the lessons they have learned from their own experience.[7]

Thus the EPP has a pioneering role. But its development and internal structure, and its working methods, are entirely comparable to those of the European Liberals, the European Social Democrats, and now the European Greens. This is particularly the case when it comes to certain specific problems facing the party confederations. One thinks, for example, of communication problems between those members of European and national authorities; or the relationship between the European party organisation and its group in the European Parliament. So taking the EPP as an example will yield insights which also – with some qualification – shed light on the other party confederations.

The transnational or international formations of the three 'classical' party families – the Social Democrats, the Liberals, and the Christian Democrats – have in common that all three had made their first entrance onto the political stage well before the mid-1970s. Their cross-border co-operation in each case has a pre-history[8] without which the magnitude of the developments described in this book do not really make sense. The birth and development of European parties really do bring in their train radical changes, and those too do not come into focus without examining the pre-history. So the following analysis starts with a description of the origins of structured co-operation between Christian Democrats in Europe.

Part II
Co-operation Between Christian Democrats and the Birth of the European People's Party

3 The International Secretariat of Democratic Parties Inspired by Christianity, 1925–1939

Political parties with Christian-inspired ideologies found each other in the early 1920s. They had begun to establish themselves as various European countries gradually became democratic over the 19th century; others came later, not until after the First World War.[1] A more or less formal trans-European co-operation started in 1925.

By contrast the Socialist International was already in place before the establishment of Socialist parties (in many cases inspired and organised by the International). The reverse was the case for the international Christian Democratic movement: it was created by the national parties. This remains the key both to the identity of the Christian Democrat International, and to its *modus operandi*. The same goes for the CDI's regional organisations, including the European Union of Christian Democrats (EUCD), from which the European People's Party (EPP) emerged. The particularities of its origins and development underlies its political programmes and the federal structure of organisations serving international co-operation and common action by Christian Democrats.

The recent experiences of World War I, coupled with the looming threat of fascism in various parts of central and western Europe in the twenties, led to the conviction among leaders of Christian-based parties that overcoming nationalism was the decisive pre-condition for preserving the peace. And political parties, especially Christian-based parties, had a moral obligation to make a concrete contribution to this.

As far as organised co-operation was concerned the first initiative came from Don Luigi Sturzo, who in 1919 had established the Partito Popolare Italiano (PPI/Italian People's party). This was no coincidence: he had personal experience of fascism, and had gone into exile after Mussolini seized power.

31

CATHOLIC PARTIES

A refugee in London, in the autumn of 1924, Don Sturzo made contact with the leaders of 'Christian' parties in different European countries to organise a meeting.[2] A few years before, he and a PPI delegation had dropped in at the offices of various party leaders to sound them out about founding an International of People's Parties (Internazionale Popolare). He was determined to establish international co-operation between all Christian-based parties. During the twenties, however, any party which could realistically be considered as a partner, or was prepared to co-operate in the way Sturzo had in mind, was without exception Catholic: meaning these were parties of Catholics, or were parties which represented political Catholicism. In these countries Catholicism's inherent internationalism, the international character of the church, and its natural ties across frontiers, all encouraged such party leaders to co-operate with each other.

The meeting Don Sturzo had striven to set up took place in Paris on 12 and 13 December 1925. The invitation came from the Parti Démocrate Populaire (PDP/The Democratic People's Party), which had only been founded the previous autumn. The delegates from five countries were all senior figures. As well as the French PDP, the Italian PPI, the Ligue des Travailleurs Catholiques de Belgique (the Workers' Section of the Belgian Catholic Union), the Polish Christian Democrats, and the German Centre Party were represented. Invitations to like-minded parties in the Netherlands, Switzerland, Czechoslovakia, Lithuania, and Spain were not taken up.

The delegates who came to Paris reported on their parties in general, their principles and their political tasks. With 'due caution and restraint'[3] a debate took place about the political situation and developments in Europe, the twin menaces of fascism and Communism, and current foreign policy issues. It soon became clear how difficult it was, given national allegiances, to agree common positions. Nor was a single one decided on. Indeed it was agreed this was impossible, and that even the fact that the meeting had taken place was to be kept secret. The French, especially, feared that there might be internal political repercussions. Such reticence was exactly the opposite of Don Sturzo's intentions: he had planned common action which would have a public éclat.

> The father of the emerging Christian Democrat International must understand from this preliminary conference how difficult it would be to go beyond the simple exchanging of information and to get parties to the point of having joint political meetings or joint action.[4]

The discussion highlighted two opposing conceptions of future co-operation: the Italian idea of a 'Union interparlementaire permanente' and the French proposal of a 'Bureau central d'information'. It was eventually decided that an 'International Secretariat of parties (or political organisations) inspired by Christianity' should be established in Paris. Its task would be to organise a network and a flow of information between parties. Another meeting was to take place in Brussels in May 1926; parties which were not at the Paris meeting were to be encouraged to come.

The Brussels meeting confirmed and formalised the substance of what had been decided in Paris, although on this occasion – the Polish delegation being unable to attend – only four of the five 'founder parties' were represented. There were apologies for absence from Lithuania (Christian Democratic party), Austria (Christian Social Party), Switzerland (Conservative People's Party), and Czechoslovakia (People's Party), which can be counted as applications for membership, since these parties more or less regularly took part in subsequent meetings.[5]

THE FRENCH INFLUENCE

The Parisian secretariat was now given an official name: Secrétariat International des Partis Démocratiques d'Inspiration Chrétienne (SIPDIC/ The International Secretariat of Democratic Parties of Christian Inspiration). The French conception of a 'Bureau' had triumphed over that of creating a union. It was true that the bodies responsible for the work of the secretariat were to be made up of agents of the parties, not individual figures. But it is explicitly stated that:

> This grouping is not, at the present time, aimed at creating a federation of the participating parties.[6]

Even the name, which avoided the 'Christian Democratic' concept, can be traced to the French influence, which was intended to remain decisive. Since Paris had been chosen as the seat of the Secretariat, it also became the PDP's job to man it. To begin with, Raymond Laurent and Philippe de Las Cases led it, and then Henri Simondet from 1928 until the Secretariat was closed down.[7]

A 'Comité central' formed the political executive body; later its name was changed to 'Comité exécutif'. Every party had a delegate to this, who had the right to send a substitute. This executive committee usually met twice a year, one of these taking place on the margins of conferences or party congresses taking place from 1926 to 1932. Member parties would each send several delegates to these.[8]

All such meetings and sessions were private. The decisions or conclusions reached over the years on topical or fundamental issues were confidential, intended only for the internal use of member party bodies. There was only one, single, exception to this rule. In January 1931 the executive committee published a declaration on securing peace which referred to 'the difficult international situation caused by rigid nationalism and the difficult economic crisis.' The statement condemned any use of force, either in domestic or foreign policy, and affirmed member parties' commitment to 'effective organisation of peace by the League of Nations, and to a rapprochement between peoples which must be achieved through both economic and political co-operation.[9]

Simondet justified the SI's departure from its principle and previous practice by saying it was necessary to make a public declaration or the SI would be untrue to its task ('mission'). It would demonstrate its fruitlessness ('stérilité') if its member parties did not, in the current situation, publicly show themselves to be 'une force au service de l'oeuvre de paix et de collaboration internationale'. Another reason for making its view public was to stop public opinion from becoming used to the idea that the movement for peace and rapprochement between peoples was purely something that concerned Socialists, Radicals, and the extreme Left.[10]

THE INTERNATIONAL SITUATION

Remonstrations and proposals from Italian representatives were instrumental in ensuring there was more and more discussion of these ideas. However, no change was made to the practice to which the Secretariat had adhered from the beginning. Even initiatives aimed at stronger organisational co-operation were not pursued. One reason was no doubt to avoid giving any impression of imitating the example of the Socialist International. In general, especially among parties from smaller countries, there was a degree of nervousness and diplomatic caution about any statement which could be interpreted as interference in the politics of a foreign power. So it was scarcely possible to develop policies beyond general statements of principles.

The Secretariat's member parties were also pursuing different agendas, and there was no procedure for producing consensus:

> While the Italians want to give this structure an unambiguously anti-fascist character, and the French above all seek dialogue with the Germans, most above all fear having to take on board too clear a political position; they prefer to deal with the traditional, less political, themes of Christian social politics (the family, workers' profit-sharing schemes etc.)[11]

The time had not yet come for creating international democratic structures which could act together to defend common political positions. Even at national level, democracy and its institutions were still extremely weak. In Italy they had already been crushed; in Austria and Germany they would not survive much longer.

> A hard nationalism of a kind we can hardly conceive of today dominated inter-war Europe, and left practically no space for internationalism. International relations, and 'trans-nationalism' could survive and be practised to an extent, but only discreetly, ashamed of themselves. They were widely suspected of being unpatriotic. It was within this kind of 'discretion' – un-public, confidential – that the 'Internationale' of Catholic Christian Democratic parties organised by SIPDIC tried to operate.[12]

Against such a backdrop it took special far-sightedness – something few politicians had at the time – to realise that democracy, democratic forms, and democratic procedures, also made sense as a basis for political relations in the international context. Without question, Don Luigi Sturzo was one of these rare men. But his proposals and representations mostly fell on deaf ears. He complained to Francesco Luigi Ferrari, who in 1929 succeeded him as representative of the Italian PPI, that 'the endeavours made from the beginning to give [the Secretariat] an international democratic orientation have progressively lost their influence.' [13] Transnational relations between parties therefore remained stuck in the tramlines of international diplomacy. The League of Nations which, during the twenties and thirties, was the institutional framework for international co-operation between states, offered democratic forces no possibilities of making their influence felt. It wasn't a league of nations but a diplomatic structure.

THE EUROPEAN PERSPECTIVE

The most active and serious of those taking part in the work of SIPDIC were representatives from member parties in Belgium, France, Italy, Luxembourg, the Netherlands, and (until 1932) Germany. It is no doubt hardly a coincidence that these were the countries which would later found the European Community. After World War II, Christian Democratic politicians from these countries who began the process of European integration, could draw strength from the common lessons and experiences of co-operation between 1925 and 1939.

The evidence of the congresses organised by the Paris Secretariat shows, at this much earlier stage, both a well-developed sensibility to, and positive interest in, uniting Europe and the business of putting integration in train. In the thirties all this was politically impossible. However, SIPDIC's last congress, held in Cologne in October 1932 – a few months before the National Socialists seized power in Germany, and under the chairmanship of Konrad Adenauer, did vote for this final declaration:

> We must strengthen and encourage comprehensive co-operation between all European nations in order to achieve a Common Market for production and the free movement and consumption of goods.... Full union, which is the final goal, cannot be achieved immediately or directly. So we must gradually remove customs barriers, and trade and financial barriers preventing the regular exchange of goods, in order to realise as quickly as possible the free movement of goods, capital, and people.[14]

That proposal for overcoming the crisis in Europe was the forerunner of the projects which, after World War II, led to the creation of the European Community.

A TEMPORARY HALT

After 1933 it was impossible for the Paris Secretariat to organise any more large-scale conferences. There were still fairly regular meetings of a more limited kind, mostly in Paris; but they had no effect in terms of politically relevant action. The tools were not there, nor the political will. People stayed in contact, and kept each other informed. An initiative to re-establish the 'International Union of Parties of Christian Inspiration', again coming from Don Sturzo, found no support. The SIPDIC's last sign of life was a confidential memorandum to the Pope in January 1938 asking him to speak out about the dangers facing Europe, and to use his moral authority to rescue the peace.

Fascism, National Socialism, increased tensions between governments, the spirit of revenge, and the dictator's obsession with power, all eventually led to World War II. And that, for the moment, ended co-operation between the Christian Democratic parties. The Secretariat ceased to exist in 1939. The outbreak of war crushed, for the time being, any worthwhile democratic efforts to shape the Continent.

In London, in the winter of 1940/41, the 'International Christian Democratic Union' was founded by British and exile politicians. Again Don Sturzo was involved and together they tried to continue the tradition of the Paris Secretariat. The initiative was linked to the 'People and Freedom Group', an organisation set up by Don Sturzo in 1936. Thanks to personal contacts and spreading information, it made a substantial contribution to maintaining connections between Christian Democratic figures during the war, and ensuring they could flourish afterwards. But they could do little more that had genuine political relevance.[15] Only after the terrible experience of national totalitarianism, with its contempt for human beings, and its destructiveness, would it be possible to take further steps on the road to international democracy, and with it international party work.

4 The 'Nouvelles Equipes Internationales', 1948–1965

The leaders of re-established or newly-founded Christian Democrat-oriented parties made contact with each other soon after World War II was over. Many were old friends from the twenties and thirties and had worked together under the arrangements made by the Paris Secretariat in 1925–39. Some kept up connections in exile, or in the resistance movements.

The initiative came from the Conservative People's Party of Switzerland. Thanks to Swiss neutrality it had been the only sister-party to survive the war unscathed. An invitation to a meeting in Lucerne from 27 February to 2 March 1947, was accepted by all those invited. Delegates arrived from Belgium, Great Britain, France, Italy, the Netherlands, Luxembourg, Austria, and Switzerland. No-one was able to come from Czechoslovakia or Hungary. And no invitation was sent to Germany, where the political situation remained unclear.

There was general agreement at this meeting both about the logic of co-operation, and its intrinsic value. But once again there were quarrels, familiar from the founding of the 'International Secretariat' in 1925, about what form or organisation such co-operation should take. This time it was the Swiss, supported by the Italians and the Austrians, who argued for an 'Entente organique' of parties going in the same political direction. They meant, an organisation capable of hammering out a common position, and securing common action, among the member parties. The Belgians, supported by the French and Dutch, insisted that there were both domestic and international reasons for limiting an international association to one in which, at most, representative Christian Democratic figures could work together. The parties were not to be involved. This argument finally won the day.[1]

Giving the organisation a name also proved controversial. Eventually, following the determined wishes of the French and Belgians, it was decided that the association should be called: Nouvelles Equipes Internationales (NEI/ New International Teams). The Belgians had anticipated this and already founded an association with this name which they now offered as a structure, and invited everyone to join. Their farsightedness was rewarded and they were given the task of co-ordinating the first Congress.

A CURIOUS NAME

The curious name deliberately echoed the Nouvelles Equipes Françaises, which just before the war (1938/39) had tried to bring together committed democrats in various French parties and groups.[2] The name also exposed a dilemma, one which would long haunt Christian Democracy's organisation and identity in Europe. It also pointed to a possible direction which was to prove important later.

The dilemma was that some parties prepared to co-operate in the NEI, and actually wantingto be Christian Democrats, did not wish to be called that. In France, particularly, the idea 'Christian Democratic' was used only with the greatest reticence, and hardly ever in public. It was feared it would be misunderstood as referring to something clerical. It was absolutely no part of the Christian Democrats' post-war idea of themselves to be the political wing of a religious authority, nor uncritically to defend the church(es) or their interests. They did not even want to be suspected of this. However, in France at least, no-one dared publicly to refute public misunderstanding created by liberal and Socialist propaganda.

The possibility foreshadowed by the name was that a Christian-inspired political movement could be open, and stay open, to like-minded political forces, but coming from other ideological traditions. So neutral names were chosen; in France, the post-war Christian Democratically-oriented parties were called Mouvement Républicain Populaire, Centre Démocrate or Centre des Démocrates Sociaux, or (from 1995) Force Démocrate.

So what did 'Equipes' mean? They could, for instance, be teams of members and activists all formed by the same parties in the various countries. They might be other groups, independent of parties, who had come together to work with like-minded people at international level. In fact, the NEI was not really a union of parties, but a mixture. Parties belonged to it, but alongside them political figures who had joined national teams. Among these were a series of French MRP and Belgian PSC members who joined individuals following their parties' refusal to become corporate members.[3] Robert Schuman, Georges Bidault, Henri Teitgen, André Colin from France, and the Belgians Paul van Zeeland, Auguste De Schrijver, Theo Lefèvre, were all energetic proponents of the NEI. Great Britain too was represented by an Equipe composed of figures from both the main parties, Conservative and Labour.[4] In Holland, the three Christian (confessional) parties – KVP, ARP, CHU – formed a joint Equipe which became a member as such. The constitution provided for 'only one Equipe per country'. 'Like-minded national groups forced to work in exile' also counted as Equipes.[5]

The founding congress of the NEI took place in Chaudfontaine, near Liège between 31 May and 3 June 1947. As in Lucerne, there were not only western European parties present, but also the Polish Workers Party (already in exile) and the Czechoslovak People's Party. The Frenchman Robert Bichet was elected president, and the Belgian Jules Soyeur secretary-general.[6] The goal of the association was laid down in the constitution:

> to arrange regular contacts between political groups and personalities from various countries who are informed by the principles of Christian Democracy; they will scrutinise both their own national situations and international problems in the light of these principles, compare experiences and political programmes and, following international agreement, strive to achieve democracy and social and political peace.[7]

The leadership was the 'Comité directeur', which met three times a year composed of representatives of each national Equipe. Decisions were reached by a two-thirds majority of those present; but there was a determined attempt to achieve consensus. The ruling committee elected a presidium (Bureau Politique) annually. This consisted of the President, four vice-presidents, and the secretary-general. To begin with, the NEI secretariat was based in Brussels, and after 1950 in Paris.

Alongside it, there were intermittent meetings of a cultural committee, an economic and social committee, and an East/West committee. Working groups concerned themselves with parliamentary matters, propaganda, international political problems, and political programmes. The 'International Union of Young Christian Democrats' was established in 1951, as the successor to the NEI's youth commission, founded in 1947. Attempts to publish regular papers were frustrated by financial difficulties.

What was new in the Nouvelles Equipes Internationales, compared to the pre-war International Secretariat of Christian (Catholic) parties, was the ecumenical element. It made possible both reconciliation and reconstruction out of the ruins of the national states. What was completely new was the vision of the future, the union of Europe, which led to overcoming the old system. Finally, the post-war Christian Democratic parties were different from their 1920s predecessors in one crucial way: they were genuine people's parties, having emerged from elections as the leading forces in their countries, and having taken government responsibility.

THE GOAL: UNITING EUROPE

The NEI also co-founded the International European Movement, and was an active partner in it. The Nouvelles Equipes was among the initiators and organisers of the legendary Europe Congress in The Hague in May 1948.[8] The NEI described itself at that time as follows:

> the NEI fulfils a simple task of especial urgency following the end of the Second World War: on the one hand, the realisation of European Union as a first step to a united world; on the other hand, the union of people and parties inspired by Christian Democracy. In this way, with the help of vital international organisations, the NEI wants to make an effective contribution to an enduring peace.[9]

A large number of conferences and colloquia followed the founding congress in Chaudfontaine. In truth, the NEI's main activity consisted of organising the annual congresses and study conferences at which topical European issues were thrashed out. The resonance of these meetings was considerable in the first years; directly or indirectly they involved members of governments, party leaders, and other important figures.[10]

The agendas for debate reveal not only the major problems of the time, but also what expectations were entertained, and particularly the hopes invested in European union to bring peace and to preserve it. However, they also demonstrate that co-operation in the NEI in those days was mainly about trying to make progress by means of classical diplomacy. That corresponded with how things were at the state level. It was only later, and very gradually, in the 1950s, that the perspective changed. That was after the European Coal and Steel Community had been successful, and people were prepared to build on it. Only then did awareness of the possibility of integration grow, and alongside it the vista of supranational and federalist inter-party co-operation as well.

These first steps in political co-operation under the aegis of the NEI are marked by the situation at the time it was founded. Following the experience of national totalitarianism and the catastrophe of the European war, Christian Democratic parties in many parts of the continent offered a convincing spiritual/political alternative. That was the reason Christian Democracy became a decisive political movement. As majority or governing parties they took responsibility for the political and socio-economic reconstruction of their countries. They were increasingly determined to bring about the political integration of European national states into a supranational community, and they sought common security in the Atlantic Alliance.

Agreement on such key questions had a powerful cohesive effect; developing a clear common political line became possible, despite the absence of an organisational infrastructure. Stabilisation and progress were given a powerful boost by joint political activity aimed at the common goal of uniting Europe during an extremely difficult time. Europe had been shattered by war, and suffered in the 1940s and 1950s from raw nerves and numerous insecurities. International co-operation between Christian Democratic parties was gaining coherence in this way during the first post-war years. And it was far more cohesive and substantive than the International Secretariat in Paris had been between the wars.

In its first years the development of the NEI was attended by informal, confidential meetings at the highest political level; they became known as the 'Discussions in Geneva'.[11] This was how Konrad Adenauer and Georges Bidault met for the first time, as did other pro-Christian Democratic politicians who were either in government, or party leaders in their countries. It was here that NEI co-operation was given a degree of political underpinning. In particular, these meetings prepared the ground politically for the reconciliation of France and Germany. European union was propelled onwards by the success of the understandings reached in this way about the peculiarly delicate questions of the German-French relationship.

WORLD-WIDE CO-OPERATION

What is certain is that Christian Democracy's global perspective advanced and influenced co-operation in Europe. The 'European Union as a first step towards a united world' was a fundamental driving force for the NEI. Its internationalism was expressed by its name and also in the sub-title – though it was rare for recourse to be made to it – 'Union internationale des démocrates chrétiens'.[12]

Christian parties were banned in central and Eastern Europe once Communist rule had been imposed. In July 1950, their representatives who had fled to the West, and had been involved in the NEI from the start, established the Christian Democratic Union of Central Europe (UCDEC/ Union Chrétienne Démocrate de l'Europe Centrale'). It included representatives from the following countries: Czechoslovakia, Poland, Hungary, Lithuania, Latvia, and Slovenia/ Jugoslavia. Their political, journalistic, and propaganda activity was mainly focused on fighting Communism, attacking the Soviet Union, and on liberating and democratising their countries. Their representatives did not just raise their voices in the NEI but in UN bodies, in international Christian associations and organisations, and obviously in public as well.[13]

Christian Democrats driven out of Central European countries, who had gone into exile in North and South America via western Europe, and also political emigrants from Franco's Spain, were especially important. They contributed considerably to the spread of the intellectual heritage, and the establishment of an inter-continental network. They had connections with like-minded groups in the US, Venezuela, Argentina, Chile, and other Latin American countries, as well as with the Christian Democratic Organisation of America (OCDA/ Organizacion Democrata Cristiana de America) founded in Montevideo in 1948. In the fifties they succeeded in forging the connection between the European and Latin American Christian Democrats.

The first inter-continental conferences involving leading Christian Democrats from Europe and Latin America took place in Paris in 1956, and in Brussels two years later. A third meeting (1961) in Santiago de Chile saw the foundation of the Christian Democratic World Union (CDWU), which brought together the European NEI, the Central European exile organisation UCDEC, and the American regional organisation ODCA, and the International Organisation of Young Christian Democrats (IUYCD).

EVOLUTION AND MEANING

The German Christian Democrats were already on board by the time of the NEI's second congress in Luxembourg, between 28 January and 1 February 1948. The subject was: the German Question. Konrad Adenauer, then scarcely known abroad, led the CDU delegation. He spoke about the future shape of Germany in a united Europe. He made a very strong impression, laying the foundation of his future credibility, and that of his party and his country. It was the first time that an office-holding politician in the new Germany had been invited to present himself abroad at an international forum. That was in no sense routine; there had been internal opposition, though it was quickly overcome. The NEI was the first post-war association to accord a German delegation membership on equal terms.

The Germans became active members of the NEI. As things developed, they pushed more and more strongly – like the Italians, but against the counter-weight of the French – for a tougher organisation, and especially for more NEI influence on national parties.[14] The CDU leadership, in particular Adenauer, exploited the possibilities offered by the NEI connections as much as possible. This was both to advance their own interests and to reach agreements on especially contentious issues, notably with the French.

The possible routes along which the NEI could develop were limited by lack of enthusiasm on the part of the French and Belgians, who shared the job of running it. The organisation, its resources, and its possibilities, all remained weak. Even Konrad Adenauer's impatience could not change that. His analysis, delivered to the CDU leadership in summer 1951, was that:

> We must create a federation with the Christian parties in the other European countries which is able to look after our common interests better than the NEI. The NEI should also have a different name, and be pulled out of the rut it is in. We should work on creating the Christian International as soon as Ems.[15]

The NEI was supposed to hold a Congress in Bad Ems on 14–16 September; the CDU federal leadership set up a committee made up of Ministers Kaiser, Kiesinger, Simpfendörfer and Süsterhenn. They were 'to prepare the idea of a Christian International for [the conference at] Ems',[16] but did not manage to do this. Adenauer, who argued forcefully for the International during the congress, did not get his way here either:

> But in one respect, I have regretfully to say, we are behind parties which – unlike ourselves – do not believe in the victorious force of Christian thinking. They have been much more effective than we have in organising international co-operation. Please reflect on the Cominform, or on the re-established Socialist International. We, my friends, the Christian parties, cannot at the moment compete with them, either in terms of our strength, or as effective propagandists. I openly admit that the German Christian parties' commitment to the common effort has been inadequate. Note, ladies and gentlemen, that the name we go under doesn't even show what we want. It is a completely neutral name, which can mean absolutely anything. When I think that the Christian parties... could forge a stronger alliance by constantly exchanging information and working together: what an amazingly strong effect that would have on what happens in Europe, on the renaissance of Europe... Stronger links between the Christian parties would decisively advance our work, work which is in a common cause, and so helps all of us. But above all, stronger co-operation by Christian parties would advance the political integration of Europe.[17]

From the middle of the fifties onwards, the NEI steadily lost its relevance. With the establishment of the Coal and Steel Union (1952), and then crucially with the foundation of the European Economic Community (1958), practical co-operation among Christian Democrats gradually moved to the Christian Democratic groups which had evolved in the Common Assembly, or European Parliament. Furthermore, several Christian Democratic parties had held on to power over this whole period; their interest in the weak NEI structures progressively declined. The machinery of government offered such party leaderships perfectly adequate means to communicate, and reach agreement, with their partners in other countries.

The fact that the NEI crisis reached its climax at the beginning of the sixties is explained by the growing tensions inside the Mouvement Républicain Populaire, and the difficulties created for French Christian Democrats by the return to power of General de Gaulle.

Despite the increasingly obvious weaknesses of its construction, the NEI's efforts during its later years, meaning from 1955 to 1965, contributed a great deal to preserving what the member parties had in common, and to the emergence of a consensus about political programmes. The NEI was a vital forum for the identity of Christian Democracy as an influential international force. It created important preconditions for the success of European political integration, and for the development of solidarity between the member parties. Therefore it is legitimate to say that the fact that the EPP exists today owes much to the fact that the NEI existed before it.[18]

5 The European Union of Christian Democrats, 1965–1976

The European Economic Community, in operation since 1958, proved to be a great success. But attempts to push forward political integration met with setbacks. Negotiations about the statute for a European Political Union had collapsed in 1962, and Italian and German initiatives to breathe new life into these proved fruitless. Great Britain's entry was blocked by French President Charles de Gaulle.

Despite the tensions which had arisen within the Community, the EEC Commission – energetically led by the German Christian Democrat Walter Hallstein – refused to be flustered, and continued with its integration programme. Support came mainly from Christian Democrat-led governments. De Gaulle, who questioned the supranational development of the European Community, faced resistance from those who, like the Christian Democrats, remained faithful to the founding fathers' federative model. The break between de Gaulle and the Christian Democrat-oriented French party, Mouvement Républicain Populaire (MRP), came in 1962.

This was the backdrop to the transformation of the Nouvelles Equipes Internationales in 1965. It now called itself the European Union of Christian Democrats (EUCD), a name which signals a change in the character of the organisation. It was designed to develop into a single, united body pursuing common aims. The phase of consultation and co-operation was to be abandoned in favour of 'defining genuine common policies', at the centre of which was 'removing obstacles on the road to creating a European community'.[1] Mariano Rumor, under whose leadership the transformation of the NEI to the EUCD had taken place, observed in hindsight:

> Our co-operation in those days attained a new level of effectiveness and initiative at European level. There also developed intensive and dynamic relations with the parliamentary group; these took on a structured and permanent character. It was because of this development that it was obvious that we must choose a new, challenging name for our European organisation.[2]

RENEWAL AND CONTINUITY

With the decline of the French MRP, the secretariat, based in Paris since 1947, was moved to Rome in 1964. This was immediately before the transformation of the NEI into the EUCD, and the move itself encouraged new, bolder thoughts about the form and content of co-operation between Christian Democratic parties. The French element, despite the remarkable contributions of individual Frenchmen from the ranks of the MRP, had always been strongly focused on national affairs: it had remained Franco-centric. The Italians, by contrast, had from the start argued for a tougher supranational organisation with more authority over member parties.

At a meeting of the Executive in Brussels on 3 May 1965, it was decided to make the transformation, and the Congress at Taormina in the same year confirmed it. The Belgian deputy Leo Tindemans, elected first secretary-general of the EUCD, drew up the relevant report. For all the intended reforms, the EUCD stressed very clearly not only continuity, but even its identity with the NEI. That first EUCD congress, held in Taormina on 9–12 December was counted as the XVII Congress of the EUCD; the last NEI congress on 21–23 June 1962, held in Vienna, had been its sixteenth.[3]

The EUCD was given a constitution with stronger unitary elements than in the NEI's. But, as before, member parties retained full autonomy vis-à-vis the international bodies, and relations between them were confederal. The members of the organisation were the parties; the recognition of an 'Equipe Nationale' made up of individual political figures now looked anomalous. The concept of an 'Equipe' was also applied to cases where there were several Christian Democratic parties in one country who had to unite as a national Equipe to belong to the EUCD. That suited the German parties, the CDU and CSU, and even more the three Dutch Christian parties, KVP, CHU, and ARP, though they were rivals in domestic politics.

It was again the French, but only the French – the Belgians having accepted the new order in the early sixties – who could not decide whether their party should join the EUCD. The MRP's successor party, the Centre Démocrate, led by Jean Lecanuet, wanted to be an 'open' party. And in fact prominent figures from the liberal camp (though pro-gressively fewer of them) joined. This fact excluded their being tied into the Christian Democratic family of parties. Until 1976, the French Equipe was led by Senate President Alain Poher; after that, the Centre des Démocrates Sociaux (CDS) was founded, and immediately joined the EUCD.

Over the first decade of the EUCD's existence, the following parties were members: the Christlich-Demokratische Union Deutschlands (CDU) and the Bavarian Christlich-Soziale Union (CSU), the Italian Democrazia Cristiana (DC), the Austrian Volkspartei (ÖVP), the Swiss Christlich-Demokratische Partei (CVP/PDC), the Parti Social-Chrétien (PSC) and the Christelijke Volkspartij (CVP) in Belgium, the Luxembourg Christlich-Soziale Volkspartei (CSV), the Partito Democratico Cristiano (PDCSM) in San Marino, the Maltese Partit Nazzjonalista (PN), and the Dutch Katholieke Volkspartij (KVP), the Christelik Historische Unie (CHU), and the Antirevolutionaire Partij (ARP). In 1972 a Spanish Equipe consisting of Castillian Christian Democratic groups and parties (Izquierda Democratica, Federacion Popular Democratica) was accepted into the EUCD, along with the Union Democratica del Pais Valenciano, from Valencia, the Catalan Union Democratica de Cataluna (UDC), and the Basque Partido Nacionalista Vasco (PNV). And in 1974 the Portuguese Centro Democratico Social (CDS) joined too.

There was a simple procedure for electing new members: the Political Bureau nominated from its ranks a small committee to look into the principles, programme, politics, meaning, and behaviour in coalition of applicant parties. The Political Bureau made its decision on the basis of the report's findings, and the committee's recommendations.

There are no permanent alliances between the parties, rather natural ties, as were found in the NEI period between German-speaking parties (CDU, ÖVP, Swiss PSC), between Benelux countries, and between Italian, French, and Spanish parties. By contrast, political alliances evolve as a result of concrete problems. Beyond that, it is also worth remarking that medium-sized parties – as with medium-sized states – often have more enthusiasm for international co-operation than many large parties, which are in a stronger position to pursue an independent foreign policy.[4]

STRUCTURE AND WORKING METHODS

The constitution laid down the EUCD's tasks: deepening the Christian Democrats' guiding maxims, and encouraging political studies; nurturing the tradition of Christian humanism, democracy, and social justice; spreading ideas and information about the achievements of Christian Democracy. It should be the aim of the EUCD to:

to develop a permanent, close co-operation between Christian Democratic parties in Europe, leading to a common policy of creating a federated Europe.[5]

The congress to lay out political base-lines was supposed to be convened every three years. There were four EUCD congresses between 1965 and 1978: in Taormina (1965), in Venice (1968), in Bonn (1973), and in Berlin (1978), that is, twice in Italy and twice in Germany. This is an indication of the growing influence of Democrazia Cristiana and of the two German 'Union' parties, especially the CDU, in international and European co-operation. The choice of personnel also reflected the dominant role of the Italians and Germans: Mariano Rumor's successor as President in 1973 was Kai-Uwe von Hassel, while Tindemans was succeeded as Secretary General by the Italian Arnaldo Forlani (1974–8).

Within the political guidelines laid down by congress, the Political Bureau decided all practical and political questions, meeting at least twice a year, but in practice usually three or four times annually. The Bureau also elected the President, Vice-Presidents, and the Secretary General. The President, four Vice-Presidents, Secretary General, President of the European Union of Young Christian Democrats (EUYCD), the Chairmen and two further representatives of the Christian Democratic groups in the European Parliament and the Council of Europe, former EUCD Presidents, Presidents of European bodies who belonged to member parties, and five delegates (originally: Chairman, Secretary General, international secretary, and two representatives of national parliamentary groups) per member party or Equipe, independent of the strength or political importance of the group in question.

This last condition led, for instance, to the San Marino party alone having as many votes as the two German Union parties together, since they formed a single national Equipe. It underlines the fundamentally accepted, but in practice much-criticised confederal character of the EUCD's structure. But as things stood, the rules on representation were eventually irrelevant. The stronger, politically more important parties – whose larger financial contributions kept the organisation going – made their weight felt anyway. Finally, co-operation in the EUCD framework did not in practice mean formulating, and certainly not implementing, practical policies with substantive content. Rather, it served as a forum to exchange thoughts and information, to formulate ideas and strategies, to forge a certain consciousness and consensus.

One substantial innovation was that the EUCD, unlike the NEI, specifically took into account the possibilities offered by the now functioning European institutions. It was not just the representatives of national parties or national parliamentary groups who co-operated in EUCD bodies. Those who held office at European level, especially the leading figures in the two Christian Democratic parliamentary groups, in the Assembly of the Council of Europe, and in the European Parliament, also participated. This markedly improved internal communication and the everyday vitality of the organisation. Particularly the Christian Democratic Group in the European Parliament took over more and more tasks from the EUCD.

The EUCD's resources came from member party contributions calculated according to rules laid down by the Political Bureau. In practice, however, the organisation's work and many of its activities were made possible only because of considerable extra financial support and services provided by Democrazia Cristiana, whose offices housed the EUCD secretariat.

CONGRESSES

Political debates during the XVII Congress in Taormina (1965), whose slogan was The Democratic Future of Europe, concentrated on defending Community orthodoxy against Gaullist attacks on supranational institutions. What was demanded was a European Commission independent of governments, 'exclusively committed to the common good and to the community of nations,' the introduction of majority voting for decisions by the Council of Ministers; and a more important role for the European Parliament, along with direct elections.[6]

The theme of the XVIII Congress in Venice (1968) was Renewal of National Societies for the Benefit of an Integrated, Modern Europe. Decentralisation of state power, participation by citizens in democratic life, reform of economic structures, worker participation in decisions made by their enterprises – these were the catchphrases in debates and resolutions. They were supposed to answer the challenge 'of the yearnings of a younger generation, whose dissatisfactions are expressed in protest campaigns'. The congress insisted on classical demands relating to the Community's political and institutional development, but also stressed the need to 'improve co-ordination of measures taken by democratic parties'.[7]

The slogan of the XIX congress in Bonn (1973) was: The Christian Democrats for Progress in Freedom and Solidarity. At the centre of debate were the fundamental political issues thrown up by a changing society. Richard von Weizsäcker delivered the introductory report: his handwriting is also evident on the final resolution, which talks, *inter alia*, of satisfying the 'ethical hunger', the demand for 'an authentic reason for human existence', the improvement of the 'quality of life', concern for the fate of foreign workers, environmental protection, and the preservation of the cultural heritage.[8] Topical political problems, by contrast, were on the margins of the congress debate.

EUCD President Mariano Rumor, handing over office to Kai-Uwe von Hassel at the Bonn Congress, summarised his eight years at the head of the EUCD as follows:

> The Union has no leadership role as far as the member parties are concerned; common positions emerge from 'open debates aimed at reaching agreement on essential points in order to put them into practice together'. At the same time, it must not degenerate to being a mere 'club ... in which points of view are exchanged'. The EUCD must be open 'to the cultural and political project which has given the most fruitful impulses to action in the various countries'.[9]

A CHRISTIAN DEMOCRATIC DOCTRINE

A centrepiece of EUCD activity was, from the beginning, the attempt to create a consensus about Christian Democratic 'doctrine'; this was seen as a precondition for any joint effort to advance the cause of European union. The traditions and ideas of the member parties differed considerably, as did the spiritual and cultural climate in each of the countries in which they had to operate.

The Rome-based Christian Democratic Information and Documentation Centre (CIDCID) played an important role in this connection. It had been established as early as 1960 in conjunction with the setting up of the Christian Democratic World Union. To secure financing it had been 'Europeanised', so to speak, in 1968, and incorporated into the EUCD. It remained under the control of Karl-Josef Hahn, a Dutchman, who was to do the job from the institute's inception until it folded in 1978.[10] The institute took on the task of organising ideological, philosophical, and theoretical reflections and discussions about a Christian Democratic programme which was in tune with the times. To this end, it organised meetings of officials from the various member parties in charge of publications and education. In the course of the 1970s, it published *Christian Democratic Panorama*, a cultural magazine, which appeared in several languages. *Cahiers D'études*, which appeared at the same time, contained numerous studies and reports. It focused on basic social and political issues, and Christian Democratic parties' different political programmes and experiences. All these efforts were also put to the service of advancing dialogue with the Latin Americans in the framework of the World Union. Later, Roberto Papini, a leading contributor over many years to the work of the CIDCID, declared:

> The overriding importance of the centre is that it made possible the deepening of Christian Democratic culture at an international level, attempting to reconcile European parties' positions with those from Latin America.[11]

One important achievement in this area was that, on 12 February 1979, the EUCD Political Bureau, meeting in Paris, was able to agree on the Manifesto of Christian Democrats in Europe.[12] A little later, on 16 July 1976, the World Union's Political Bureau followed suit by passing the 'Political Manifesto'.[13] Much of this text was drawn up by an enthusiastic CIDCID working group (Idea and Action). It involved a compromise, in that it included the various elements that the parties insisted was part of their specific tradition: personalist-communal, Christian-social ideas, along with conceptions that were Christian-conservative, and pragmatic-centralist.

BETWEEN AN EC ORIENTATION AND THE 'CONSERVATIVE QUESTION'

From the early seventies onwards the EUCD was increasingly compelled to address itself to the question of whether, and how, the Conservatives should be involved in Christian-Democratic joint activities. The issue moved centre-stage after the United Kingdom joined the European Community in 1972. In the 1960s the British Conservatives, no doubt anxious to avoid isolation as well as to secure some kind of leading role, had adopted the practice of holding 'interparty conferences'. They took place on the fringe of the party conference proper, and developed into a forum for informal debate. Usually attended by Conservative representatives from the Scandinavian countries, there were also delegates from German, Austrian, and Swiss Christian-Democratic parties. As the EC took shape and its membership grew, British and Scandinavian Conservatives and Christian Democrats from the neutral countries felt a greater need for a more intensive flow of information and co-operation. The idea of establishing a grouping of parties making up the broad European centre had been mooted for quite some time.[14] The EUCD accordingly began to debate whether a 'democratic centre' should or could be created. The argument ended in stalemate at about the same time as the Christian-Democratic-oriented European People's Party (EPP) was set up in 1976. Prompted by similar practical considerations, the European Democrat Union (EDU) came into being too. Members of the latter body included all conservative parties, but only a smattering of EUCD parties.

As all these developments were in train it became apparent that the European party system would have to undergo radical changes. Spurred on by the continuing integration process, parties in EC countries were paying more attention to Community-related policies and institutional and procedural matters. Proceedings in EUCD bodies were increasingly overshadowed by the European Parliament's Christian Democratic Group, or by the parties represented in it. EUCD member parties from non-Community countries, and in particular the neutral Austrians and Swiss, felt increasingly that their interests were being neglected, and their views relegated to the sidelines. The 'Standing Conference of the Six', set up within the EUCD in 1970, failed to allay such anxieties. Nor did the 'Political Committee of CD Parties from the EC Countries', which was established two years later. However, both made for clarity and a rational division of tasks. The precarious situation brought about by these developments was exacerbated still further when the European People's Party was founded in 1976, and a crisis within the EUCD followed. It was a crisis destined to continue until the watershed year of 1989, when the collapse of communism opened up a new field of activity in Central Europe and the EUCD had a new *raison d'être*.

These two problems – the turbulence produced by rapid progress towards EC integration, and relations with the conservatives – sorely tested the EUCD's consensus. There was an incipient awareness of the need to form a 'European party'; it grew more and more evident as the EC's distinctive political system gradually emerged. The urgent questions became: which forces needed to be incorporated into such a party to ensure it carried as much weight as possible? And what would be its politics? These questions directly affected Christian Democracy's idea of itself, and had implications for its survival and the influence it might hope to wield in the future.

Following the EPP's foundation in 1976, the German member parties (CDU and CSU) were particularly anxious to include conservative parties in this 'Federation of Christian-Democratic Parties of the European Community'. Their goal was a common basis for action for large, representative, centre-right people's parties right across the Community.

6 The Christian Democratic Group in the European Parliament, 1952–1978

The grouping together of parliamentarians by political groups in the General Assembly of the European Coal and Steel Community (ECSC) was quite simply revolutionary. The mandate of those MPs nominated by national parliaments came from voters in member states; it gave them the right to represent them politically at home. The basic treaties for the European Communities provided a distribution of the seats only by member states. It had evidently been assumed that the Assembly would in practice divide up along national lines. The fact that this did not happen is why the Assembly became a politically influential body and, after the founding of the European Economic Community (EEC) and the European Atomic Community (EAC), would become the European Parliament.

BUILDING PARLIAMENTARY GROUPS IN THE EUROPEAN ASSEMBLIES

The Consultative Assembly of the Council of Europe was founded in 1949. Only much later, in the early 1960s, did like-minded parliamentarians from the different member countries unite in groups. It is hardly a criticism of the Christian Democratic Group that – compared to the group in the General Assembly or the European Parliament – it played a relatively minor role in building up a transnational party structure. One reason for this was evidently that this Assembly met less often, and co-operation imposed far fewer obligations on anyone.

The establishment of groups in the ECSC General Assembly was formally recognised in the resolution on 16 June 1953.[1] The first European Christian Democratic Group met on 23 June; it had 38 members (out of a total of 78 deputies). When the European Parliament (EP) was established in 1958 as the parliamentary organ of the three Communities (EEC, ECSC, EAC), Article 36 of the rules of procedure explicitly included the right to form parliamentary groups. The EP Christian

Democratic Group, which consisted of 66 deputies, stated in its own rules of procedure that membership was open to those belonging to a Christian Democratic party (according to their own definition of the term, and of the party's values).

Thanks to its smooth running and the first successes of the EEC, the European Parliament grew in importance. The group too became increasingly keen to improve inter-party co-operation. Members' national parties which had come together at European level did not automatically pursue the same policies, even if there was ideological agreement. The constant effort to find common positions led to the discovery of common fundamentals, and their importance to common action; it also led to better information, growing understanding, and finally to appreciation of how different the parties were from each other. The joint debate with opponents or competitors encouraged the feeling of belonging together.

> In building political will and establishing a common will, the central focus – in the Christian Democratic case, as elsewhere – is the plenary meeting of the whole group, and other group meetings'. [Their logic and purpose reside in] the political integration of the group, which is after all composed of various parties and nationalities. [An important function] of the group executive is to establish political goals, as well as determine parliamentary strategy. Composed of the leader, his two deputies, and seven members acting as spokesmen for the national delegations, the group executive has both a narrow and a broad form. The latter includes eight further members, all holding positions in the group (members of the parliament's presidium, committee chairmen, and former Presidents of Parliament). Group committees, working groups, and study seminars, all serve both practical parliamentary work and its preparation and discussion within the group. On the one hand, group committees...help to mould group opinion and political will in connection with issues dealt with by European Parliament committees. On the other, their job is to report to the group on committee work and results, and to use their expertise to prepare the group position for the plenary debate and votes. Working groups within a parliamentary group concern themselves...with fundamental and long-term political issues and problems.... Special meetings of the whole group, normally held twice a year in member states, have value as study days or conferences, a forum for thrashing out fundamental problems of European policy. But they are also a means of familiarising members with the special regional problems of the country in which the meeting is being held.[2]

CO-OPERATION WITH THE EUCD

For far too long, during the 1950s and 1960s, the European parliamentarians were exposed to the danger of isolation in Strasbourg and Luxembourg. The dual mandate which meant they had to be present at both national and European level placed a huge burden on everyone: in intellectual, practical, and physical terms. If something important was going on in a national parliament, the deputy could often be absent. And for the most part national problems overshadowed European issues because they were more urgent, and because they directly impinged on a deputy's position in his constituency, his party, or his parliamentary group. Colleagues in national parliamentary groups or parties were rarely in a position to deal with the complexity or range of European problems. As for the public, it was even more bewildered by the European dimension. Dialogue between European parliamentarians and their national parties and groups was the exception; co-operation was completely inadequate. Beyond that, the Nouvelles Equipes Nationales (NEI) had neglected to include the European Parliament element. Worse, inside the organisation there was a great deal less co-operation between the parties from the mid-1950s onwards. The European Christian Democratic Group found itself in a thoroughly unsatisfactory situation. It had no organic connection with an appropriate party organisation to support and encourage it. Its members had to operate without any solid substructure.

Until the creation of the European Union of Christian Democrats (EUCD) in the mid-1960s, nothing changed. The EUCD made increasing efforts to support the group in the European Parliament in facing up to the new tasks of the European Community as it developed and grew in importance.[3] Close contact with the EUCD was maintained through Alain Poher, President of the European Parliament from 1966 to 1969, and the chairman of the CD Group, Hans August Lücker (1969–75). At the same time, EUCD bodies were being properly established by its president, Mariano Rumor. Co-operation between the group and the federation of parties was eventually given institutional form with a new statute on 18 July 1971.

THE POLITICAL COMMITTEE

The constant improvement of integration in the European Community and the simultaneous, and growing, need to reach agreements between member states meant there had to be closer co-operation between their representatives. The next development, in April 1970, was an informal 'Standing Conference' of leading figures from EUCD member parties from EC countries. In April 1972 a special body was set up in the context of the EUCD: the 'Political Committee of Christian Democratic Parties from member states of the European Communities'. Its goal was

> a permanent link between the parties and parliamentary groups at national and European levels, as well as a basic political consensus about the deepening and further development of European integration.[4]

It really was about:

> creating an appropriate political structure, as a 'structure d'accueil' which could be used for a possible future European Christian Democratic party.[5]

The presidents of the EUCD and the CD Group co-chaired the executive of the Political Committee. This consisted of leading figures from parties in the EC and members of the group's executive in the European Parliament. This soon led to more and more contact and co-operation, which in turn encouraged single-minded political action. Joint conferences of the CD Group and representatives of national Christian Democratic parliamentary groups were organised. Working groups were set up involving a mixture of representatives of the CD Group, EUCD bodies, and/or member parties. Together they elaborated political programmes, forged a consensus in every area relevant to European policy, and clarified the main points of Christian Democratic ideology.

The leader of the parliamentary group in the European Parliament was *ex officio* on the EUCD Executive Committee as well. This offered the permanent possibility of consulting the EUCD leadership, and of maintaining contact – with chairmen of national parties and parliamentary groups, and with Christian Democratic heads of government and ministers. Hans-August Lücker was adept at exploiting all these possibilities in order to achieve the breakthrough to a 'European party'. It had been his goal, and that of a number of others, for some time.[6] On his re-election he assured his audience:

> that in the course of his new mandate he would continue to devote himself wholeheartedly to the interests of the parliamentary group and the European Union of Christian Democrats so that a European Christian Democratic Party could be founded, a party with a single political programme.[7]

The organic co-operation which had been achieved in this way was deepened and intensified during the presidency of Kai-Uwe von Hassel, who in 1973 succeeded Mariano Rumor as leader of the EUCD. However, the EUCD was still a relatively loose association of parties, many of them from non-EC countries. The founding of the Political Committee had already underlined the fact that it was not an adequate organisation as far as promoters of a 'European Federation'[8] were concerned. Members of the European Parliament were particularly dissatisfied. They badly missed an active party organisation at Community level.

Direct elections were in the air, and the EC political system was taking shape. The heads of state and government, at their meeting in Paris in 1972, had given notice that they intended to 'transform the totality of relations between member states...into a European Union before the end of this century.' The Community admitted a series of new members on 1 January 1973: Great Britain, Ireland, and Denmark. European Political Co-operation (EPC) was put in place, and discussion began on establishing an economic and currency union. A new European Community financial statute was to be agreed, and in this connection too it was argued that there should be 'no federal treasury without federation'; there must be reforms which would give Community institutions a federal shape.

FOCUSING ON DIRECT ELECTIONS

As early as 1970, during a study conference of European deputies from the Dutch Christian Democratic Equipe,[9] Tjerk Westenderp had recommended founding a European Christian Democratic party as both possible and necessary. He explained that European parties were needed for much the same reason as national parties: to enable citizens to participate, to formulate alternatives, to choose candidates, and to serve as a channel for new ideas.

> By the general election of the European Parliament in all member states at the latest all pre-conditions for the foundation of European parties will have been met.[10]

In the Dutch parliament a few days before, Westenderp had proposed for the prompt introduction of direct elections for national deputies to the European Parliament, as provided for in the Community treaties. The matter was becoming ever more urgent, both for European and for democratic reasons, he said. Soon afterwards, a parallel initiative for direct election of German European deputies was proposed by several CDU/CSU parliamentarians in the Bundestag. In several other countries there were similar attempts to ensure that direct elections to the European Parliament should follow national electoral laws until such time as European regulations had been agreed. There was evidently another motive for all this – to put pressure on governments to get moving on the issue of direct elections and democratisation.[11]

On 1 January 1973, parliamentary group leader Lücker sent EUCD president Rumor a note concerning 'the political activity of the CD Political Committee of the European Community in connection with the decisions of the October 1972 Paris Summit'. In this he demanded:

> an intensification of co-operation in the Political Committee as well as in the EP group's communication with groups in the national parliaments...But this alone will not be enough. Such work must be pursued more systematically, make a far more effective impact on the activities of national parties and parliamentary groups, and eventually be carried into popular political consciousness. This is impossible without appropriate personnel and financial resources. It is true that the existing organisational structures can be used, but not that they take on the whole of this new task, for which the organisation was not intended, and for which it is not equipped. [A political programme had to be elaborated] whose declarations on all the important areas in political life can be jointly presented by parties across the Community as their joint election manifesto for the direct elections to the European Parliament. [To get through the work needed to prepare for the European elections] the Political Committee must engage its own Secretary General, based in Brussels. [The rule that the parliamentary group's Secretary General should double as Secretary General of the Political Committee was also less and less sustainable: increasing demands were being made of the parliamentary group. He also indicated that the CD Group in the EP intended to create a political institute in the form of a foundation, which might be given the honorary designation of, for instance, the 'Robert Schuman Foundation'.][12]

The idea of giving the Political Committee its own Secretary General in order to take a further step towards independence and the creation of a 'European party', was not put into practice. The move was vetoed by the group's Secretary General, Alfredo De Poi, who saw a threat to his own political function, and a risk of damaging co-ordination between the two bodies. All in all, Lücker's proposals proved premature. But they did show the way things were supposed to develop, even if realising those plans was to be delayed for a while.

ON THE WAY TO BECOMING A EUROPEAN PARTY

It was indeed 'already in the logic of things that Christian Democrats were thinking of building a European Christian Democratic party – it emerged from all the forms and processes of their European co-operation ... and the external impulse for this' would be 'the direct elections to the European Parliament'.[13]

From the start, there was not enough agreement about how to proceed with constructing this 'European party', and particularly about its political/ideological profile. The European Union of Young Christian Democrats, for instance, took the revolutionary position that national Christian Democratic parties should be replaced by 'one large Christian Democratic party'. This emerged from a declaration made at their meeting in Malta on 15 May 1972:

> A party which will give popular expression to political participation in the framework of free, communal institutions; it should be marked by a progressive spirit and find coherence in the anti-fascist tradition. This party will solve current problems which national political forces cannot deal with because they are too small.[14]

The dominant doctrine, by contrast, was expressed in a contribution by Robert Houben, head of the Belgian member party's scientific educational institute:

> Both political integration of the kind we are striving for, and the fact that the European Parliament exists, pose the question of forming parties at European level....At the same time, to be realistic, we must assume that a party at European level will only take shape gradually, and in fact will start from what exists; just as European union can probably only come about through the development of the Common Market to an Economic and Currency Union, and then on to political integration, which will have to take into account a transition period and a great deal of patience....Building a party at European level, and the further development of European integration, have to develop in parallel and at the same pace.[15]

Starting from what existed, that was how the 'European party' of Christian Democrats was to take shape. What existed was the European Union of Christian Democrats, the Christian Democratic Group in the European Parliament, and the Committee of Christian Democratic Parties in the member states of the European Communities. The latter brought together the two traditional structures, the union of parties and the parliamentary group. And it was above all in this committee that decisions were reached which would finally lead to the foundation of the European People's Party.

7 Founding the European People's Party, 1976–1978

European Community heads of state and government decided in December 1974 to fix the date of the first direct elections to the European Parliament for 1978.[1] The 'Political Committee of Christian Democratic Parties from EC Member States' began discussion of the practical preparations for these as early as spring 1975. Discussions about ideas were going on everywhere. In Bonn, for instance, acting on behalf of EUCD President Kai-Uwe von Hassel, Heinrich Böx, head of the CDU's office for foreign relations, was the man behind a small study group. With the foundation of a 'European People's Party' in its sights, it discussed questions of strategy, a political programme, and an organisational structure, and it prepared documents for the German delegation in the Political Committee.

STAGE BY STAGE

In September 1975 an *ad hoc* working group with the name 'European Party' was set up under the joint chairmanship of Wilfried Martens, president of the Flemish CVP, and Hans August Lücker.[2] Members were the Deputy Secretaries General of the EUCD, Karl J. Hahn (NL) and Heinrich Böx (D), the Secretary General of the CD Group Alfredo De Poi (I), and the Executive Secretary of the EUCD, Josef Müller (D). The working group was given the task of 'elaborating the basic documents for founding a Christian Democratic party with reference to direct elections to the European Parliament', in other words' a constitution and a programme. The working group met several times between November 1975 and January 1976, and in Paris on 20 February and was able to present the Political Committee with a draft constitution.[2]

Having checked the draft, which was rapidly agreed, the Political Committee meeting in Brussels on 29 April 1976, decided to found the 'European People's Party. Federation of European Community Christian Democratic Parties', and the constitution was accepted.[3]

The formal foundation of the European People's Party took place in the framework of a meeting of the Political Bureau in Luxembourg on 8 July 1976.[4] Representatives of the following parties took part: Christelijke

Volkspartij (CVP) and the Parti Social Chrétien (PSC) from Belgium; Christlich-Demokratische Union (CDU) and Christlich-Soziale Union (CSU) from Germany; Centre des Démocrates Sociaux (CDS) from France; Fine Gael (FG) from Ireland; Democrazia Cristiana (DC) from Italy; Christlich-Soziale Volkspartei (CSV) from Luxembourg; Catholic People's Party (KPV), Anti-Revolutionary Party (ARP) and the Christian-Humanist Union (CHU) from the Netherlands.

Leo Tindemans, Prime Minister of Belgium (and former Secretary General of the EUCD) was unanimously elected President. The EUCD president, Kai-Uwe von Hassel, and the Chairman of the CD parliamentary Group, Alfred Bertrand, became (in accordance with the rules of procedure) *ex officio* Vice-Presidents of the EPP. Further Vice-Presidents were elected: Norbert Schmelzer (NL), André Colin (F), and Dario Antoniozzi (I). Former Bundestag and European Parliament member Josef Müller had been the EUCD's executive secretary in Brussels since 1973 (while the general secretariat was in Rome) and was given the task of building up the general secretariat. He would for the time being run things in tandem with the CD group Secretary General, Gianpaolo Bettamio.

This did not complete the ground-breaking phase of the party. It included agreement on the political programme by the EPP's first congress in Brussels on 6/7 March 1978. The proposal elaborated by rapporteurs Martens and Lücker was accepted without amendment: it had already been agreed by the Political Bureau, which had discussed it several times.[5] On the margin of the congress, at the initiative of those present, the Political Bureau also elected a Secretary General, Jean Seitlinger. A member of the French National Assembly, he had in the early 1960s been the last Secretary General of the Nouvelles Equipes.

Alfred Bertrand had meanwhile been succeeded as group chairman by Egon Klepsch, and was elected treasurer, completing the leadership. On 14 March a week later, the Christian Democratic Group decided to rename itself the 'Group of the European People's Party' – and the structure of the EPP was complete.

The need for the EPP was above all felt by Christian Democratic deputies. In the early days they had worked together to unite as a parliamentary group in the Assembly of the Coal and Steel Community, and later in the European Parliament. As things progressed they felt a greater need for a European party organisation. On top of that came the interest of national parties to run a co-ordinated campaign for the first direct elections to the European Parliament. Party leaders were also more and more aware of the political and operational possibilities offered by closer co-operation in an increasingly integrated Community.

THE CONTROVERSY ABOUT THE NAME

Agreement had quickly been reached about the structure of the new party, and how it would be built up. From the outset there was a consensus about the goal – the creation of a political party. But naming the baby was more difficult. The draft constitution put before the Political Committee had not resolved the issue. It had not yet been discussed, and it remained contentious – the name would define the party's ideology, its alignment, and its political profile. A name signals not only who is delivering the message, it also gives an idea of whom the message is for.

The quarrel was detonated by the strategic question of whether the British and Danish conservatives – whose deputies in the European Parliament had formed their own 'Democratic Group' – should be invited to join the future European People's Party. Those in favour argued for a choice of name which avoided the description 'Christian Democratic', which they felt was too narrow and exclusive. Those against such an invitation, in other words those who wanted to give the party an unambiguously Christian Democratic character, argued that this should also be reflected in the name. There should be no possibility of misunderstandings.

Above all the Germans favoured a 'strategy of opening'. Their arguments were evidently based on their own experience and tradition. Both CDU and CSU owed their strength relative to sister parties elsewhere in Europe to being able to integrate conservative (and liberal) forces. Against them, the Italian representatives of Democrazia Cristiana, along with the Dutch and Belgian parties, insisted on emphasizing a Christian Democratic identity. They saw this as important to the party's *raison d'être* and political direction, and essential if their action in helping to found a European party was to be successful in their own countries. Its identity, its political profile – and therefore the party's whole coherence and effectiveness would, it was argued, be hopelessly compromised if the conservatives were allowed to join in at this crucial early stage. The other founder parties, from Luxembourg, Ireland, and France agreed with this.[6]

To compromise with the Germans it was accepted that soundings would be taken among other like-minded parties in order to establish a common platform, the 'Democratic Centre committed to European unity and social progress'. This was not meant to be a party:

> What we had in mind was rather an association, like a political club, to provide the framework for meetings and discussions between the leading political figures in member parties and parliamentary groups. The final impulse for these ideas was the political alliance of the

Socialists with the French Communist Party, as well as the development of some EC Communist parties to 'Euro-Communism'. These were plainly efforts to achieve a joint political structure involving both Socialist and Social Democratic parties.[7]

In no circumstances was such an initiative to be pursued at the cost of the effectiveness of the European party of Christian Democrats. In September 1975, following a proposal by Hans August Lücker, a working group with the name 'Democratic Centre' was set up alongside the European Party working group. However, it achieved nothing.

There was, therefore, a clear majority against bringing in the conservatives. But as far as the name question was concerned, a compromise was found. The idea of a 'People's Party' signalled both the openness the Germans wanted and connection to the Christian Democratic tradition. Numerous past and present Christian-inspired parties, and parties with a Christian Democratic or Christian Social orientation, had similar names. For example, (to mention only parties in EC member states), there was the Italian People's Party, in France the Democratic Peoples Party (PDP) and the Republican People's Movement (MRP), Belgium's Christian People's Party (CVP), the Dutch Catholic People's Party (KPV), and the Christian-Social People's Party (CSV) in Luxembourg.

To safeguard identity, and so to speak as a 'guarantee', below the official title 'European People's Party' was a sub-title, the description 'Federation of the Christian Democratic Parties of the European Community'. Since this was clumsy, however, the sub-title was understandably rarely used. Indeed it was soon forgotten.

A FEDERATIVE PARTY

Apart from its compromise character, the name did express a bold challenge and an honest judgement by the founders. It was bold since they were aiming high by calling the EPP a party, and setting a goal whose realisation seemed to many, at the time, a chimera. They were honest in that the sub-title expressed what it was all really about, namely an association of parties. There was a dynamic tension between that forward-looking claim to being a European party 'in the making', and the realistic insight that it could for the moment be no more than a European association of national parties. And it was out of that fruitful tension that, over the coming years, the EPP was to develop.

The EPP could not and did not want, as a European party, to copy any national model. Unlike national parties, no single model informs every part of its organisation. The EPP respects the existing, established, and valued structures of its member parties. It builds on them and depends on them. In other words, the EPP is a federative party which organises common action by its members at European level, and seeks to ensure they are politically supported. That is also expressed in the constitution.

> The parties and 'équipes' which are members of the party retain their [own] names, their identities, and their freedom of action within the framework of their national responsibilities. (Article 2)

> The party ensures close, permanent co-operation between its member parties and 'équipes' in order to realise a European federation through joint policies. In particular…it advances, co-ordinates, and organises European actions by its members. (Article 3)

Two categories of membership were foreseen for the various party bodies, the Executive Committee, Political Bureau, and Congress. One sort of membership would be the representatives of member parties or – where there was more than one member party in a country – the national Equipe. Their number would be determined by the proportion of national deputies in the EPP Group. The other category would consist of elected deputies or office holders belonging to member parties in the European Parliament, the European Commission, the EPP Group, and associations recognised by the EPP, as well, obviously, as the President of the EPP itself, its Vice-Presidents, Treasurer, and Secretary General. Every decision would require an absolute majority of members present, a rule which reflected the party's supranational and democratic character.

THE POLITICAL PROGRAMME

The political programme decided by the EPP's first congress evinced considerable consensus about almost all European political issues, many of them with profound socio-political implications. The programme expressed a joint intention to develop and complete integration in the context of the European Community, leading to a political union equipped with federal and democratic institutions.

The rapporteurs, Wilfried Martens and Hans August Lücker, had been able to base their draft on productive preparatory work and agreed, documented common positions. The years prior to the foundation of the EPP had been fruitful for the Christian Democrats in terms of developing political programmes. Nearly all European parties had discussed basic and action programmes, and either decided on them or were in the process of doing so. The reasons for this can be traced, above all, to the general change in the socio-political climate resulting from the revolt of 1968. This especially affected Christian Democratic parties because it was those parties which had generally been in government since the war. But at the same time new questions were being raised by developments in European politics and their cultural, economic, and socio-political implications.

Beyond that, particular internal-political circumstances, in Germany and the Netherlands for instance, necessitated intensive – and extensive – efforts. In Germany, where the CDU and CSU had been in opposition since the autumn of 1969, it was a matter of a radical new direction. The first phase of this would come as a result of the second edition of the 1968 Berlin Programme (Düsseldorf Party Congress, 1971); the party congresses in Hamburg (1973) and Mannheim (1975) completed this text with important decisions on socio-political issues, as well as with up-dated domestic and foreign policies. A Basic Programme Committee had been working since 1973, and made its draft proposals in 1976. In the Netherlands, the three Christian confessional parties (ARP, CHU, and KVP), looking ahead to uniting as one Christian Democratic party, had conducted an intensive debate about the inspiration and contents of their policy; they published the results in 1975.[8]

All these multifaceted labours yielded the raw material for the rapporteurs, and for everyone else involved in developing the policies of the EPP or participating in the debate. This material included specialised programmes as well as important statements on key issues, election programmes, and – not least – work done by the Christian Democratic Group in the European Parliament. Thanks to the work of the Konrad Adenauer Foundation, synopses and comparative analyses were available. The 'Manifesto of European Christian Democrats', passed by the EUCD Political Bureau in Paris on February 21, 1976, served as the basic document. The 'Political Manifesto of the World Union of Christian Democrats' was also helpful. This had been passed by the EUCD Political Bureau in Rome on 16 July 1976. Both texts, in whose formulation Lücker had an active hand, contained detailed expositions of basic precepts of Christian Democratic policy; they also set out the basic conceptual framework.[9]

The EPP Political Programme declarations were arranged into five chapters under the slogan 'Together for a Europe of Free People'. These were: Our guidelines for Europe, Europe in the world, European Community policy, The Community's institutional dynamics, and Our goal – a united Europe. Starting from a consensus on principles about man and society, the political chapters contain an action programme which –

given the exercise had never been tried before – is already unusually concrete and detailed.[10]

Compared with equivalent texts passed at the same time by the European organisations of the Social Democratic and Liberal parties, the EPP's Political Programme is unique in its attempt to respond fully and in detail to relevant issues. The Social Democrats' Appeal to the Electorate, passed by the federation's Congress in Brussels in January 1979, 'does not go … beyond a brief presentation of global aims'. As for the Liberals' Election Programme, voted through by the federation's congress in Brussels in November 1977, 'only general theses [are] binding…. Statements offering detailed proposals and solutions to political problems are, as far as the parties are concerned, optional and subject to interpretation.'[11]

THE EUCD CRISIS

The CDU and CSU delegates had failed to win adequate support from other parties for 'opening' the EPP, though they had reached a compromise on the question of the name. But this was not the end of the matter. The Germans sought other ways to unite the forces of the centre. Within the EUCD and the EPP, they called for a dialogue to be established with conservative parties, reactivating the 'democratic centre' idea. A working party to foster such a dialogue held two meetings, in December 1977 and in April 1978, under the chairmanship of the EUCD President (and EPP Vice-President), Kai-Uwe von Hassel. A draft 'dialogue paper' submitted by the CDU/CSU delegation stipulated that member parties had to pledge primary support to the EPP, since this was the only Europe-wide federation of parties to which they belonged. It was proposed that a 'working group' be set up in parallel to the EPP to provide a platform for co-operation among all non-Socialist, anti-collectivist centre-right parties across the whole of Europe.[12]

Once the EPP had been founded, a degree of pressure to establish relatively formal links between Christian Democratic and conservative forces was also exerted by EUCD parties that felt excluded from the EPP. An express stipulation had been made in the EPP Constitution (Article 4) to the effect that only parties from Community member states were eligible to join. On 28 October 1976, the EPP Bureau decided that no other parties should be granted associate membership or even observer status. In this matter too, the parties that set particular store by their Christian Democratic identity proved to be the most hawkish. They set their faces against any dilution of the supranational and federalist approach that had inspired the formation of the EPP as a party designed to operate in the EC system.

The Austrian People's Party and the Christian Democratic People's Party of Switzerland responded by drafting a joint memorandum on 23 November 1976. They wanted a revision of rules and decisions which they regarded as discriminatory, and they wanted a mechanism allowing EUCD parties to work with the EPP.[13] They were turned down.

Apart from the negative psychological effects this had, there was the practical consequence that the EUCD developed into a 'waiting room club'.[14] The result was that some of those affected – namely the parties from Austria, Switzerland, Portugal, Spain, and Malta – felt the need to look for an alternative. They found it in the EDU, whose champions commended it as an alternative:

> The downgrading of the EUCD to a rump could be averted by the creation of the European Democratic Union (EDU), which would include conservative and other centre parties alike. The EUCD could operate under the EDU umbrella as a grouping of Christian Democratic parties.[15]

The effect was the awkward situation that the tough insistence on a federal European ideal helped ensure that the EDU model, the very model they were trying to resist, had a real chance of success.

THE FOUNDING OF THE EDU

The EDU project of closer co-operation between Christian Democrats, conservatives, and other 'like-minded parties', was in the tradition of so-called 'inter-party conferences'. These had convened regularly since the 1960s, informally bringing together leading personalities from interested parties. The Austrian People's Party (ÖVP) was particularly keen on fleshing out this idea and creating an organisation; it was to play a leading part both in founding the EDU and developing it. The German parties were very enthusiastic too, as was the British Conservative Party.

On the basis of their own experience, the Germans were trying to 'normalise' things at European level. No doubt they thought it utterly perverse that they were not able to work together in the same grouping as their natural partners, the British Conservatives. This was a party in a member state which was a key player both in European policy and policy on the German Question. The principal British concern was to break out of their isolation. But in the end they too were looking for a new order, one consonant with the adversarial nature of their system of government – an order which pooled together anti-Socialist forces. A resolution at the 1975 British Conservative Party Conference called for the party to cultivate European allies:

> Recognizing that the United Kingdom is now a permanent member of the European Community…[the party] should work more closely with our political allies in Europe with a view to forming a moderate centre-right alliance (a 'European Democrat Party') that could effectively counter Socialist coalition tactics in the European Parliament, and take positive initiatives on European construction.[16]

Immediately after the EPP was set up, preparations were put in hand to found the EDU as an 'association of Christian Democratic and other non-collectivist parties'. The constitution was agreed at a meeting in Munich in October 1977; December the same year saw agreement, at a meeting in Vienna, on the issue of finance, and the European Democrat Union officially came into being at Schloss Klessheim, near Salzburg, on 24 April 1978.[17]

Once the EDU was in place, it became pointless for the EPP member parties to make any further attempt to agree a joint strategy for organised dialogue with the Conservatives. Belgian, Dutch, Italian, and French members of the EPP felt basic mutual trust had been put in question, and protested. There was a 'time-consuming and heated discussion about the EDU' at the May 1978 meeting of the EPP Political Bureau in Dublin, where the final version of the Political Programme was supposed to be decided on the basis of the EPP Congress debates and resolutions. It was true that the founding of the EDU, within a few weeks of the EPP's successful first Congress, had an extraordinarily 'negative, divisive effect, tarnishing the image of the EPP'.[18]

'Simultaneous membership of the EPP and the EDU is bigamy', was the view of the Walloon PSC leader, Charles Ferdinand Nothomb. Henning Wegener, head of the CDU department of foreign relations from 1977 onwards, quoted Nothomb back to his party leadership. 'The formation of the EDU has caused serious ill-feeling in the EPP', he said. 'Patient, painstaking explanation will be required to dispel it'. Addressing EPP bodies, he defended his party's view that the CDU considered the foundation of the EDU to be necessary:

> to forge links with like-minded parties in European countries where, for historical reasons, the Christian Democratic movement had not taken root; to pave the way for solid, non-collectivist, majorities in

the future European Parliament, and to offer a home to sister parties from European countries that did not yet belong to the European Community.[19]

So the advent of the EPP as a specifically Christian Democratic European party, with supranational ambitions, led to a crisis within the EUCD, from which the EPP had sprung. It also led to the founding of the EDU, which was intended both as an alternative and a complement to the EPP. Subsequently, the EPP, EUCD, and EDU – as was to be expected given their common origin – behaved like communicating vessels. There were frictions. By their nature, like national political organisations, international ones strive for autonomy, for a distinct identity, and for dominance. They invariably find subordination to, or dependence on, rivals hard to bear. In practice, a balance of sorts was struck, based on – generally – respecting a division of responsibilities. Things calmed down, but relations remained volatile.

Part III
The Evolution of the European People's Party

8 Congresses and European Elections, 1979–1990

Congresses and elections are the highlights of a political party's life and of its history. Congresses bring out the festive, stately sides of a party's character, and elections its combativeness and sense of adventure. Congresses serve parties' need to present themselves, reassure themselves, to reinforce their self-confidence. Elections are a time for parties to stand up to their rivals and their opponents, and for others – namely the voters – to weigh them in the balance. Elections are the moment of truth.

That was how things began for the European parties, which came into existence because of the first direct elections to the European Parliament. Their development has remained tied to the results of European elections held every five years since 1979. The strength or weakness of a European party is essentially the function of the number of deputies it has in its European Parliamentary group, in other words, the member parties' electoral success, or lack of it in the individual countries.

Primarily it is national parties and their candidates who are up for election. European elections are elections in member states; they are run according to national electoral laws, sometimes radically different from each other. This corresponds to the character of the European Community's political system. It is made up of nation states, and is thus largely determined by the various national systems. That is why, despite several attempts during the 1980s, it has still not been possible to introduce a common electoral system, although Article 138 of the EC treaty gives the European Parliament the right to propose one.

However, even if a single electoral system were introduced, national member organisations of the European Parliament would be the protagonists in any European election. They are on their own turf, know the voters and their specific problems. They speak their language and last but not least, they have the resources and the machinery needed to mount an election campaign.

The EPP leadership knew all this, and from the start decided to limit its activities at European elections to what member parties were not in a position to do, but which the EPP could. There were two. First, there was the elaboration of, and forging agreement on, common electoral programmes as a basis for common policies. These served as a demonstration of the solidarity of the

73

various member parties, and the coherence of what they had to offer. Second, the EPP could facilitate communication and consultation between parties on preparing and executing election campaigns, and making sure member parties in individual countries did not give an excessively different account of themselves. At the very least, this was designed to ensure that the way national parties presented themselves was, as far as possible, in line with the same ideas – or at the very least, compatible with them.

II   CONGRESS AND THE FIRST DIRECT ELECTIONS TO THE EUROPEAN PARLIAMENT, 1979

The EPP's II Congress took place on 22 and 23 February 1979, again in Brussels. Its central task was to prepare the imminent first direct elections to the European Parliament, above all to decide on the electoral platform. This had tightened up and updated large parts of the 1978 political programme. Congress approved a text proposed by rapporteur Hans August Lücker, voted through by the programme committee chaired by Wilfried Martens, and agreed by the party's executive bodies.[1]

The individual chapters of the electoral platform were put to Congress and justified by Garret FitzGerald: A Europe of Freedom and Solidarity; Pierre Pflimlin: A Responsible Europe; Luigi Granelli: A Democratic Europe Open to the Outside [world]; Pierre Werner: A Europe of Economic and Social Progress and Full Employment; and Alfons Goppel: A Europe of Freedom, Security, and Peace.[2]

Member parties, to varying degrees, tried to appear consistent in the campaign, making reference to the EPP platform and the common political programme agreed by the I Congress in March 1978. The EPP leadership could exercise a certain influence as far as uniform presentation was concerned in individual countries. This was thanks to the financial resources the European Parliament put at the disposal of parliamentary groups, or the political forces of which they were made up. These were intended to pay for spreading information and publicity about the direct elections. The Political Bureau and the EPP secretariat tried to co-ordinate the publicity campaigns. Some events with a European flavour with well-known politicians of different nationalities could be run jointly with national parties.

EPP parties were very successful in these direct European elections. Altogether they attracted 32.6m votes, 29.6 per cent of the electorate; it was a better result than the Socialists, who managed only 29.3m votes (26.6 per cent), even though the EPP was not represented in Great Britain or Denmark, and the Social Democrats had member parties throughout the EC.

The divergent electoral laws, and the fact that obtaining a mandate required very different numbers of votes in different member states, had the curious effect of putting the EPP Group and its 107 deputies in second place in the European Parliament – behind the Social Democratic Group, which had 112 members.

III   CONGRESS, COLOGNE 1980

The III EPP Congress took place in Cologne on 1 and 2 September 1980, a full year after the first direct elections. At issue was the process of staking out a position. The overall theme was The Christian Democrats in the Eighties – securing Freedom and Peace, Completing Europe. The main speakers were Flaminio Piccoli, the Democrazia Cristiana Political Secretary, and Jean Lecanuet, President of the Centre des Démocrates Sociaux. Their subjects were: East-West relations, the energy crisis, the international currency and financial issues, the further development of the European Community to Political Union. Agreeing on the principal party lines, but with different emphases, they analysed the problems and marked out the political framework with which Christian Democrats would have to face up to the challenges of the next decade.

This Congress took place in Germany, not least because of the imminent Bundestag elections on 5 October. In that sense it was an EPP contribution to the Union parties' election campaign. Their candidate for Chancellor, Franz-Josef Strauss, used the opportunity to present his programme to an international public. He appealed to Europe's Christian Democrats and particularly to those with government responsibility in their countries:

> to accelerate the realisation of European Union despite all the well-known difficulties. Thus Europe, as a strong second pillar of the Atlantic Community of values within the Nato alliance, can be true to its historic calling and to its role on the world political stage. On that too depends the free and peaceful future of Europe and of its peoples.[3]

With the greater responsibilities it now bore as a result of the direct elections to the European Parliament, the EPP – like the other parties, and parliamentary groups – needed to develop clear, concrete policies within the European Community. That meant that the Congress – for all the agreement on basic issues – pointed out political differences, too. For instance, the consideration of measures to overcome unemployment was referred to the Political Bureau, since no agreement could be reached.[4]

Much of the debate concerned the future of the EPP itself: organisational and financial problems were handled in the same way as questions of internal coherence and the party's profile in terms of its political programme.

IV CONGRESS, PARIS 1982

The IV Congress took place in Paris between 6 and 8 December 1982, under the slogan Preserve Peace – Create Peace – Unite Europe. Several programme texts were discussed and agreed:

> two on foreign political subjects (Freedom in Peace and Security; Development Policy, a Duty of Solidarity and a Vital European Responsibility), two on social policy (Internal Peace – Economic and Social Policy; Action Programme for Small and Medium-sized Businesses in the European Community) and a resolution on the institutional strategy of the EPP.[5]

For the first time, CDU chairman Helmut Kohl took part at an EPP Congress as Chancellor, having won this office for the first time a few weeks before. On 1 January 1983, the new federal government he led would take its turn as President of the EC Council. Kohl used his appearance at the EPP Congress to signal initiatives which would advance the Community on the road to European Union:

> If we fail to make the decisive step forward during this decade, we will have wasted a historic opportunity; we must not delay European unity in the hope that better times and conditions will arrive and allow us to start all over again.[6]

Paolo Barbi had succeeded Egon Klepsch as chairman of the EPP Group at the beginning of the year. Both critical and constructive, his fiery speech to Congress called for a better-organised EPP operation, and a beefed-up secretariat which must be set to work continuously. In particular, he said, the EPP secretariat must be in a position – on the basis of precise knowledge of the problems, and of mainstream opinion in the member parties – to take responsibility for identifying common positions, and drafting practical proposals.[7]

V CONGRESS, ROME 1984

With imminent direct elections to the European Parliament in June 1984, the V Congress held in Rome on 2 to 4 April 1984, was mainly concerned with agreeing and presenting an action programme. A proposal by Arie Oostlander, director of the Dutch CDA's Scientific Institute, had been elaborated by a programme committee chaired by the secretary-general. After exhaustive discussion, the Political Bureau unanimously approved the text. Neither the text, nor proposed amendments, were to be discussed. Indeed the whole point of the Congress was to have the action programme endorsed by acclamation. Speakers also had to limit themselves to commenting on, and publicising, the policies set out in the programme.

This process demonstrated not just anxiety about being seen to agree. It also showed an aversion to open, democratic debate – in other words, a lack of mutual trust. The unanimity rule flagrantly contradicted the EPP's pretension to being a party. However, it didn't matter very much. Public consciousness, and so the electorate, was very far from being sensitised enough to take offence. And the competition, the Social Democrats and the Liberals, had not yet got any further along this road. On the contrary. The EPP Action Programme was designed to be comprehensive, omitted no important issue, and was also very progressive in its statements on European policy. Both the Social Democrats and the Liberals had little more to offer than general declarations.

The four chapters of the Action Programme for the Second Legislature of the European Parliament dealt with the principal tasks and goals of European policy. These were: More Jobs and Employment in Europe – For Human Development in a Viable Europe – For a Stable Peace based on Justice and Solidarity – More Democracy and Unity in Europe. An introductory chapter dealt with the basic convictions which informed the programme: Opting for Europe – More Jobs through Economic Recovery – Possibilities for the Citizen – Caring for the Environment and Nature – A Just Peace.[8]

The detailed text again reflects serious efforts to deal with a series of existing problems. There had to be proposals which were as specific as possible. So, apart from analytical observations and statements of principle, every chapter also contained lists of demands which were binding on the party. Compared to the 1978 Action Programme, which was conceived more like a basic programme than as an action programme, this text evinced a new kind of consensus. It reflected systematic and continuous co-operation in the EPP structures, notably in the EPP Group during the previous legislature.

The Action Programme's closing sentences expressed a new confidence which had come from the experience of unity and acting together:

> The EPP occupies a key position in the European Parliament, with the political power of substantially influencing the decision-making process.

The EPP is the party which steadfastly, determinedly, and unanimously stands for the creation of a United States of Europe.

Christian Democrats in Europe are federalists. Their efforts are directed towards social justice and harmonious co-operation. They are guided by the realistic conviction that only a united Europe will advance the well-being of its citizens.

The Congress was held in what, for these purposes, was a thoroughly unsuitable hotel on the periphery of Rome. Proceedings suffered not just from public indifference, but from the fact that the leadership of the Italian host party seemed neither politically engaged, nor over-interested in organising the event. Ciriaco De Mita, their Political Secretary, carried the final responsibility for this. Throughout his entire period of office, from 1982 to 1990, he had shown not even a mild interest in co-operation in the framework of the EPP.

But the Congress was successful as far as its content and the participation of delegations was concerned. That is – with the exception of the Italians, who mainly distinguished themselves by their absence. In any event, this Congress helped greatly in giving member parties a political steer, and shaping the EPP's internal cohesion. Crucial in this respect were the committed speeches of EPP President Leo Tindemans, and government leaders Helmut Kohl, Ruud Lubbers, Wilfried Martens, Jacques Santer, and Garret FitzGerald.

However a political-cultural demonstration at the Rome opera house, designed to open the European election campaign, was a fiasco. Those responsible in the DC leadership had neglected to invite potential participants, namely Christian Democrats and sympathisers from Rome and the surrounding area.[9] About 400 delegates and Congress guests were marooned in the huge hall with the stars of culture and politics: there was enough space for 2000 people. But the Italians were able to make good such organisational deficiencies in the gastronomic department, and eventually there was the kind of atmosphere in which friendship thrives.

THE SECOND EUROPEAN ELECTIONS, 1994

Once more, ahead of the second European elections, in June 1984, the Political Bureau and the general-secretariat attempted to co-ordinate member parties' campaigns. But this time there was substantially less by way of resources available from the EP budget. Moreover, the EPP Group was far less willing than in 1979 to hand over a part of the available resources for the kind of campaign proposed by the party. Since the winter of 1983/84, there had been an 'Election Campaign' working group. Chaired by the Secretary General it had regularly brought together the responsible party workers from member parties to ensure a flow of information, and to discuss common projects. The result, as can be imagined, was not a unified election campaign – not even a co-ordinated one. But mutual awareness brought very good results in terms of harmonised efforts and specific ideas. Moreover, there was long term benefit and integration arising from this kind of practical co-operation between experts and senior officials from different national party headquarters.

The result of the 1984 European elections was disappointing for the EPP; far from increasing its lead *vis-à-vis* the Social Democrats, the gap became larger. After the first direct elections of 1979, it had been 107 to 113; it was now 110 for the EPP Group, while the Socialists had 130. Once again, however, the EPP had a larger absolute share of the vote than the federation of Social Democrats – 31 million against 30 250 000. But the EPP's result was two million less than in 1979, and its 3 million-vote advantage melted to 750 000.

VI   CONGRESS, THE HAGUE 1986

The VI Congress fell during EPP president Piet Bukman's term of office: he was also chairman of the Christen Demokratisch Appel (CDA). So it was obvious that this Congress, due to run from 10 to 12 April 1986, should be held in The Hague. This time it was not a matter of preparing a European election, but of presenting the growing movement.

The process of European integration had been palpably enlivened by Spain and Portugal joining the Community in January. The EPP had admitted the Christian Democratic parties in both countries as members; from Spain the Partido Democrata Popular, the Unio Democratica de Cataluna, and the Partido Nacionalista Vasco; from Portugal the Centro Democratico Social.

Jacques Delors, President of the European Commission since 1985, had re-enlivened the European debate with his 'Europa 1992' initiative aimed at creating a large single internal market. Christian Democratic-run governments in Italy, Germany, Belgium, Ireland, Luxembourg, and the Netherlands lent powerful support to this tendency.

The organisational and material conditions in the Congresgebouw in the Hague were excellent. The Dutch host party, had ensured that, with the help of social events under their aegis on the margins of the Congress, the context was right too. This was also the first EPP Congress in which a number of representatives of non-European parties from the Christian Democrat International federation took part, notably from Latin America, among them the CDI President Andres Zaldivar (Chile) and of the ODCA, Ricardo Arias Calderon (Panama), as well as the Secretary-General of the ODCA, Aristides Calvani (Venezuela).

The Congress focused on two large subject areas: economic development, and environmental problems. Two comprehensive Congress documents had been prepared, and were used as the basis of discussion, and – with amendments – voted through. Two working groups, chaired by Fernand Herman and Hanja Maij Weggen, carved out intensive debates. The rapporteurs were Elmar Brok and Reinhard Klein. The various aspects of the problems under discussion were introduced by Beniamino Andreatta and Karlheinz Narjes (economics) and Marcelle Lentz-Cornette and Siegbert Alber (environment).

A whole raft of proposals for resolution were discussed, in part proving controversial. Overall, this Congress allowed for much more debate than previous Congresses: there were not just speeches, but spontaneous contributions.

As at all previous Congresses, EPP party government leaders were once more the stars of the show. Ruud Lubbers, Wilfried Martens, Jacques Santer, Garret FitzGerald, and Helmut Kohl, all spoke at a concluding demonstration to which, apart from the delegates, CDA members from far and wide had been invited. Only Ciriaco De Mita was conspicuous by his absence.

VII   CONGRESS, LUXEMBOURG 1988

Another European election, that of June 1989, was imminent at the time of the VII Congress, and the meeting was conceived as a prelude to the consciousness-raising and mobilisation campaign being undertaken ahead of the election campaign proper. The Congress was held on 7–8 November 1988, in Luxembourg, under the chairmanship of Jacques Santer. It was used to discuss and vote on the action programme for the 1989–1994 legislature. The Programme Committee, chaired by Lutz Stavenhagen, minister of state in the foreign ministry, had prepared a very detailed document. Congress was also presented with numerous proposals for amendments and additions.[10]

In contrast to 1984 in Rome, Congress itself became a forum for debate and decision making. The individual chapters of the draft were debated in four parallel study groups. Decisions were reached on a two-thirds majority about proposals from member parties, the EPP Group, and associations.

Understanding orders, proposals which were neither accepted nor rejected by the study groups were put to the vote in the plenary session; a simple majority decided their fate. Since the study groups had been given the right to made decisions for the whole Congress, their composition had to mirror that of Congress. That meant that each group had to contain a quarter of all the members of individual delegations with the right to vote. This procedure ensured lively, sometimes heated debate. It did not just involve the classical issues of practical European policy, but socio-political problems such as the permissibility or otherwise of artificial insemination. The answers to such questions challenged fundamental positions.

The Action Programme's chapter headings contain the essential message which Christian Democrats in the EPP wanted to send to the voters in European Community member states:

We are strengthening democracy in the Community and creating the European Union.

We are creating Europe as a modern, effective, and humane economic and social space.

We are shaping a humane society in a Europe of citizens.

We are strengthening Europe's security and World peace.[11]

The Action Programme, entitled 'On the Side of the Citizen' was passed, as was an election manifesto containing, in abbreviated form, the main EPP demands and a call to the citizens of Europe to support the EPP in realising them.

Alongside the logo introduced at the time the party was founded (the green E with a circle of stars), the Luxembourg Congress was presented with a new logo (the blue heart containing a circle of 12 stars). This was to illustrate the Congress slogan 'EPP – the Heart of Europe'. Since then, this logo has been that of the EPP Group in the European Parliament.

A public event, a Euro-Show with folkloric entertainments and popular music, marked the conclusion of Congress, graced with the presence of EPP heads of government. About 2000 people took part. Mostly they had travelled from Belgium, the Netherlands, France, and Germany. They were joined by a good number of Italian, Greek, Spanish, and Portuguese party supporters living and working in these countries.

THE THIRD EUROPEAN ELECTION, 1989

The European campaign was prepared and executed in the same way as before in the first direct elections in 1979. Once more a working group met early on, bringing together fairly regularly the responsible member party officials. Given that the institutional context of the election remained identical, everything took a familiar course. Nor did the EPP, any more than its rival European parties, have additional resources, let alone new instruments at its disposal. It could do no more than before: put in place the basic political programme and ensure a degree of consensus on how to proceed between the member parties.

The EPP secured 121 seats. It was a relatively low score, given that, for the first time parties from Spain and Portugal took part in the election under EPP colours. With only modest results in these countries, they managed to win only 19 mandates, 15 of them for the Spanish Partido Popular. Just before the election it decided to withdraw its deputies from the Conservative Group and join the EPP Group instead.

The modest booty of this election was mostly attributable to the ill fortune of the largest EPP member party. Compared to 1984, the CDU lost nine seats; other EPP parties did about the same as then. The Social Democrats had, in Spain and Great Britain, once again had considerable success. The effect was badly to weaken the EPP against the Social Democrats, the gap now widened to 121 against 180.[12]

VIII   CONGRESS, DUBLIN 1990

The importance of the VIII Congress, in Dublin on 15–16 November 1990, was the new perspective created for the Community and for Europe altogether by the political watershed of 1989. The Central and Eastern European countries had freed themselves from Communism and Soviet hegemony. The Berlin Wall had fallen, the reunification of Germany had become a reality. The foundations had been laid for a new and decisive move towards European Union, a union which must be equipped to take the newly-liberated countries.

A meeting of the European Council had been fixed for 15 December. On the basis of this vision it was to call for an Intergovernmental Conference to revise the Community Treaties. The EPP's ideas on this were to be discussed at Dublin. A draft document written by Paul Dabin had been worked on by a committee chaired by EPP vice-president Alan Dukes, then chairman of Fine Gael, the Irish member party. It contained not only a description of the form the desired European Union and its institutions should take, but also suggestions on how to proceed to reach this goal. One chapter was devoted to each of the two pillars of the European Union: Political Union, and Economic and Monetary Union.

This was the first Congress chaired by Wilfried Martens, then still Prime Minister of Belgium, and President of the EPP from May 1990 onwards. The Congress was incidentally held under the rules tried out in Luxembourg two years before. Two working groups discussed and passed the two chapters presented by the Programme Commission along with amendments to them. The result was published under the title: A federal constitution for the European Union.[13]

This document would, in the weeks and months that followed, have a considerable influence. It set the direction not only for the EPP Group, but for the majority in the European Parliament. Indeed, there was a consensus between the majority parliamentary groups along the lines of this document at the so-called Assizes, an informal meeting (a more or less formal affair) of MEPs and national parliamentarians held in Rome on 30 November. Christian Democratic heads of government and ministers involved in negotiating the new treaty largely followed the ideas developed in the paper.

While the Congress was over-shadowed by the leadership crisis in the EPP's Irish member party, the simultaneous leadership crisis in the British Conservative Party attracted particular attention to the Congress. The imminent resignation of Margaret Thatcher re-activated expectations of a closer association between the British Conservatives and the EPP. Several Conservative politicians were present as observers. The British press paid particularly close attention to the discussions and to the result.

It was the first ever EPP Congress attended by delegates invited from Central European countries. The Slovene prime minister and leader of his country's Christian Democrats, Lojze Peterle, addressed Congress, which clearly articulated the new dimensions of European politics.

9 The Conference of Government and Party Leaders, 1983–1995

A first meeting of EPP party leaders was called by EPP President Leo Tindemans, and held in Strasbourg in spring 1980. The main topic was the possibility of strengthening the voice of the EPP in the European Community's decision-making processes. The idea was that Christian Democrats in responsible positions at different levels should co-operate and co-ordinate their work. The arenas were to be: in the executive bodies of the EPP and its member parties, in the EPP Group in the European Parliament, and in the national parliamentary groups, in the EC Commission, and in member state governments:

> We should make efforts to establish a system for consulting each other on important national, European, and international problems.[1]

There was general agreement on the paramount importance for the EPP's leading figures meeting regularly to consult with one another. So it was therefore decided:

> that there would be a meeting of the Bureau at least three times a year in which all party leaders, our Prime Ministers, and the most important ministers, would take part. These meetings of the Bureau should if possible take place before the convening of the European Council.[2]

This decision was only put into practice in the autumn of 1983. However, it took a different form from what had originally been intended. Party leaders were not to meet in the context of the regular sessions of the executive (Bureau), but independently of them, with a separate agenda, and only party and government leaders.

The party leaders met on 3 October 1983 in the Val Duchesse Chateau in Brussels, under Leo Tindemans's chairmanship. There were three items on the agenda:

the further political and institutional development of the European Community; EPP tactics ahead of the 1984 European elections; Co-operation of Christian Democratic parties in the EPP, EUCD, and the Christian Democrat International.[3]

At the suggestion of Helmut Kohl, federal leader of the German Christian Democratic Union (who had been Chancellor scarcely a year), it was decided to call a conference to which heads of government belonging to member parties should also be invited. And only a few weeks later, on 26 November, the first conference of party and government leaders was held, again in Brussels, but this time in the Palais d'Egmont. Every party leader, and all the Christian Democratic government leaders, were there: Helmut Kohl, Wilfried Martens, Ruud Lubbers, Jacques Santer, and Garret Fitzgerald. The meeting was the prelude to a series of such conferences,[4] which for the time being had an informal character. They were not provided for in the EPP statutes, nor were there any internal rules setting out either a procedure, or what the conference was for.

THE AGENDA

It became a tradition that the first item on the agenda dealt with the development of the European People's Party, and organisational and political problems which had arisen in the party's work. The debate would regularly be introduced by the president's report. These conferences of party and government leaders set a political direction which was of the greatest importance for the development of the party's structures, for its sense of identity, and for the EPP's political strategy.

The second item on the agenda was, as a rule, European Community politics; over the years the agenda of the next meeting of the European Council came to dominate the discussion. The 'EPP Summit' really did become, over time, a welcome opportunity to prepare for the official Summit meeting of the European Community. Irrespective of the negotiating positions of governments, and especially of foreign ministries and the diplomatic corps, it was possible – among friends, so to speak, and not in the context of binding negotiations – to exchange ideas, and to test reactions to proposed solutions to problems. It was also a forum for agreeing tactics.

For party leaders in opposition at home, attending such meetings was not merely a chance to put across their own points of view. It was also their opportunity to inform themselves about positions and ideas to which they would not otherwise have access. These meetings also sometimes afforded an insight into the strengths and weaknesses of their own countries' negotiating positions: which was especially useful to members of the European Council. In any event, both government leaders and opposition leaders benefited from these exchanges, which of course also included the leadership of the EPP Group in the European Parliament.

Such meetings would normally be prepared with an aide-memoire from the secretary-general which summarised the agreed position of the EPP on agenda items, and in some cases recommended a line to take. Only rarely would resolutions connected with meetings of party and government leaders be made public. Especially when discussions were taking place ahead of European Council meetings, it was not in the interests of government leaders to be tied down; they needed to retain as free a hand as possible in their discussions with other government leaders. Since 1988, when Jacques Santer took over the Presidency of the European People's Party, it has been the practice for the party leader to give his summary of the results of the conference to the press.

HIGHEST AUTHORITY

Looking back on the 23 conferences of this kind between 1983 and 1995, there are two discernible highlights. One concerns the involvement of party and government leaders in a key matter relating to the EPP. Another concerns the actions of party and government leaders ahead of the Maastricht Treaty.

The first highlight was bringing the British and Danish conservatives into the EPP Group in the European Parliament – which immediately raised the issue of whether the People's Party should be open, as a matter of principle, to members coming from outside the Christian Democratic tradition.[5]

The issue was one which goes to the core of the group's identity, and which defines itself as Christian Democratic. The majority of its members consciously distance themselves from conservative positions, especially from those held by British Conservatives under the leadership of Margaret Thatcher.

On the other hand rapprochement with the conservatives offered particularly big advantages to the EPP: the possibility of a presence in Britain, and of influencing British politics, looked especially promising after the departure of Margaret Thatcher and her replacement by John Major in the autumn of 1990. With the entry of the British

Conservatives, Danish conservatives could be won over, and later, once the Community expanded to include Sweden, Norway, and Finland, so could conservatives from those countries, in none of which there was a strong Christian Democratic party. In truth, the application by the conservative MEPs to join the EPP – even if it was for the moment confined to the group and not the party – posed the fundamental question about the future political profile of the EPP, and whether or not it would accept non-Christian Democratic parties.

Since the issue was so fundamental, and – this was connected – so controversial, it was impossible for the parliamentary group alone to decide it. Its leadership turned to the leaders of the party. But it soon became clear that, even if the party leadership had the right to do so under the constitution, it too could not cut the Gordian knot. The president therefore decided to pass the problem over to the conference of party and government leaders. This took place at a special meeting, solely devoted to this issue, at the Chateau Val Duchesse, Brussels, on 13 April 1991. The result was a clear confirmation of the EPP's Christian Democratic identity, and its commitment to European federalism. But a signal was also sent out, that the EPP was ready to engage in closer co-operation with all popular parties committed to 'a similar social project, and with the same goals in terms of their European policy'.[6]

On this basis, the EPP Group was recommended to undertake a process of 'orchestration' with conservative deputies which was supposed to resolve various matters both of substance and of practice. If this proved satisfactory, the creation of a 'Fraktionsgemeinschaft' (an alliance of parliamentary groups, as found in the German Bundestag between CDU and CSU) was to be considered. The conference of party and government leaders studied the results of this on 14 February 1992, and concluded that they were adequate 'for the Fraktiongemeinschaft to be brought into effect on May 1'.[7]

ON THE ROAD TO MAASTRICHT

The second highlight of these conferences was connected with the part they played, in 1991, in the origins of the Maastricht Treaty. There were three meetings of party and government leaders that year. On Wilfried Martens's initiative, Christian Democratic government leaders or their agents met twice that autumn – as a sub-committee of the summit, so to speak – to ensure there was agreement on the Union Treaty project.[8]

It was no coincidence that the two key EPP summit meetings since 1983 fell during the same period. Both concerned vital decisions that had to be made in two inextricably connected processes: the establishment of European Union, and the Europeanisation of the party system.

The backdrop to the 13 April conference, which focused on the issue of co-operation with the Conservatives, was already the:

> perspective of a federal, democratic European Union and its later enlargement to the countries of Scandinavia and Central Europe....The evolution of the European Community into a federally structured Political Union, including a common currency and common security, is a high priority goal for the EPP.[9]

At this point, Helmut Kohl – always the driving force in the conferences of party and government leaders, and especially so at this stage – could still hope to win over the new British Prime Minister to the EPP's European federalist ideas. Had he not promised to lead Great Britain 'to the heart of Europe'?[10] The attention devoted to the British Conservatives is largely explained by this hope; the success of the imminent intergovernmental conference on European Union depended greatly on the preparedness, and ability, of John Major to take a different direction from that of his predecessor.

The meeting of the Christian Democratic party and government leaders in Senninger Castle near Luxembourg was wholly devoted to preparing the meeting of the European Council (Luxembourg, 28–9 June). Six government leaders were present; all of them would be at Maastricht: Helmut Kohl, Giulio Andreotti, Ruud Lubbers, Konstantin Mitsotakis, Jacques Santer, and Wilfried Martens. Austrian Vice-Chancellor Josef Riegler was there for first time, along with the Maltese Prime Minister Edward Fenech Adami, since the Austrian Volkspartei and the Maltese Nationalist Party had been accepted as associate members of the EPP. The summary of what had been agreed read:

> The EPP explicitly supports the unity of the European Union and categorically rejects all proposals which boil down to placing the Community, along with other forms of co-operation, under the intergovernmental tutelage of the European Council. The EPP therefore insists that the parallelism between Political Union and Economic and Currency Union is thoroughly justified; they are two different aspects of the same structure, namely European Union.[11]

Just before the meeting of the European Council in Maastricht (9–10 December 1991), there was a further EPP summit in The Hague on 6 December, following which Wilfried Martens could declare that:

We in the EPP agree unanimously that Maastricht must be a success. However, we are not ready to agree to a compromise which puts in question the democratic and federal development of the future Union, or the irreversible character of this development. In particular we emphasise
– our commitment to increasing participation and co-decision by the European Parliament over a wide jurisdiction;
– an extension of Community competencies in areas which are important to economic cohesion and the development of a social dimension.[12]

In agreement with Ruud Lubbers, who would chair the summit in Maastricht, Martens had drawn up a list of the most important demands. The EPP heads of government were committed to a man to defending these. The demands related to the following fifteen points:

– the irreversibility of the timetable for establishing the Union, and its democratisation;
– the indivisibility of the institutional structure;
– the investiture of the Commission and the extension of its mandate to five years;
– European Parliament co-decision in legislation;
– the agreement of the European Parliament for new actions and for changes in the Treaty;
– the independence of the Central Bank and Parliament agreement to statute changes;
– the creation of an advisory Committee of the Regions;
– strengthening of the statutes of the Court of Auditors;
– more majority voting in the Council;
– the extension of Community competences;
– qualified majority voting in Common Foreign and Security Policy;
– economic and social cohesion;
– the number of German deputies in the European Parliament;
– recognition of the role of the European Parliament.[13]

A comparative analysis of the results of Maastricht and the EPP demands shows that only on one point is there no progress at all, namely on the '*avis conforme*'. Ten of the demands were satisfactorily met. What was achieved on four further points left open the hope of a breakthrough at the conference to revise Maastricht, pencilled in for 1996. At all events, it could be stated at the conference of party leaders and heads of government on 14 February 1992, 'that the results of Maastricht owe much to orchestration between Christian Democrats'.[14]

SETTING IMPORTANT GUIDELINES

To emphasise the highlights of 1991/1992 is not to belittle the contributions of party and government leaders before and after that. For example, the conference on 20 June 1985, in Rome, a week before the European Council meeting in Milan (28–9 June 1985), was important. It decided to call an intergovernmental conference in order to bring a clear advance along the road to European Union.

Without Christian Democratic support, Italian Prime Minister Bettino Craxi would scarcely have risked following foreign minister Giulio Andreotti's advice, and in Milan put to the vote the proposal to hold an intergovernmental conference. It was a move fiercely resisted by British Prime Minister Margaret Thatcher. The support of five Christian Democratic heads of government (Kohl, Lubbers, Martens, Santer, FitzGerald), and of Andreotti – who, with Craxi, was a key player because of the Italian Presidency – was indispensable.

The conference in Pisa on 17 February 1990, was also of considerable historical importance. It had the following points on the draft agenda:

Reform and further development of the EPP structures; The challenge resulting from the new democracies in central and eastern Europe; The consequences of the new situation for the European Community/priorities for 1990 and longer-term perspectives.[15]

A report was prepared on the first point summarising the conclusions of a working group set up with the object of strengthening EPP structures, and Europeanising member parties.[16]

The second (and third) points related above all to the reunification of Germany. The Wall had fallen. It had become clear that the population of the GDR wanted unification with the Federal Republic as well as democracy. In a few weeks there would be the first democratic elections to the GDR Volkskammer. Chancellor Kohl had returned from Moscow only days before with an assurance from Gorbachev. It was foɪ the Germans themselves not only to resolve the question of unifying their country, but also to decide what form of government it should have, and how reunification should proceed.

In Pisa, Helmut Kohl turned on all his persuasive powers to explain to his colleagues that German reunification did not pose any danger to the process of European integration, but on the contrary offered numerous opportunities. Restoring the unity of the German state could only succeed if it was embedded in the political/institutional framework of the

Atlantic Alliance and the European Community. The Federal Republic was firmly anchored in Western Europe, especially in the economic sense. There would be absolutely no danger of Germany playing 'see-saw politics'. If reunification succeeded, there would be a gut German predisposition to make European unity work too. Both processes, the European and the German, were bound up with each other, and each affected the other.

The overwhelming success of Helmut Kohl's efforts at persuasion became evident the same evening. The Young Christian Democrats (EYCD) were holding their congress in Pisa. At their press conference, the Rome correspondent of the *Frankfurter Allgemeine Zeitung*, Heinz Joachim Fischer, asked the Italian Prime Minister Giulio Andreotti whether he still took the view that the existence of two German states was an important element in Europe's security. Andreotti conceded that he did now see things differently. The political context had changed, he said, and he could see no reason to doubt the assurances he and his colleagues had been given by the federal Chancellor.

The feeling of confidence engendered in Pisa no doubt ensured absolute loyalty of Christian Democrat-led governments, as well as both national and EP parliamentarians who belonged to EPP member parties, during the process of German unification. In their own countries they helped to persuade public opinion to accept unification and to support it.

AN EPP BODY

Only after the revisions to the 1976 statutes, made at the Dublin Congress in 1990, did the conference of EPP heads of party and government leaders become a party body. Membership of the conference was now laid down:

- the President and the Secretary General;
- the Chairman of the EPP Group in the European Parliament;
- the President of the EUCD where he belongs to a member party;
- chairmen of member parties (party leaders);
- the members of the European Council (heads of government) who belong to a member party;
- the President of the European Parliament, if he belongs to a member party;
- the President or a Vice-President of the European Commission representing members belonging to member parties.[17]

The statutes say nothing about the tasks of the conference, merely stating that the President should report to the Executive on the results of such meetings and what lines are to be followed as a result of them.

The first job of the leaders' conference was and remains that of developing common positions and a common line for meetings of the European Council which, usually twice a year, bring together national and government leaders. Between 1986 and 1994, six of the 12 members of this supreme body belonged to the EPP. Their common position, to which were always added the voices of several natural allies, was crucial to the European Council's capacity to take decisions.

The conference of party and government leaders is limited to making recommendations, which reflects sensitivity to the Executive, whose composition is based on democratic and federal principles. As the statutes made clear, the Executive is not supposed to forgo the right to make decisions and to draw the practical consequences of what the 'chiefs' have decided. But it should be remarked that this sensitivity is of a somewhat theoretical nature. Practice has shown that the Executive has more respect for the party leaders than *vice versa*.

The significance of the regular meetings of party and government leaders for the EPP's development as a European party is not to be found purely in its function as a leadership body. The other element is that such meetings were the public manifestation of the EPP as a united, powerful organisation, one which was able to make a difference. The 'internal' effect was that the conference of EPP leaders crystallised a feeling of integration, and was an opportunity to identify with the wider movement.

One demonstration that this was a positive exercise was the fact that, when they founded the European Socialist Party (SPE) at the start of the 1990s, the European Social Democrats copied the example of the EPP and established a regular 'party leaders' meeting.[18]

10 Attempts to Merge the EUCD with the EPP, and the Revision of the Statutes, 1985–1990

Soon after its foundation, the European People's Party politically outweighed the European Union of Christian Democrats, from which it had sprung and with which it remained institutionally bound. It was natural, then, that the EUCD member parties which also belonged to the EPP concentrated more and more of their work in the framework of the EPP. Among the parties which could not become members of the EPP, because their countries were not members of the European Community, a number and most importantly the Austrian People's Party, found another field of activity in the so-called European Democratic Union (EDU). It suited their aspirations better, now that their most important partners in the EUCD were dancing at another wedding, a wedding to which they had not been invited.[1]

At the start of the eighties the draining away of the EUCD's importance became obvious. Its then President, Diogo Freitas do Amaral, took a first step towards merging the two organisations. However, the impulse faltered because it was far too ambitious, seeking to include in the new organisation the Christian Democrat International (CDI), which operated at a global level. In 1982, Freitas do Amaral, and soon afterwards the Secretary General, Guiseppe Petrilli, both resigned, for different reasons. No succession had been considered. It signalled a crisis which could not be entirely concealed by the energetic and determined leadership of the EUCD's bodies by the former EUCD President, Kai-Uwe von Hassel, who took over the leadership as a commissar in his capacity of First Vice-President. EUCD activity had for some considerable period not amounted to anything more than organising meetings for its constituent bodies.

FUSION OF THE SECRETARIATS AND INTEGRATING THE EXECUTIVE BODIES

The first step in resolving this situation was to make the same person Secretary General of both the EPP and the EUCD and, as a logical extension of this, to fuse the secretariats of the two organisations. Thomas Jansen, Secretary General of the EPP, who had been appointed in April 1983, was elected Secretary General of the EUCD as well a few months later.[2] The EUCD's general secretariat in Rome was dissolved, and its functions taken over by the EPP general secretariat in Brussels.

Jansen's intention was to unite the leadership of both organisations, both in terms of resources and politically. At the same time, efforts would be made to clarify the specificity and particular value of the two federations. They are differently constituted and their functions are different. The EPP is a supranational, federative party active in the political system of the European Community, and takes on responsibilities at both parliamentary and executive levels. The EUCD by contrast, is the organisation of Christian Democracy, in principle uniting all the members of this political family from every country in Europe.

The single leadership was supposed to ensure that Christian Democratic parties in Europe followed a coherent political line – irrespective of whether their field of activity was in the European Community, the Council of Ministers, or other European and international connections. It was also hoped that this would help ensure that the expectations, points of view, and interest of 'the Other Europe' would be taken into account when decisions were made in the EPP. And as far as EPP decision-making was concerned, the point was *vice versa*: to formulate policies appropriate to the whole of Europe which did not lose sight of the European Community perspective. Joint meetings of the executive bodies (Political Bureaux) and the setting up of joint committees and working groups also served this purpose.

A special effort was needed to keep alive the EUCD's sense of its own value in relation to the EPP, with its increasing importance as an effective force in the framework of the EC. This was not just a matter of justifying the existence of the EUCD to members who were simultaneously EPP members, and whose political advantages as EPP members made the EUCD less and less interesting to them. The EUCD was also supposed to be revived as a forum for action and co-operation for those members who were not in the EPP, and who felt discriminated against by the EUCD's neglect.

WHEN AND HOW TO MERGE THE ORGANISATIONS?

The issue of merging the EPP and the EUCD re-emerged when Spain and Portugal joined the European Community in 1986.[3] The effect was to increase the number of parties in the EPP, and further deplete the ranks of EUCD Parties not in the EPP as well. This time the prospect was of a further round of EC enlargement in the medium term, an enlargement heading in the direction of including every country in western Europe. Fourteen of the EUCD's 21 member parties, in other words two thirds of its members – among these the largest and more influential – were already in the EPP. In the circumstances, it no longer seemed sensible to retain two organisations. Especially given the joint general secretariat.

Practice had shown that integrating the EPP and EUCD (while retaining the fiction that they were distinct) had not resulted in any political problems at all. In particular, there had never been an attempt either by a single member party, or a group of EUCD parties, to undermine or dilute any position taken by the EPP, either in relation to further development of the European Community, or in Community policy.

None of the seven EUCD parties[4] which could not join the EPP insisted on the survival of the EUCD as a distinct organisation. Indeed: all of them were interested in having as close a relationship as possible with the parties of the European Community, and in imposing similar rules on themselves as already existed in the EPP.

There was another factor: the co-existence of two organisations at European level muddled the public image of the movement and did not inspire confidence in its ability to act. The image problem, made worse by the parallel existence of the EDU, could hardly be resolved by the fusion in 1983 of the EUCD and EPP secretariats. The same was true of the inefficiency resulting from duplication. These headaches would remain as long as there continued to be two (even three) presidents, presidencies, and executive bodies, required to arrange separate events for the EPP and EUCD (and EDU), and of course their own separate representation (not to mention their separate needs for financial resources).

INITIATIVE, DEBATE, AND DECISION-MAKING

In 1984 the European Union of Young Christian Democrats, a recognised association of the EPP and EUCD, had made a powerful case for the fusion with their organisation of two previously co-existing federations.

They pushed for their mother organisation to follow suit. They made the point that the united Europe the Christian Democrats were striving for had also had to overcome differences in the way integration was achieved – here the EC, there the Council of Europe, and so on. And at the EUCD Madrid Congress in 1985, they formally proposed that:

> attempts should continue to be made to combine, more than at present, the political and technical work of the EUCD and the EPP.[5]

This was unanimously accepted, and led to discussion in EUCD and the EPP bodies. Initially these bore no fruit. But a year later, at the EPP conference in the Hague, there was once again an EYCD proposal. This time there was an explicit demand for fusion of the EUCD and EPP:

> The VI Congress of the EPP requires the Secretary General of the EPP and EUCD, in agreement with the Presidents of both organisations, to present to the EPP Political Bureau, before the end of 1986, a proposal for changes to the EPP statutes which would above all allow for admitting to membership parties from outside the EC, and prepare the way for the complete fusion of both organisations, while taking into account the wishes of all member parties, and of EPP work specifically developed for the Community.[6]

The motion was rejected, but it was passed on to the Political Bureaux for further consideration. Both presidents and the Secretary General were assigned the task of taking soundings and then proposing how to proceed. The soundings and detailed discussions in the course of 1986 and 1987 revealed a general agreement with the project, though a number of party representatives tended to be sceptical about the conditions.

Passing the resolution was held up by the continued opposition of the EUCD President and the Italian delegation. The reasons for this related both to political issues and to personalities. For the Italians the reasons were on the one hand the worry about the identity of the EPP as a party confederation relating to the European Community. They also assumed that the fusion of the EUCD and EPP would lead to the demand, especially from the Germans, to admit the conservative parties. It was something they had always refused to do. On the other hand they no doubt also feared losing the post of President, occupied since 1985 by Emilio Colombo (and before that, from 1983 onward, by Giulio Andreotti).

However, in the summer of 1988, it was finally decided to set up a commission to look into the merits of merging or integrating the EUCD and

EPP, and to weigh up other methods of strengthening Christian Democracy as an active force in Europe. The commission was also asked to draft a statute for a renewed federation of European parties, one capable of taking effective action.[7] The Secretary General was to chair the committee which would be made up of a representative from each member party, a representative of the CD faction in the Parliamentary Assembly of the Council of Europe, a representative of the EPP Group in the European Parliament, and representatives from both the EUCD and EPP presidencies. The results were to be presented for decision by, at the latest, Autumn 1989.

A 'BIG' EPP

The commission's mandate was kept very general out of sensitivity to the Italians' reservations. But it did amount to creating a new structure for a 'large' EPP, in which all European parties with a Christian Democratic orientation could co-operate as equals. There had for some time been an understanding that fusion would take place on the basis of the EPP statutes, meaning the EUCD would be absorbed by the EPP. It was assured that this would be effected by absorbing the last non-EPP members of the EUCD.

To do this the EPP statute would have to be changed in two ways, in terms of conditions for and in the matter of voting rights. But the opportunity would also be taken to undertake a radical revision of the 1976 statute.[8]

In accordance with earlier EPP decisions, this reform should be made in the light of 'the perspective opened up by the Single European Act', as well as 'the experiences and achievements of co-operation within the EUCD and the EPP', and finally 'the political developments of the European Community since direct election of the European Parliament'.[9]

Such ideas gave rise to proposals for a new statute. Which were repeatedly debated by the Political Bureaux of both organisations, and in principle approved by them. Given that parties from countries which did not belong to the European Community had the right to vote, the proposal envisaged that such parties should take part in all discussions, and on all matters. But they would not be allowed to take part in decision-making about the constitutional development of the Community, or Community political issues generally.

The period leading up to the final discussion of the proposed statute coincided with the revolutionary events taking place in Moscow and in other capitals of eastern Europe. Suddenly the possibilities for co-operation across the whole of Europe opened up. In the light of the new situation, the EUCD Political Bureau decided in spring 1989 to postpone the merger project. Instead, a radical reform of the statutes, strengthening both the EUCD's independence and its capacity to act, was designed to prepare the organisation to take in the Christian Democratic forces of Central and Eastern Europe as soon as they had succeeded in forming themselves into parties. These forces were now free again, and were making the first moves to organise themselves.[10] The setting up of groups, clubs, and forums – the stage leading up to the foundation of actual parties – was proceeding apace in several countries.

Looser and less binding, the EUCD framework seemed more suitable than the EPP for dealing with the expected influx of new parties from countries in which a political system based on the rule of law, and with democratic structures, had not yet developed. In any event, from the EPP's point of view it was quite unthinkable to take in as members or associate members parties from Eastern and Central Europe about which it was still impossible to know anything. Furthermore, the countries in which they were preparing themselves to take over political responsibility would have no chance, in the short or medium term, of joining the European Community.

All this brought to an end the mandate to effect a fusion of the two organisations. The constitutional commission now set about using the work it had done to develop new statutes for both the EPP and the EUCD.

THE NEW CONSTITUTION

The revision of the EPP's constitution had for some time had a momentum of its own, independent of the merger project. On 2 December 1983, immediately after taking office, the Secretary General had written a note identifying the source of a number of deficits in EPP working methods and the way its various bodies saw themselves. These were the result, he said, of structural problems which above all showed themselves in the fact

that there is a striking gap between the demands of the EPP statute as far as the composition and the role of the Political Bureau is concerned, on the one hand, and reality on the other. This circumstance in turn cor-responds to the gap between the pretension evoked by the name 'European People's Party' and our association's real circumstances: they remain, as ever, not much more than a 'Federation of the Christian

Democratic Parties of the European Community'. I do not want to draw the conclusion from this that we should withdraw this pretension. On the contrary. We should fortify it by taking in the fact that we can only reach the goals embodied in the name 'EPP' if we don't behave as if we had already reached them.[11]

This in turn gave rise to the proposals for a careful medium-term reform of the statutes, in order to:

bring the working methods of the EPP bodies into line with the actual state of the EPP's development as a federation of national parties and to be able 'by this means to avoid many a frustration produced by exaggerated expectations, and many an absurdity created by the distance between pretension and reality, and eventually to get better political results.[12]

On 26 June 1984, the Political Bureau decided to revise the constitution which came into force with the founding of the EPP in 1976

because of the development of the EPP since then; because of the experience we have had of the constitution since then; because of our appraisal of the political situation and continued development of the community towards a European union. The constitutional reform, if it is to be effective, must be thoroughly prepared. It must not be the fruit of more or less accidental considerations dictated by the moment. The Secretary General is therefore tasked with laying before the party's responsible bodies, by the end of 1984, proposals for such constitutional reform; these will serve as the basis of a comprehensive debate.[13]

This task was quickly overtaken by the discussion about fusion with the EUCD which soon afterwards blotted out everything else. Reflections on how to revise the statutes were swamped by the debates about a new constitution for the 'big' EPP. And that in turn was connected with a proposed revision of the EPP constitution being elaborated by a working group chaired by the Secretary General from spring 1989 onwards. The text had been discussed and voted through at the Dublin Congress in November.[14] It introduced a series of important innovations:

– the sub-title of the name (correct up to now, but clumsily expressed: 'Federation of Christian Democratic Parties of the European Community') was simplified. The name of the party was now officially 'European People's Party. Christian Democrats' (Article 1);

– member parties were obliged to 'represent the policies taken up by the EPP in the context of the European Community in their national policies' (Article 3);

– the expression 'associated member' would apply to Christian Democratic parties, which are in the process of negotiating their entry to the European Community (Article 4);

– the possibility of attaining the status of 'permanent observer' would be offered to parties of similar political orientation (Article 5);

– 'individual membership' would be introduced (Article 6);

– conference of heads of party and government would be recognised as a constituent part (Articles 7 and 10);

– the elected presidium would replace the Executive Committee made up of a large number of *ex-officio* representatives and presidium members (Articles 7 and 11);

– the Secretary General's role would be strengthened and recognised as a constituent part (Articles 7 and 14);

– representation in the Executive (previously 'Political Bureau') and Congress would be re-organised in accordance with political realities (Articles 8 and 9);

– conditions would be imposed on speaking and voting rights, committees and working groups, associations, the treasurer, and finances would either be renewed or transferred from standing orders into the constitutions (Articles 12, 15, 16, and 17).

The constitutional reform meant adapting the standing orders[15] as well as – for the first time – revising the financial regulations (equally applicable to the EPP and EUCD). These, *inter alia*, laid down the levels of contribution, the conditions for grants to associations, as well as the method of calculating them, and also the accounting rules and the financial control of the general secretariat.[16]

The new statutes, the documents relating to how it should be run and financed, gave the EPP a 'constitution' which clearly stressed its claim to be a 'European party'. The conditions it contained did not – as did some paragraphs of the 1976 constitution – exaggerate the extent to which the member parties or their representatives could or should be present or participate. Beyond that, the party bodies and system of rules remained flexible enough to adapt to the effects of more intensive political and institutional integration of the European Union in the years ahead.

11 Shaping the Programme 1989–1993

From the start, efforts to develop a clearly-defined party programme were crucial to the EPP's development. Working out a political programme will always mean developing a consensus. And establishing consensus between the member parties and their leaders is central to all EPP undertakings. That consensus will initially be forged between member parties' leading figures and elected representatives, but eventually between their active members as well. Indeed it is part of the EPP's *raison d'être*. A European party can ultimately achieve nothing if it does not know, or can't express, what it wants to achieve.

Work on a political programme, being a matter of forging a consensus, also tends towards political integration. Common programmes contribute to European integration and to uniting peoples and states. That too goes for the efforts needed to formulate those programmes – of which overcoming national or cultural differences is an inescapable element.

MODERNISING CHRISTIAN DEMOCRATIC 'DOCTRINE'

The process of enhancing co-operation in the framework of the EPP during the 1980s, made one thing clear: constant attention to the party's spiritual foundations was of the essence. Without that, the EPP would, over time, not be in a position to establish the political consensus without which it could not hope to act effectively. That in turn was urgent. These were years when the EPP was poised to take on ever greater political responsibilities: in the European Community as it moved towards European Union, as well as at parliamentary and government level.

In 1985, Leo Tindemans ordered a joint EPP and EUCD working group to be set up to study the 'spiritual foundations of Christian Democratic politics'. They worked on the assumption that Christian Democracy drew its political force from the situation in Europe after the Second World War. Peoples liberated from fascism and spared the oppression of Communism found the Christian Democratic value system suited their social, political, economic, and cultural situation. But there had been a continuing shift in values. The reduced influence of the church, widespread questioning of the validity of the Western political order, and numerous other crises all contributed to the erosion of almost every tradition. And Christian Democracy had lost much of its original attraction.[1]

Another factor was that the inevitable pressures of gaining and holding on to power squeezed into the background basic questions about the nature and direction of policy. That held good too for the Christian Democratic parties which, in the 1950s and 1960s, enjoyed extraordinary success. The result was a loss of self-confidence. In constant fear of being pigeon-holed as intolerant, intransigent, or reactionary, the Christian Democratic movement was reticent about mounting a proper defence of its values. Such a retreat was especially marked during the 1970s, when Social Democratic doctrine became more and more dominant.

Things were not improved by reluctance to consider theoretical questions, or to formulate a specific Christian Democratic 'doctrine'. Such weakness in terms of political theory is no doubt the flip-side of the strength of Christian Democracy in Europe; even in the hey-day of ideology, the movement never fell into the ideology trap.

The 'spiritual foundations' working group, chaired by the EPP and EUCD secretary-general, resolved at its inaugural meeting to mount a series of colloquia, to examine the problems of Christian Democracy in detail and depth. The first of these events took place in Amsterdam in April 1986. As the basis for subsequent work, the initial task was to go into the tradition of Christian Democratic thought. Questions such as the limits of the welfare state, and moral and practical aspects of development aid, would be examined prior to going into Christian Democracy in practice.[2]

Further colloquia[3] followed: on 'International Solidarity' in Praglia, northern Italy, in autumn 1986; on 'Federalism, as an Element of Christian-Democratic Thought' in Vienna in spring, 1987; on 'The Social Market Economy, a Christian Democratic Idea' in Paris, autumn 1987[4]; on 'What is a Christian View of Humanity, and what Political Relevance does it Have?', Madrid, summer 1990; on 'The Future of Europe, and the Contribution of Christian Social Teaching[5] in Chantilly, autumn 1990.

THE EPP'S POLITICAL PROJECT

But in 1989 the political upheavals in Europe and the world in general meant re-thinking and re-formulating positions taken by the European People's Party since it was founded. This was a practical political necessity. The international context of the European unification process had altered with the ending of the ideological conflict between East and West.

That had implications for political priorities. At the same time the climate of opinion had altered. The change enshrined in the Maastricht Treaty, the evolution from the Economic Community to the European Union, also meant a reappraisal of ethical values, and a political redefinition.

The EPP's continuing attraction as a European party was largely due to its federalism. The Christian Democrats of the immediate post-war period had bequeathed a spirit of reconciliation, solidarity, and community, and spirited it into international politics. They were the values from which initiatives to unite Europe had grown, initiatives which had been further and further developed over the last 40 years. Since its foundation, the EPP's winning formula had included a commitment to transform the European Community into a federal Union. That union was to be both an economic and currency union and a political and security union; it would then be equipped to deal with the member states' problems in the future, and to enable the Community to take in the states of western, central, and south-eastern Europe which would join in the years to come.

This project finds expression in the federal conception, and the supranational working methods, of the EPP. As a 'European Party' the EPP is part of the Union's political system. It sees its role as helping to build consensus and political will, and to take on responsibilities. The EPP's consensus about European federalism, strengthened and deepened by co-operation between its members, has bound them together. The party has permitted Christian Democrats from the various Community countries to participate actively in European politics' practice and operation.

All this is in part the result of a general, basic agreement on political methods and goals based on a 'Christian view of humanity'. Irrespective of their various national or cultural background, it is usually easy enough for Christian Democrats in Europe to do without any particular ideology or intellectual schemas. In general, they orientate their proposals according to practical possibilities and imperatives, and at the same time apply where possible Christian teachings and their own experience.

So the EPP evidently did not want to jeopardise its Christian Democratic identity or its role as a mass popular party occupying the political centre ground. That applied to the vast changes taking place from 1989 onwards and – especially – to the issue of opening its doors to other, notably conservative political forces. This was the well-spring of the party. And it was assumed that the EPP's position at the political centre would also be the main attraction to conservatives. The EPP then, was prepared to join forces with the conservatives only on condition that the party's essential Christian Democratic direction – and in particular its federalist European stance – were not brought into question.

THE BASIC PROGRAMME COMMITTEE

During its IX Congress, held in Athens between 11 and 13 November 1992, the European People's Party agreed a new basic programme.[6]

Party and government leaders had called for such a document to be drawn up. In April 1991 they decided that, while the party would be opened up to the British and Scandinavian conservative parties, the EPP's Christian Democratic identity should also be deepened. The more parties there were to be working together, all from different traditions and ways of thinking, the more urgent it would be to accentuate the party's identity. That was the way to ensure political cohesion and effective common action.

The resolution of EPP party and government leaders on 13 April 1991, took the line that the EPP:

> saw itself as 'a Christian Democratic-inspired force of the political centre' and (would) 'make determined efforts' to preserve and develop its Christian Democratic identity and political programme.[7]

The EPP Executive duly decided on 3 July 1991, to set up a Basic Programme Committee with the following mandate:

> The Basic Programme Committee will elaborate a new Basic Programme reflecting the consensus reached in the EPP. The Basic Programme will place in practical context the programmes agreed at EPP Congresses, and develop them further....The Basic Programme Committee will concentrate on articulating and formulating the principles which guide the EPP in specific [policy] areas.[8]

This work was so important it was decided that the Basic Programme Committee chairman should be the EPP president Wilfried Martens. The fruits of its labours would be presented to the autumn 1992 Congress to be debated and voted on. This Committee, which included representatives from member parties, recognised associations, and from the EPP Group in the European Parliament, met several times between autumn 1991 and autumn 1992. Its discussions were based on texts for individual chapters or paragraphs proposed by Jos Van Gennip and Cees Klop, Paul Maertens, Tomas Gauly, Paul Dabin, and Léon Saur.

Originally it had been thought policy areas of key importance to European integration should, along with other matters, be dealt with under the heading of 'fields of application'. This included foreign and security policy, development aid, social and economic policy, policy towards business, including domestic, environmental, and cultural policy. However, this idea was abandoned during the course of discussions. The Basic Programme, it was decided, should not be cluttered up with individual policies. Rather, these should be dealt with later in an Action Programme.

IX CONGRESS, ATHENS, 1992

Congresses had by now been held in all Community member states with EPP member parties – all except Greece. It was Athens's turn and the Greek Nea Demokratia was keen to host the event. Following the summer 1990 elections, the party, under Konstantin Mitsotakis's leadership, was once more in government. The legendary hospitality of the EPP's Greek member party was a good augury for a splendidly-organised Congress and an appropriate venue.

Discussion of the new Basic Programme was the main focus. Member parties and the EPP Group in the European Parliament, as well as the recognised associations (Women, Youth, Workers, and Independent Business) had proposed a large number of amendments and additions to the document. These were discussed in working groups and in the Congress plenary session. The vote – as had become routine since the Luxembourg Congress in 1988 – was by simply majority. Obviously an attempt was made to secure broad agreement on controversial issues.

The first chapter contained a new, up-to-date description of Christian Democratic philosophy based on the Christian view of humanity. It set out this philosophy's basic values, and what these meant in terms of ideas about society and the political system. A fresh description of the basics of Christian Democratic thinking had become necessary in the light of the new socio-political order in central and Eastern Europe following the watershed of 1989, and the knock-on effect on European integration policy. But there was another reason too. That was the change in western European values since 1968. By setting out what was supposed to inform EPP policy, a picture emerged of the Christian Democratic conception of how society and the political system altogether should evolve.

The second chapter was devoted to the European Union. It set out proposals for its future federal and democratic constitution. This chapter contained the EPP's federal European creed, and its vision of the future shape of the European Union once the Maastricht Treaty was signed. Maastricht had by now been negotiated and signed, but not yet ratified. The referendums in Denmark and in France had shown how extremely difficult the ratification process would be. However, Congress fastened on the Maastricht Treaty as the starting point for all further developments.

These two chapters were introduced by a chapter penned by Wilfried Martens in which he analysed the situation of European society and the challenges it posed. Taking this as his starting point, he attacked the various (new and old) ideological temptations. It was a way of pointing out, at the same time, the emerging dangers, for example as a result of population growth, increasing interdependence in the world economy, the gap between rich and poor, the exhaustion of natural resources, the revolution in media technology, the growth of criminality, and the resurgence of racism and nationalism. Against all these dangerous developments he set out:

> the chances of a lasting peace after the end of the east-west conflict, and the possibilities of the consensual western model which connected the Social Market economy with democracy.... Christian Democracy wants to contribute to this development. Firmly rooted in its traditions, the movement wants 'the best' and seeks to evoke man's constructive qualities by giving up-to-date expression to our ideals of Christian-social personalism.[9] Finally, Congress discussed topical issues relating to the development of the Community and European politics, above all the difficulties arising in various countries from the process of ratifying the Maastricht Treaty. The Congress's Athens Declaration confirmed traditional Christian Democratic position and expressed the EPP's firm intention of doing everything it could to ensure the success of Maastricht.[10]

The British and Danish conservative MEPs had been admitted to the EPP Group in the European Parliament in May 1992, and it was intended to bring the Scandinavian conservatives into the EPP. So it was important for the EPP leadership to restate unambiguously both the party's Christian Democratic identity and its commitment to a federal Europe. There were also important tactical reasons for this. There had been resistance on the part of a number of member parties, notably the Dutch, Belgians, and Italians, to 'widening' the EPP's membership. Agreement had only been reached by a commitment to 'deepening' it as well.

Tensions between representatives of the various ways of looking at things (and different cultures) were centre-stage in Athens, and were still evident in the debates. This was both because of the strategic and tactical implications mentioned above, but also because of the exceptionally difficult and extensive text of the draft programme. However the work was eventually done, and the various protagonists could see that worries about being done down by their partners, or pushed down the wrong track, were mainly groundless. Tensions abated, giving way to general agreement about what had been achieved.

Along with that went a tacit or explicit recognition of the achievement of Wilfried Martens, whose authority and commitment were applied as a mediator, and also in his decisive role in the programme committee and the Congress altogether. They were essential to the agreements which were reached and the quality of the results.

X CONGRESS, BRUSSELS 1993

The Athens Congress also instructed the Executive to set up a committee to prepare a draft Plan of Action based on the results of the Congress. Wilfried Martens was once again in the chair, with almost exactly the same members as those in the Founding Principles committee. Work began in spring, 1993. It had to be completed by the summer if the text was to be debated and voted on in the next EPP Congress, scheduled for December 1993.

An 'Action Programme', in the EPP tradition, is not merely an electoral platform containing a few hard-hitting demands. It contains detailed policies for all key problem areas, and is in effect the party's and the parliamentary groups' 'breviary' for the next parliamentary session. But of course it must be available in time for the electoral campaign so that candidates and campaigning parties can refer to it. And it must also be in time for member parties to include its contents in their own campaign preparations. Even more important, they must be able to take it into account in their own policy statements.

The debate in the programme commission was able to base itself on a series of texts prepared in connection with the Founding Principles committee, in particular on the text – postponed at the time – called 'areas of application'. This was largely integrated into the new draft. The rapporteurs for the individual chapters were Klaus Welle, Jacques Mallet, Fernand Herman, Ferruccio Pisoni, José-Maria Gil-Robles, along with the President and the Secretary General.

At the EPP's X Congress, held in Brussels from 8–10 December 1993, working groups and the plenary session debated amendments to the programme committee's draft text. They eventually decided the final version by majority vote; the procedure[11] was by now tried and tested. Changes and additions had, as before, come from member parties, the associations, and the parliamentary group.

The dates of the EPP Congress coincided with the meeting of the European Council at the end of the Belgian Presidency (9–10 December 1993). This had been preceded by a conference of party and government leaders. Jean-Luc Dehaene, Ruud Lubbers, Jacques Santer, and Helmut

Kohl spoke at the first meeting. And although Brussels was full of journalists from every leading country because of the Summit, neither this
opening session, nor Congress itself made any noticeable impact in the
press. Attention was concentrated on national affairs. Journalists or their
editors had clearly not yet registered that a Congress held by a European
party in this context – or indeed any other context – might have any relevance at all. Reporters were also distracted by the appearance of Salman
Rushdie at the European Socialist Party Group, meeting at the same time,
in the 'Espace Léopold' in Brussels. This too gives an insight into how
opinion-formers saw European parties.

THE ACTION PROGRAMME 1994–1999

The Brussels 1994–9 Action Programme was entitled 'Europe 2000: Unity
in Diversity'.[12] It should be seen as the application to the new realities in
Europe of the principles set out and explained in the Athens programme.
The first Article sets these out as follows: The collapse of the Communist
system, which defined itself as real existing Socialism, and the end of the
division of Europe, is the prelude to a new historical epoch in our continent. The end of the east-west conflict and the post-war order has permanently altered the context of international politics. The chance now exists
to establish freedom and democracy for all the peoples of Europe. At the
same time, new dangers have arisen. A barbaric war is being fought in the
middle of Europe which demands our engagement. Beyond that, the countries of central, eastern, and south-eastern Europe need extensive economic and political support; without democratic, economic, social, and
security stability, the threat remains of internal disorder, and ethnic
and inter-state conflict which would directly endanger the interests and
security of other countries.

The text consists of seven chapters, each dealing with one policy area.
The subject of the first chapter is 'Peace and Security in Europe and the
World'. And it is of course no coincidence that it begins with demands and
proposals for a Common Foreign and Security Policy, on conflict resolution, and on reform of the European Union's instruments of security
policy. For the EPP saw the question of Europe's ability (or inability) to
act together, communally, over the Bosnian war as the topical and decisive
challenge after Maastricht. That challenge was above all to the governments of member states.

The second chapter calls for 'an open and responsible Europe' and contains a definition of common European interest in world politics, of which

the most important are: carrying through reforms to ensure democracy, the rule of law, and the free market in central and eastern Europe; the successful shaping of an enlarged European Union, and advancing and supporting economic and social progress in the Third World.

The third chapter describes the conditions 'for an economically powerful Europe'. Taking as its starting point an analysis of the crisis, this chapter examines the conditions for restoring the credibility of a currency union, so that the possibilities for extending the basis of economic recovery can then be demonstrated. Finally, it also sets out proposals for making the European economy competitive again. The argument includes a determined plea for a global solution, taking all aspects of the crisis into account. But this can only succeed if the measures are decided at Community level – even if they are to be implemented at national level in accordance with the subsidiarity principle.

The fourth chapter, entitled 'For a Social Europe', is not concerned with classical social policy, but rather with job-creation, improving working and living conditions, combating poverty, and the possibilities which European policy should offer the old and the young.

Chapter Five, 'For a Europe based on the Rule of Law and on Humanity', is also very complex. It assumes an obligation to defend human rights throughout the world. It sets its face against xenophobia and racism, and is equally determined in its support for the rights (but also the duties) of minorities. Finally, this chapter deals with the fight against crime and drugs, and the problems connected with immigration policy.

Chapter Six, 'For a Europe Worth Living In', is both about cleaning up and protecting the natural environment, and about looking after our cultural heritage.

Chapter Seven, the last, contains 'The Institutional Requirements'. It succinctly outlines the main EPP proposals on constitutional development of the European Union. These are based on three primary principles: subsidiarity, efficiency, and democracy.

The document concludes by making a number of commitments on the contribution of social forces and of political parties. Among these is the following:

> The European parties have a decisive role in building political will and giving shape to 'the common good'. The EPP is therefore determined to see a European party statute enacted, based on Art 138A of the Maastricht Treaty, and giving a legal framework to European parties' activity, financing, and rules of procedure.

12 Bringing in the Conservatives, 1989–1995

Historical developments which both the Christian Democrats and the conservatives had to accept underlie the rapprochement between the conservatives and the Christian Democrats. That was why the EPP could not remove itself from the arguments on this issue, which had bedevilled it since the party had been founded, and which were a constant source of controversies and quarrels in the EPP's ranks.

A RAPPROCHEMENT DETERMINED BY HISTORY

The internationalisation of politics and, more precisely, the Europeanisation of all political life and political cultures in the European Union, has had a number of consequences. One is that any party seriously intent on accomplishing its tasks or fulfilling its mandate has to have a presence at European level. It follows that it must belong to a Europe-wide organisation of like-minded parties. But the British and Scandinavian conservative parties could find no partners in other European countries outside the EPP or the EUCD – none, anyway, with whom an alliance would bring political gains, or which could be justified to the electorate at home. In spite of the different cultural traditions, the Christian Democratic parties of continental Europe are their natural allies. Ultimately they share the same values, and represent the same electoral constituency.

Beyond that, the long standing co-operation in the EDU between conservative parties and a number of EUCD and EPP member parties had, over time, led to a remarkable degree of political harmony. This was especially true of European policy and international relations, but it held good too for basic economic and social policy issues. The conservatives (though not to the desired extent in the British case) had thus become more and more sympathetic both to Christian Democratic thought and to EPP policies.

The collapse of Communist regimes in central and eastern Europe, the unmasking of the Communist brand of Socialism as an illusion, and the resultant slump in the stock of political ideology – all this had a clear effect on political attitudes. Christian Democracy, and with it modern Conservatism, had an undeniable new allure. It was boosted above all by

European integration and the social market economy, successes which are both credited in equal measure to Christian Democratic and conservative parties.

The appeal of Christian Democracy was spectacularly demonstrated when Central and Eastern European people's parties embraced Christian Democratic ideas as well as the structures in which Christian Democrats organise their co-operation at European level. At the time they were founded, many of these parties had been unable to draw on a Christian Democratic tradition. Either it did not exist at all in their countries, or the movement was only embryonic. According to the accepted yardsticks, such parties had to be described as 'conservative'. Almost all of them, as a matter of course, applied to join both the EUCD and the EDU. It was a demonstration to their western European partners that, in the new circumstances in Europe, a rigorous distinction between conservative and Christian Democratic positions had become a dispensable luxury.

THE EUROPEAN DEMOCRATIC UNION

The desire to include the conservative parties was present right at the beginning, at the time the EPP was founded in 1976. The hope was to create a 'federation of Christian Democratic parties in the European Community'. The hope was to create one functional unit of the large, representative people's parties of the centre right from across the European Community.[1] The German member parties were especially enthusiastic about this project. But it was most fiercely opposed by the Italian and Benelux member parties. They saw in the inclusion of the conservatives a threat to the EPP's Christian Democratic identity.

The advocates of including them argued that there were no Christian Democratic parties in Great Britain or Denmark with which the EPP could forge an alliance. The party should take the only available option, which was to open its doors to conservatism. Otherwise, ran the argument, the EPP Group in the European Parliament would continue to lack both British and Danish MEP's. Once the Community expanded, the EPP's position would be dramatically inferior to that of the 'federation of Social Democratic parties in the European Community'. If the EPP continued to accept only parties with a Christian Democratic tradition, then it could expect no reinforcements worth mentioning from Greece, Spain, or the Nordic countries.

The prospects of including the conservative parties were not good; the majority was against. The German member parties, with the strong support of the Austrian People's Party, founded the European Democratic Union (EDU), designed to forge organised, systematic co-operation and durable links between Christian Democrats and Conservatives. The EDU brought Conservative and Christian Democratic parties together. It developed at a pan-European level as a sort of parallel organisation to the EUCD, but one that was distinctly different.[2] Its working method contrasts with that of the EUCD, which favours a parliamentary style of procedure; the EDU tends to follow the rules of diplomacy, as practised in inter-governmental co-operation. And in reality the EDU was mainly concerned with the machinery of communication and consultation in the service of foreign policy – that of the governments led by EDU-member parties. Putting into practice a common political project inspired by an idea came, at best, a poor second. The Executive is a steering committee which meets every two to three years. This is made up of member parties' international secretaries. The EDU's highest authority is the party leaders' conference, held every two years.

The Christian Democratic parties working together in the EDU are all major people's parties with complex identities. They largely incorporate their countries' conservative and liberal elements as well as Christian Democrats. Their programmes and policies reflect this fact, which means they avoid rigorous positions. They are more concerned with practice than with ideology. These characteristics, while evidently more or less pronounced in different parties, are increasingly the same for both Christian Democratic people's parties and conservative parties.

The dissent evident from the fact that some EPP and EUCD parties also joined the EDU, and the resulting tensions, were smoothed over. By carefully avoiding discussing what had happened in either EPP or EDU bodies, conflict could be avoided. But that also delayed hammering out a consensus.

Until the mid-eighties nothing at all changed. Questions about the EDU, and indeed about the relationship with the conservatives altogether, were ignored. In any event they were not answered. The issue remained burdened with a profound misunderstanding. The effect was to produce mutual mistrust between those in favour, and those against, bringing the conservatives into the fold.

There was not even any discussion after the Nea Demokratia (ND) deputies joined the EPP Group in the European Parliament after Greece entered the Community in January 1981. Nor was there a debate when it was resolved to accept the ND's application to join the EPP as a full member – this in spite of the fact that the ND is unambiguously a conservative party. It is in any event a party with no Christian Democratic tradition, nor a Christian Democratic party programme. But it has to be said that this party, only founded once democracy had been restored in the 1970s, was neither politically nor ideologically compromised. And its political direction was unambiguously European.

PARTIDO POPULAR

Not until 1988 did opening up the EPP to the Conservatives become an urgent item on the agenda. The issue was the situation in Spain. After their country's accession to the Community in January 1986, the MEPs from the Conservative Alianza Popular (AP) became members of the European Democratic Group (EDG), where they joined the British and Danish Conservatives. Only MEPs from the small Spanish member parties of the EUCD – the Partido Nacionalista Vasco, the Unio Democratica de Cataluna and the Partido Democrata Popular – joined the EPP Group.

The last of these, now renamed Democracia Cristiana, did not win a single seat in the first Spanish elections to the European Parliament in June 1987. The same fate befell the Basque party; one lone female deputy from the Catalonian party managed to win a seat.

The leader of the AP, Manuel Fraga, himself a Member of the European Parliament, and his group, soon began to seek an alliance with the EPP Group. The Spaniards did not feel particularly at home in an EDG dominated by the Tories, where they were alone with the British and Danish. It also became clear quite quickly that they were far less 'conservative' than their British EDG partners. That did not just apply to their policy on Europe, but also to their views on, for instance, issues of social policy. And as a result of the close links they maintained with the Bavarian CSU, in particular, they increasingly acquired a taste for the EPP.

The secretary general of the Council of Europe, Marcelino Oreja, although an independent, was known for his Christian Democratic views. And it was under Oreja's influence that Fraga agreed, in the run-up to the 1989 European elections, to re-form his party and thus to enable political figures with a 'centrist' profile (like Oreja and his friends) to play a part in it.[3]

Fraga had repeatedly been worsted in elections by Felipe Gonzales and the socialists. He had obviously become convinced that there was no chance of winning elections in Spain on a clearly 'right-wing' ticket. He agreed to a change in his party's profile and programme, its acceptance of the political forces of the centre, and its 'Europeanisation' on the model of the EPP – which his party, thus reformed, would join. The credibility

of this operation was to be sealed by his resigning from the party leadership, and his withdrawal from national politics.

In these circumstances and in view of the hopelessness of a solo effort
by the Democracia Cristiana, its chairman, Javier Ruperez, decided that
his party should be dissolved and integrated into the People's Party
(Partido Popular), a process which was intended to give the party a completely fresh start. He was vigorously supported by the EPP. At a meeting
in Luxembourg in January 1989 between the party leadership (represented
by the President, Jacques Santer, the Group chairman, Egon Klepsch, and
the secretary-general) Oreja and Ruperez agreed that the parties should act
together, and mutually assist each other.

The right-wing Conservative Allianza Popular was now transformed
into a party of the centre-right: it was renamed Partido Popular/PP in
spring 1989. And the Christian Democrats were prepared to join the PP.
Everything was now in place for integrating the PP into the EPP. The PP
went into the 1989 European elections with a manifesto based on the EPP
programme. Its MEPs – including some Christian Democrats like Oreja,
who headed the list, and José Maria Gil-Robles – were admitted to the
EPP Group following the elections. This was in line with a decision by
EPP party leaders before the elections that any MEP who had stood for
election on a list shared by Christian Democrats should automatically be
allowed to join the EPP Group.[4]

Soon after being elected to succeed Fraga as party leader in April 1990,
José Maria Aznar, made contact with the EPP leadership to discuss what
steps had to be taken to join the party. Aznar himself would have to overcome internal – right-wing Conservative – opposition to entering the EPP.
Within the EPP, the resistance of the Catalans and Basques in particular
was another obstacle. For internal Spanish, or Catalan, or Basque reasons,
they opposed letting in the PP. The Italians, Belgians, and Dutch, *inter
alia*, had to be convinced that the Spanish party had undergone a genuine
conversion, and that the conditions existed for co-operation in a spirit of
mutual trust, and for a common policy at European level based on
Christian Democratic principles.

In the EPP, Wilfried Martens, then still prime minister of Belgium, had
been elected president in May 1990. From the outset he had been a strong
advocate of opening up the EPP and so actively supported the PP's admission. His own party, the Flemish CVP, was guarded to negative.

In autumn the same year, the PP was granted observer status. A year
later, it became a full member of the EPP. And as with the Greek party,
Nea Demokratia, it soon became clear that the integration of 'conservatives' did not have to affect the EPP's Christian Democratic orientation or
identity.

THE STRATEGY OF OPENING UP THE PARTY

A strategy was needed to persuade those who were hesitant, apprehensive, or suspicious, to accept the policy of opening up the party and including the conservatives. Above all, given the differing self-images and perceptions, there had to be a framework of principles which would ultimately convince, or at least reconcile, everyone concerned. Given that the relationship between Christian Democracy and Conservatism was a sensitive and, historically speaking, highly-charged issue, the aim had to be to prevent irreparable breaches within the EPP or between member parties.

It was the expansion of the Community itself that compelled the EPP to ask itself whether it was willing and able to open itself up. These potential partners, though sharing the same common ground on essentials, had nevertheless grown out of a different tradition. The Political Union was destined to grow to include the northern European countries in the relatively short term, and the Central and Eastern European countries in the longer term. The EPP, being a European party, naturally had to have a presence in all Union member states if it was to remain credible and capable of making its mark. That also held good for countries where, for historical and cultural reasons, Christian Democratic parties had failed to emerge, or had not developed into mass people's parties.

Further important reasons for pursuing a strategy of openness became apparent. The EPP is a party that has to fight for majorities if it is to translate its ideas into reality. The EPP is a people's party and must not shut itself off from individual groups, classes, strata, or movements, least of all when they see themselves as having something in common with the party, or wish it to represent them. The EPP is also a Christian Democratic party and believes its ideas to be persuasive. And the EPP is, when all is said and done, a federalist party which respects the peculiarities of its regional or national components, but seeks consensus between their different contributions in order to articulate and pursue a common policy.

The hope connected with such a strategy had to be this: to ensure that the EPP did not miss the chance of integrating forces which were allied or politically close to it. This would in turn make the party more influential in every Community country, and across the Community as a whole, and allow it to assume a leading role. But for this to succeed, the EPP had to see itself – and make sure it was seen to be – an open people's party with Christian Democratic traditions and goals. Moreover, it had to be clear that it was possible to work with those who represented other traditions and points of view, as long as they in turn respected the party's traditions and accepted its policies. Seizing this opportunity was also in line with the EPP's ambition to become pre-eminent, and as far as possible to translate its project into reality. The EPP's claims and ambitions were to a degree founded on the role which Christian Democrats had played in European unification, and the responsibility which that achievement had conferred on the present generation of leaders.

These considerations were the backdrop to the observation by the Conference of EPP Party Leaders and Heads of Government on 13 April 1991, that the EPP:

> would in future enter into closer co-operation with people's parties working towards a comparable social project in their countries, and towards the same goals as the EPP in European politics. As Europe's leading political force, the EPP is in principle prepared to admit those parties seeking membership provided that they accept the EPP's guidelines, basic policies, and constitution.[5]

This strategy of opening up the party, was intended to go hand in hand with 'deepening' Christian Democratic identity and to boost the party's self-confidence. It was convincingly and resolutely pursued in 1990 and 1991, above all by Wilfried Martens. He found his most important ally in the CDU party leader, Chancellor Helmut Kohl. The run of success ended in 1992, when the big issue was to integrate British and Danish conservative MEPs left in the EDG Group after the Spanish had left.

THE RAPPROCHEMENT WITH THE BRITISH AND DANISH CONSERVATIVES

The Conservative MEPs understood, before their party friends in Westminster or in Central Office, that Britain's future is 'at the heart of Europe'. It was they who committed themselves to a rapprochement with the EPP. Directly after the 1989 European elections, in agreement with their Danish colleagues, the EDG, led by chairman Sir Christopher Prout, applied for membership of the EPP Group in the European Parliament.

The application was so controversial that the group felt unable to discuss it, let alone to take a decision. So EPP Group chairman Egon Klepsch called together the EPP party Executive. At the time the party was chaired by Jacques Santer, this body had decided – after a lengthy debate in July 1989 – that the time was not yet ripe. This was above all because of prime minister Margaret Thatcher's policy on Europe. But Santer had urged the conservative and Christian Democratic groups in the European Parliament to intensify both dialogue and co-operation with each other. A fresh decision would be taken two years later in the light of mutual experience.

Internal opposition in the EPP Group, however, initially prevented the dialogue called for by the EPP Executive, or any closer co-operation. In the summer of 1991, Wilfried Martens began trying to fill the gap left by the EPP Group's dilatory treatment of the issue. He met more frequently with the leading figures of the EDG, especially its chairman and secretary general Harald Romer, and later also with the chairman of the British Conservative Party, Chris Patten.

It was not until the second half of 1991 that dialogue between the two groups began. This was a few months after Mrs Thatcher's resignation. Urged on by Helmut Kohl, and under Wilfried Martens's leadership, the April 1991 conference of EPP party leaders and heads of government once more considered the Conservatives' application. It instructed the group to establish by the end of the year whether, and under what conditions, a joint parliamentary group was feasible, and under what circumstances.[6]

During the second half of 1991, consultations were held on a number of sensitive issues.[7] The conclusion was that close co-operation was, in principle possible. In February 1992, the conference of EPP party leaders and heads of government was able to report that given the outcome of these discussions – there was little to prevent the Christian Democrats and Conservatives from forming a single group. The EPP Group in the European Parliament was given the mandate to set out the arguments for a 'joint parliamentary group' with the Conservatives.[8]

One of the key pre-conditions for admitting the Conservative MEPs to the EPP Group, which eventually took place on 1 May 1992, was evidently Mrs Thatcher's resignation as British prime minister and leader of the Tory Party, and John Major's willingness to pursue a different policy on Europe. But Helmut Kohl's determination was critical. Given the imminent enlargement of the European Union, he had strategic reasons for wanting to open the EPP to the Conservatives. Without Kohl, the breakthrough would not have come so soon. The decision could not have been taken at all, however, if party chairman Martens had not been so committed on the issue, and not taken political and practical responsibility for seeing it through.

After the British and Danish Conservative MEPs had joined the EPP Group, it was to be expected that in the medium term their parties would also forge closer links with the EPP. The first step was taken by the Danes when, in July 1993, they applied for the Konservative Folkeparti to be granted permanent observer status.

THE NORDIC CONSERVATIVES

As early as 1989, the Finnish Conservative party, Kansallinen Kokoomus (KK), had expressed an interest in involvement in the EUCD and EPP. In spring 1991 it applied for observer status in the EUCD. But was rejected by the Political Bureau because of opposition from representatives of various member parties, notably the Scandinavian Christian Democratic parties.

Immediately after its chairman, Carl Bildt, had formed a coalition government with the Liberals, Centrists, and Christian Democrats in the autumn of 1991, Sweden's Moderata Samling (MS) also expressed an interest. The EPP leadership now pressed hard for the necessary dialogue with the northern European conservatives to be accompanied by a special effort to reach agreement with Christian Democrats in these countries. This was essential if minds were to be changed inside the party. Any involvement of the conservatives in the Christian Democrats' European political organisation was bound to be controversial: at home they were rivals. For a number of EPP member parties, how their future partners in Scandinavia dealt with this problem would determine whether or not they agreed to extend EPP membership to them.

So the first step had to be the admission of the Swedish Christian Democratic Party. Referring to a provision in the constitution that allows EUCD member parties in countries wanting to join the EU to be admitted to the EPP as associate members, the Kristdemokratiska Samhällspartiet (KDS) had submitted an application; it was approved in the autumn of 1991.

This step was initially controversial. Unaware of the situation in Sweden, the representatives of some member parties in the EPP Bureau assumed that the KDS was a *'quantité négligeable'*. They feared that any recognition of this small, relatively young party – without a single MP in the Swedish parliament until the September 1991 elections – would hold up recognising the Moderata Samling. An additional factor was that anti-European statements by the Christian parties of Norway, Denmark and Finland were mistakenly attributed to the Swedish KDS.

Scandinavia and Finland's Christian Democratic parties are much younger than their equivalents in continental Europe. They were founded in reaction to the secularisation of public life in the 1960s and 1970s promoted not only by socialists and liberals, but also by conservatives. Apart from the Norwegian party, founded as early as the 1930s, none of them existed before the 1960s. They should be seen as 'Christian', confessional parties, making their stand for the teachings of their churches in politics. There is a limit to how far they can grow unless they can evince confidence outside matters demanding only moral rigour and ethical rigidity. One measure of this is the development of their policy on European integration. Apart from the Swedish KDS, they have so far had great difficulties in arriving at a positive attitude.

In the countries of mainland Europe, bourgeois consensus and people's parties are normally Christian Democratic. In Scandinavia, this role tends to be a conservative one. However, it is also noticeable that the Christian parties of Norway and Sweden have some potential for development and growth. They hold their own in parliament, and on occasion in recent years have taken over the reins of government. The effect is to expose them to the influences which, in mainland Europe, turn confessional parties into people's parties. In view of their weak position, the Scandinavian CD parties' concern about the conservative parties drawing closer to European Christian Democracy is understandable.

The Swedish KDS, in particular, responded in a constructive way to the sympathy expressed by the EPP leadership for their concern about this. The KDS leadership understood and accepted that the European view of things differed from their national or Scandinavian view, and that the EPP's essential concept of 'Christian Democracy' goes beyond the positions underlying the self-image and programmes of their own parties.

It must also be borne in mind that the 'Conservatism' of Sweden's Moderata Samling, Finland's Kansallinen Kokoomus, Norway's Hoyre, and Denmark's Konservative Folkeparti is not the same as that of the British Conservatives. And it is absolutely not the same as Thatcherism. They are parties of the centre that are open to Europe and advocate a social market economy. Their position is 'moderate' and 'middle-class'. This too was a factor in smoothing the process of convergence and the incorporation of the Nordic Conservatives into the EPP.

But in order to enable them to work with the party, the EPP statutes had to be changed. The rules allowed associate membership or observer status for parties from countries seeking to join the EC but only where the applicant parties were also members of the EUCD. The Athens Congress passed the required change in the statutes in November 1992. Two months later, in January 1993, Moderata Samling and Kansallinen Kokoomus were accepted as permanent observers. This decision had near-unanimous approval once the KDS representatives had signalled their agreement. In May 1993 the EPP Bureau also accepted Norwegian Hoyre's application – with no votes against, and not even abstentions. And after Sweden's and Finland's accession to the European Union, Moderata Samling, Kansallinen Kokoomus, and the Konservative Folkeparti were admitted as full members in February 1995. Norwegian Hoyre was granted the status of associate member at the same time.[9]

The British Conservative Party, whose MEPs are loyal members of the EPP Group, will probably not be joining the European People's Party in the foreseeable future. But a political solution has essentially been found to the organisational problem of integrating conservatives into the Christian Democratically-inclined European People's Party. The internal debate that accompanied this exercise was occasionally impassioned and stormy. For the issues associated with it go deep into the member parties' idea of themselves. It could not have succeeded without the simultaneous debate on the EPP's programme, which issued in a new policy statement adopted at the Athens Congress in November 1992.[10] It confirms the EPP's Christian Democratic identity in a new, modern way. The debate on the opening up of the EPP has thus not only contributed to its enlargement, but also made it politically more cohesive and more serious.

Part IV
Structures, Problems, and Perspectives

13 What is the Meaning of 'Christian Democracy' in the European Context?

What is the specific feature that marks Christian Democracy out from other non-socialist political movements, especially from conservatism of the British or Scandinavian type? The question is not merely of theoretical interest. It played a prominent role in the discussions surrounding the foundation of the European People's Party or EPP, and the issue remained a live one throughout the development, because of the recurrent problem of whether or not conservative parties were to be brought into, or excluded from, European Christian Democratic organisations.

But even if we leave that matter to one side, the question merits attention if we are to describe the making of a political party which defines itself as Christian Democratic. Indeed if one ignores the way the party is rooted in the Christian Democratic movement, the birth and development of the European People's Party makes little or no sense.

A POLITICAL MOVEMENT

What we bracket together under the term 'Christian Democracy' is a product of the political history of the countries of continental Europe, where society has largely been shaped by Catholicism. Christian Democracy has remained fairly alien to the political tradition in Britain, and indeed to political thought in the Anglo-Saxon world and Scandinavia too.

In some countries there have always been national state churches, for instance in Britain and Scandinavia. In others, the Church has been socially and politically powerful and influential until the most recent times – as in Poland or Spain. In none of these cases has there ever been much need to establish lay political movements bound to the churches, and committed to defending ecclesiastical institutions and positions. The same applies, roughly speaking, to the countries of south-eastern Europe. Here, Orthodoxy has created different cultural and social conditions, and the independent national churches have willingly subordinated themselves to those holding power at any given time.

Without exception, the Christian Democrat parties in Italy, France, Germany, Belgium, the Netherlands, and in a few other countries in Western and Central Europe, grew consistently out of confessional movements. These were predominantly Catholic. But some – for instance, in the Netherlands – were Protestant. Such movements, in certain cases already established in the 19th century, were reactions against secular or anti-clerical tendencies in the modern state. Later, inter-denominational (Christian) parties emerged from these. They freed themselves from their earlier defensive attitude, developing their own social agenda in the confrontation with Socialism and Liberalism. In this way, they prepared themselves to take on government responsibility. And it was in this way too that the reconciliation of the Christian churches and their members with the modern state was made both possible and easier.

On the basis of their experience in government, and of the responsibility that goes with power, these parties opened up further. The process accelerated as the century wore on, becoming more pronounced after the Second World War. Forces were integrated into the Christian parties which were not predominantly confessional or ideological (in the sense of an ethical conviction). Rather, what drove them was a pragmatic or rational impulse (in the sense of an ethic of responsibility). Only now could they perceive themselves as Christian Democratic or Christian Social parties, meaning parties made up of citizens inspired by Christianity, citizens who were taking over responsibility in state and society quite independently of their respective churches.

In Britain and Scandinavia, by contrast, the conflict with Liberalism and Socialism produced bourgeois people's parties. These were conservative movements committed to defending the traditional social order, its values, and state institutions. In their own countries they represent the same classes of voter, in terms of sociology and value systems, as Christian Democratic parties in continental Europe. However, they are very different in their party programmes, political approach, and style.

Today, Christian Democratic parties exist mainly in Europe and Latin America. Here as there, there are significant regional associations bringing national parties together in one continental organisation – in Europe: the European Union of Christian Democrats (EUCD), in Latin America: the Organización Demócrata Cristiana de América (ODCA). The ODCA and the EUCD work together in the framework of the Christian Democrat International (CDI). There are also some individual parties and groups in Africa and Asia which are recognised by the CDI but not (yet) organised into regional associations.

POLITICAL PHILOSOPHY

Not the least important foundation stone of Christian Democracy is a political philosophy with a conception of how politics should be conducted and what it is for, the form society should take, and how the state should be organised.

At the heart of this idea stands the human being, who is morally responsible before God, and has political responsibility towards society. This is the central form of Christian Democracy: a person is concerned as much with the individual as with human society and the national community as a whole. In other words, the point is not the interests of a particular class or the preoccupations of a specific group. That is why Christian Democratic parties see themselves as people's parties.

As people's parties they attempt to integrate the differing interests and concerns of all classes and groups by developing consensus. And so this building of consensus, meaning the constant endeavour to strike a balance and reach an understanding between divergent efforts and antinomian principles, is also a fundamental element in the Christian Democrat's approach.

This is also the driving force behind the concept of the social market economy, propounded by German scholars and politicians with Christian Democrat leanings. It concentrates on squaring economic efficiency with social justice, reconciling the laws of the market with the precept of social responsibility.

Similarly, Christian Democrats regard federalism as a suitable method of linking the need for unity with respect for diversity. Thus they do not envisage the European Union as a centralised undertaking. Quite the reverse: Christian Democrats support European unity because they believe that, in the present historical circumstances, only co-operation and belonging to a broader community will allow the identity of the various peoples and nations to be preserved and to blossom.

The need for unity derives from the fact that almost all social, economic, and political problems arising in individual European states today are trans-national. It means that they can only be resolved by common endeavour in a spirit of solidarity, and in line with the principle of subsidiarity.

Subsidiarity and solidarity are two cornerstones of the Christian Democratic credo, which is also strongly influenced by the social teachings of the Christian churches. Catholic doctrine, steadily developed in papal encyclicals on society since *Rerum Novarum* (1891), is of especial importance. Conversely, Catholic doctrine is itself greatly influenced by Christian Democratic thought and practice. This became especially clear in the papal encyclical *Centesimus annus* (1990). This for the first time holds up the social market economy – though it is not mentioned by name – as a concept which confirms the teachings of the church.

The Christian Democratic philosophy has consequences for the political attitude and behaviour of its champions; it calls for an openness to dialogue, and patient efforts to reconcile opposing positions. Christian Democrats thus find themselves in the middle of the political spectrum, seeking a balance between the antinomies which permeate the lives of both men and politics. They prefer moderate solutions and a measured approach to any form of radicalism.

This attitude involves a receptiveness to fresh ideas and flexibility in new situations. It means that Christian Democrats do not follow an ideology just because it claims to have all the answers. They know that no human being is perfect, and that is especially true of Christian Democrats themselves. They do not want to implement some ideological theory worked out by bureaucrats or academics. Their priority, rather, is to seek solutions that satisfy people's needs and are therefore accepted by them. So pragmatism, as long as it does not become an end in itself and thus ideological, is a key element in Christian Democratic thinking.

This overview of a model of Christian Democracy is in no way intended to idealise the Christian Democratic movement. However, it is important to stress that this is a living model. And it is a model that most politically active Christian Democrats with positions of responsibility in state or society keep before their eyes. It certainly is not binding upon every individual to the same degree, but it does serve as a general guideline for everyone. The evidence of that can be found in the political programmes of the Christian Democratic parties of Europe and the political action which is based upon it.

AN HISTORICALLY DETERMINED IDENTITY

Thus Christian Democracy is by its nature a political philosophy. Historically, it has developed on the back of a political movement, opposing both Socialism and Liberalism. Christian Democratic identity is thus determined not simply by its philosophy. The fact that it is a movement, and its history, are just as important. In the search for this identity, the successes and failures of the Christian Democratic parties and personalities play a role along with Christian social teaching, both Catholic and Protestant theology and literature, and a great deal more besides.

Christian Democrats in the various European countries have had different historical experiences, and the same is true of the Latin Americans. It follows that Christian Democratic identity varies too: different individual aspects or elements of it are valued and regarded differently in different places. Also, Christian Democrats have not all had the same teachers, or read the same books. It is hardly surprising that they will have different focuses, not only in theory but also in practice.

It is obvious, therefore, that the issue of a consensus-building identity plays a key role in efforts to construct global or European co-operative federations of Christian Democratic parties, or to build effective political structures out of the same material.

What remain the most decisive factors for the shared identity of Europe's Christian Democrats will certainly remain common action, and the way responsibility is exercised in specific situations. If Christian Democrats continue regularly to invoke the names of Robert Schuman, Alcide De Gasperi, and Konrad Adenauer, it is because these personalities have been examples of Christian Democratic identity – through their actions and their decisions, their successes and achievements. Not one of these 'founding fathers' was a theorist; none of them would even have dreamed of defining what Christian Democracy might be. They were Christian Democrats because that was how they saw themselves and because of how they behaved.

'Christian Democracy' cannot be understood as something abstract: there is no 'pure' form of it. Rather, it exists only as an expression of a movement or as a programme, and the action of a party that changes in unison with the people it represents, and with the circumstances it has to confront. Even the idea or philosophy underpinning the movement emerges from the conflict with realities within which it has to prove itself. Its historical character can also be seen in the fact that it bears the mark of various (national) imprints, and has been through various stages of development.

14 Working Methods of the Party Bodies

The EPP's bodies are Congress, the executive, the conference of party and government leaders, the presidency, the President, and the Secretary General. Their composition or appointment are determined by the statutes, as are their specific tasks and competencies.

The first, 1976, constitution was hardly changed in 1979, but had not been revised since.[1] Instead, a completely new constitution was elaborated by a Statutes Committee, chaired by the Secretary General, which had been working intensively on the project since 1988. It was passed by the VIII Congress in Dublin (14–16 November 1990), and it brought considerable changes.[2] Experience had shown they were necessary, and they also reflected the more intensive, and increasingly political character, of the European integration process. The changes sought to make decision-making simpler by extending the competencies of the Executive at the expense of the Executive Committee's 'grace and favour' members. This committee was abolished, as it had in practice turned out to be superfluous. But the reforms also sought to democratise the Executive and Congress by getting rid of excessive representation by the 'grace and favour' members, and replacing them with delegates from member parties. Beyond that, the party was strengthened by according the leading bodies of the body more delegated authority to act and take initiatives; it made the party better able to act, or react, in a coherent way. That was the logic of recognising both the presidium and the Secretary General as autonomous bodies. And to that should be added the informal, but already much-valued conference of party and government leaders which had been meeting since 1983.

CONGRESS

Congress meets at least once every two years, in different venues, and it is the forum for deciding the political line or programme, and for changes to the statutes. It is made up of delegates from the member parties, from the recognised associations (youth, women, workers, local and regional politicians, and SMEs), members of the EPP Group in the European Parliament who belong to the member parties, the EPP Presidency as whole, national heads of party and government, and European Commissioners who belong to a member party.

The number of delegates is weighted according to how many deputies a party has returned to the European Parliament, individual delegates being elected by the appropriate body in the member party. For example, in the CDU this vote is taken by the federal committee, to whom a list has been presented based on proposals by Länder party association. The democratic and federalist spirit of the EPP's statute are not yet found everywhere else: often, delegates are still nominated by the party leadership.

Congress organisation follows rules of procedure passed from time to time by the EPP Executive; occasionally they are adapted to take account of how these have worked out in practice. Until the VI Congress, in 1986 in the Hague, Congress documents were decided in advance by reaching a consensus in the Executive. This was done to take account of minority opinions, and with an eye on maintaining unity. Although delegates could, during Congress, discuss, propose foot-notes to, and deliver commentaries on, such documents, they were not allowed to decide any changes to them. Since the VII Congress (Luxembourg 1988) all changes or additions to the Congress document have been decided by majority vote, and this includes all changes and additions proposed by the deadlines to a Congress document prepared by a programme commission. A procedure set out in the agenda of the IX Congress (Athens 1992) applies:

> Congress meets as a plenary and also in (two) working groups; both the plenary and the working groups are permitted to make decisions. The working groups should reflect the composition of Congress. Delegations' votes in working groups in each case count for half the number of votes they hold in the Congress plenary. Proposals which, in the working group vote
> a) are supported by fewer than a third of delegates present will be definitively rejected;
> b) are supported by a two-thirds majority will be definitively accepted.
> c) fail to achieve a two-thirds majority, but are approved by over a third of the delegates present, will – after a position has been recommended by the programme petitions committee – be presented to the Congress sitting as a plenary for decision. (The vote being by simple majority).

A new quality of co-operation and integration emerges from this procedure, made possible by a growing policy consensus, and in particular the increased ability to understand each other's point of view. For it should be borne in mind that the principal problem in international or supranational understanding in a European party of like-minded parties is not in essence that individual national elements hold differing interests or ideas, and quarrel with each other. The main problem – and this goes for other transnational groups as well – lies rather in the different languages, cultures, and constitutional backgrounds of the various countries from which partners and colleagues have come and in which they have grown up. So they bring with them different ways of speaking and behaving. Styles of debate and rhetoric vary from country to country. To those who are inexperienced everything seems alien, making understanding, let alone trust, more difficult. The skill or otherwise of the interpreters does not change this.

Compared to a national party's congress, a European party congress is not lively or flexible; the reasons for this are difficult to overcome. The need for interpreters so that people can understand each other does not just palpably reduce spontaneity. Another consequence is having to adhere to strict and very limited working hours. The interpreters, according to the rules that apply at present, are not allowed to work for longer than two shifts of three and a half hours, one in the morning and one in the afternoon. In general, in order not to put any of the delegations at a disadvantage, all official Community languages are translated. To ensure there is interpretation to and from each language, a team of three interpreters is needed for each language. That means 24 interpreters for eight languages, which, for financial reasons alone, precludes extra meetings. This puts a very rigid straight-jacket on proceedings.

THE EXECUTIVE

Decisions made by the Executive (previously the political bureau) take into account the programme and policy lines set by Congress. The Executive meets at least four times a year, in practice at least every two months. Most meetings take place in Brussels, in one of the rooms allocated to the EPP Group in the European Parliament buildings.

The Executive consists of delegates sent by national parties, their number being in proportion to the number of deputies each member party has returned to the European Parliament; *ex officio* members are members of the EPP presidium, members of the EPP Group presidium and leaders of national delegations in the Group; chairmen of member parties and associations and (in so far as they belong to member parties) the European Commissioners and the President and/or Vice-Presidents of the European Parliament.

The political task of the Executive is to guarantee the unity of the party as an active body, and to influence European politics in the spirit of the party programme. It has a number of further tasks which are of relevance to organisation: it determines the budget, controls the leadership, elects the presidium including the President and (on the recommendation of the President) the Secretary General. The Executive also decides on whether or not to admit new members, and finally it is the Executive's duty to convene a Congress and decide its agenda.

That makes the Executive, chaired by the President, the most important decision-making body. It is the forum for agreement, or argument, between the party and the parliamentary group. The party representatives' ambition is as a rule to dictate to the group leadership the political line the group should take. And the group leadership's aim is to bring the party Executive over to the group's way of thinking. In so far as these conflicts are about issues requiring expertise in Community politics and experience in dealing with Community institutions, the group representatives always have the advantage. By contrast, in wider political matters of international relations or economic policy, the people from the party tend to be better at getting their way.

Evidently the Executive can decide by a majority: indeed this has been the case since the EPP's foundation in 1976. Naturally, the Executive will always try to establish general agreement. It will in any case strive to respect members' individual identities, and not make unrealistic demands of any delegation. Enormous attention has to be devoted to parties' sensitivities. Over the years it has become possible to consolidate the party's internal relations as integration and consensus grows. Eventually, from 1992 onwards, Wilfried Martens – elected EPP Chairman in 1990 – was able to make more and more use of majority voting.

The representatives of the member parties are now far more willing to back down on an issue in order to achieve a common position. Besides, experience has shown that the 'national', in particular the 'bottom line' position, is frequently made the subject of a stubborn rearguard action for home consumption only. Sometimes weakness is another motive. It is, after all, not always simple to represent a decision 'at home' which breaks with a much-loved national way of seeing things, or which conflicts with a national habit – not even when this seems the sensible and necessary course from a European perspective.

PRESIDENT AND PRESIDENCY

The President represents the party internally and externally, and leads and chairs the Congress, the Executive, and the conference of party and government leaders. The success of the EPP depends to a large extent on his political commitment and the success of his initiatives with member parties and in the relevant circles in European politics. It is demanded of him that he lead the party – by means of integration and moderation. It is therefore no coincidence that, so far, every single EPP President has been a political figure from the Benelux countries: the Belgians Leo Tindemans (1976–85) and Wilfried Martens (from 1990), the Dutchman Piet Bukman (1985–87), and the Luxembourger Jacques Santer (1987–90).

The European Liberals and Social Democrats also prefer to choose their chairmen from these countries, whose political culture has turned balance and compromise into a fine art. Belgium is certainly the leader in this respect.

The Presidency had been accorded a purely ceremonial role in the original constitution. In the new 1990 statutes it becomes an independent body responsible for ensuring the EPP's political presence at all times, making sure Executive decisions are carried out, and overseeing the work of the Secretary General, especially in budgetary matters. This put the Presidency at the head of the party, a forum in which the President, Secretary General and treasurer discuss internal, operational, and administrative proposals and initiatives with the Vice-Presidents before the Executive deals with them.

Since 1990, the election of Presidency members takes place every three years (previously every two years). Along with the Presidents, the Secretary General and the Treasurer, ten Vice-Presidents are elected.[3] The following are or were Vice-Presidents for one or more of the electoral periods after 1976: José-Maria Aznar from Spain; Garret Fitzgerald and Alan Dukes from Ireland; Jean Spautz from Luxembourg; the Dutchmen Hans de Boer, Norbert Schmelzer, Piet Bukman, and Wim Van Velzen; from Germany Egon Klepsch, Ottfried Henning, Gerold Tandler and Marlene Lenz; Marc Bertand from Belgium; Joannis Varvitsiotis from Greece; and Dario Antoniozzi, Vito Lattanzio, Beniamino Andreatta, Gianni Prandini, Giuseppe Guarino, and Bruno Orsini from Italy; André Colin, Pierre Pflimlin, and Pierre Méhaignerie from France. Two further Vice-Presidents were *ex-officio* members of the presidium: the Chairman of the EPP Group and the President of the European Union of Christian Democrats. The following have been chairmen of the parliamentary group since the EPP's foundation: Alfred Bertand (1975–77), Egon A. Klepsch (1977–81, 1984–91), Paolo Barbi (1982–84), Leo Tindemans (1992–94), and Wilfried Martens (since 1994). The EUCD Presidents have been: Kai-Uwe von Hassel (1973–81), Diogo Freitas do Amaral (1981–83), Giulio Andreotti (1983–85), Emilio Colombo (1985–92), Wilfried Martens (1993–96), and Wim van Velzen (since 1996).

May 1990 saw the first contested elections, because nine candidates had been put forward for six places. This was a clear indication of the

Presidency's enhanced powers. But it also gave expression to a new openness and the triumph of democratic procedures over diplomacy. The big improvement in the way the party was developing was above all shown by the fact that the majority turned down a proposal to increase the number of Vice-Presidents – this figure not being laid down in the statutes. The argument for rejection was that the Presidency was not a ceremonial but rather a supranational body. It did not derive legitimacy from the fact that it represented all, or as many national components of the party as possible. Legitimacy came from the fact that the party had confidence that those who had been elected were competent to represent the EPP as a whole. And the Presidency had to be able to act, and to be flexible, which meant keeping it as small as possible.

THE SECRETARY GENERAL

The Secretary General implements decisions reached by the party bodies. With the support of the general secretariat, he prepares meetings and concerns himself with co-operation and agreement with, and between, member parties, the associations, and the parliamentary group. His election is by the Executive, on the President's recommendation. The same person can, as has been the case since 1983, also be Secretary General of the EUCD, in order to co-ordinate the common action of Europe's Christian Democrats beyond the boundaries of Community countries. As a rule, the Secretary General is a member of one of the bigger parties from one of the larger countries. It can hardly be a coincidence that for most of the period during which the classical party federations have been in existence, all the Secretaries General have been German.[4] This reflects the strong position of German parties in the European formations, and no doubt, too, widespread confidence in the Germans' organisational efficiency and skill in political management.

The first Secretary General of the European People's Party, Jean Seitlinger, held an honorary post. During the entirety of his term of office, from 1978 to 1983, he was both a deputy in the French National Assembly and a Member of the European Parliament; and he was also mayor of Sarreguemines in Lothringen. He left the running of the general secretariat to the Executive secretary Josef Müller, a former Member of the German Bundestag and of the European Parliament, who had a great deal of broad political experience, particularly of European matters.[5]

This situation was generally held to be unsatisfactory. The appointment of a new Secretary General was seen as a first step towards breathing life into the EPP structure foreseen at the time the party was founded. This man should not be burdened with parliamentary duties, and available to devote his full attention to the job. Helmut Kohl, the federal leader of the German Christian Democratic Union, insisted to EPP President Leo Tindemans – who, according to the statutes, had the right of proposal – that the position must be filled by a German. The new EPP Secretary General should at the same time take over responsibility for the EUCD general secretariat, which was to be transferred from Rome to Brussels and integrated with the EPP general secretariat.

Thomas Jansen was elected in April 1983. He would remain Secretary General of both EPP and EUCD until the end of 1994.[6] In Jansen's opinion, the Secretary General had to be free to defend the interests of the EPP against the demands of member parties, those of the EPP parliamentary Group, and against individual ambitions. To ensure his independence, he, for instance, refused to have his services requisitioned by the EPP Group. (This contrasted with his Social Democratic and Liberal colleagues, who were both integrated into the staffs of their parliamentary groups).

The Secretary General is in fact the only office-holder whose election by the Executive gives him a political mandate which is exclusively an EPP one. He is also the one person able to devote himself full-time to the task of developing the party structure and organising its work. All other members of the Presidency, including the President and of course the members of the Executive, have other duties arising from their other positions or mandates. These other duties will usually take precedence for them. Such obligations will be to their national parties, to their associations, or to their parliamentary group. So it is not exaggeration to say that the Secretary General embodies the party's conscience. In any event, he is the conceptual and dynamic force behind all undertakings intended to give the party a public profile, whether organisationally or in terms of the political programme.

THE GENERAL SECRETARIAT

For the first few years of the European People's Party general secretariat's existence, the 'team' consisted of two people: Josef Müller and his colleague Trudi Lücker. It was not until 1981 that two members of staff joined. They were Guy Korthoudt, who had previously been Secretary General of the Young Christian Democrats in Flanders, and Monique Poket. It soon became clear that the increasing demands made on the general secretariat by member parties were too great for such a tiny personnel.

As along ago as 1979, the electoral campaign in the first direct elections in the European Parliament had demonstrated the usefulness, for both the leadership and the *apparat* of national parties, to have someone to represent their interests at European level. The increased requirements made of European political work led to growing demands being made of the general secretariat by member parties. The still rudimentary structures had to be developed. The advantages of its existence for the member parties and for the EPP Group could be demonstrated by the fact that the EPP proved good at organising communications and opinion-forming inside the party.

In the course of the following years it became possible, in stages, to double the general secretariat staff. It then became possible to carry out its work satisfactorily, especially the preparation, practical organisation, and follow-up of meetings of party bodies, and congresses. In particular, the member parties too could now receive documents in the languages which were most important for the EPP's work (German, Italian, French). And it became possible to correspond in a few more languages (Dutch, English, and Spanish).

In recruiting new staff, special attention was paid to getting polyglots on board, and a mixture of nationalities. But for practical reasons, in particular due to the fact that the office was in Brussels, there was a numerical dominance of Belgians on the staff. Up to the 1994 European elections, the general-secretariat staff were: Guy Korthoudt (Deputy Secretary General since 1986), Ilse Schouteden, Monique Poket, Malou Dairomont, and Danielle Buffels from Belgium; the Germans Margaret Württemburger and Alexander Bartling (external staff member and Executive secretary of the EPP/CD Group in the Council of Europe); Denise O'Hara from Ireland; Vittorio Faggioli from Italy; and finally Gerardo Galeote, the external Deputy Secretary General (1993/94) from Spain. And the following were active in the general secretariat for varying lengths of time between 1978 and 1994: Josef Müller (as Deputy Secretary General until 1986) and Trudi Lücker from Germany; Katherine Meenan (political adviser) from Ireland; Camillo Zuccoli (external Deputy Secretary General, 1986–93), Melitta Senoner from Italy; and Isabella Defeu from Belgium.

In contrast to the secretariats of the Social Democrats' and Liberals' European organisations, the EPP's headquarters were from the beginning not in the office assigned to the European parliamentary groups. They were in an 'autonomous' place, in the centre of Brussels, in the Rue de la Madelaine, then from 1978 on the Place de l'Albertine, and later (until 1995) in the Rue de la Victoire, where a building had been made available by a sympathetic foundation, the 'Fondation Internationale'. This house, known as the 'Centro Aristides Calvani', was home to the general secretariat of the Christian Democrat International (CDI). This arrangement, with separate offices for the EPP party, articulated the leadership's determination to pursue their tasks in their own way and at their own speed. In any event, the intention was to separate party business from the the the parliamentary routine and in particular from the requirements of the EPP Group.

The 'EPP Bulletin. Communiqués from the General Secretariat' has been published since 1983, to communicate with officials and members of EPP member parties, and to inform the general public. It has appeared since then on an irregular basis, documenting or commenting on the key proceedings and decisions, *inter alia* the results of the political programme being put into practice. In spite of numerous attempts and many good intentions, until 1994 this bulletin (in six different language editions, German, French, Dutch, English, Italian, and Spanish) was still not being published regularly. It is an example of one of the painful gaps in the general secretariat during those first years. For lack of money it did not have an expert on press and publicity.

THE TREASURER AND THE FINANCE STATUTE

The EPP Treasurer's functions are essentially to work out a budget in co-operation with the Secretary General and to present it to the Executive, to make sure member parties pay their dues, to make sure budgetary decisions are executed, and to look for other possible sources of finance beyond member parties' contributions.

For most of the EPP's existence, the Treasurer's job has been held by two enormously solid and reliable people, both Flemish Belgians: Alfred Bertrand (1978–85) and Rika de Bakker (1985–96). It proved sensible to give this job to Belgian politicians, as this simplifies dealings with the banks and authorities of Belgium, which is where the general secretariat is based.

During the eighties, the growth in staff, and of course other costs related to the increasing level of activity, meant there was a need for determined attempts to improve party finances. As well as the problem of increasing the level of contributions from member parties, there were a couple of other sensitive problems which had to be solved. First, not least in the interests of solidarity and cohesion, it was vital to establish some discipline about paying contributions. Second, a fair basis for calculating the levels of contribution levels had to be established, one that was acceptable to everyone.

The second problem was solved very quickly (in 1985), providing a new basis for establishing contribution levels that would prove both satisfactory and permanent. But the first problem is still with us, though there have been significant improvements. Apart from two cases, one of them leading eventually to the ejection of the party in question (the Portuguese Centro Democratico Social/CDS), all member parties fulfil their obligations in full, even if they are not all equally prompt about this.

The rules for the financing of the EPP are set down in the finance statute, which was not finally agreed until September 1993. However, this had existed in draft form for some years, was only modified in one negligible matter in 1993, and has remained the basis for how the party's finances are run. The finance statute systematises and incorporates the agreement, made over the years, to put in place a transparent and equitable structure for contributions and management of resources.

The EPP finances itself entirely from the contributions of member parties and the EPP Group, which also contributes in kind. Determining the respective contributions follows clear rules. These are based on a combination of criteria for measuring the level of contributions: the number of votes the member party secured in the last European election, and the number of deputies the member party has in the EPP party group. In this way a party's electoral strength at national level is combined with its possibilities of influence at European level. A coefficient is laid down per vote, and per deputy, expressed in Belgian francs.

Setting the individual contribution levels is done by the Executive at the same time as the debate on the budget. Inflation is automatically taken into account. Any rise of the contributions above this is done by increasing one or both of the coefficients mentioned above.

This process is fair in that it reflects the real significance and effectiveness of individual parties in their respective countries (electoral results) – and at the same time the role which it can play at the European level (number of deputies). This double assessment is made necessary by the dissimilar number of European Parliament seats attributed to each country, and also because of the different electoral systems. The sum arrived at in the first calculation is corrected by the sum reached in the second calculation.

15 The Associations

As early as the 1950s, there had been a European or international youth organisation. Originally it was connected to the Nouvelles Equipes Internationales (NEI), then to the Christian-Democratic World Union (CDWU). Once the EPP had been founded, it adapted to the changed position, so that it could be active in this new area. The Christian-Democratic women soon worked well with the EPP too, having for a long time had a good working relationship with the EUCD.

Things developed both as far as the women and youth were concerned, because every member party had either a national or a regional women's and youth association; all of them were interested in co-operation beyond national borders.

WHAT ARE THE ASSOCIATIONS, AND WHAT ARE THEY FOR?

Apart from women's and youth organisations, however, not every EPP member party has associations bringing together certain categories of members to work for the party in their field, or alternatively to press their particular cause in the party. This model of internal party associations only has an historical basis, or deep roots, in the German and Belgian member parties (CDU, CSU and CVP, PSC). The European Union of Christian Democratic Workers and the European Local Politics Association and the European Middle Class Association, as well as, later, the European Union of Pensioners, came into being because of initiatives and pressure by Belgian and German organisations which had been in existence for a long time.

The EPP's interest in the founding of such associations, and their becoming active, was essentially because they substantially increased the circle of people and groups directly involved in European work. Political figures involved in European affairs improve their knowledge and experience. Connections are forged and opportunities created for trust and solidarity to build up between EPP members from different countries. And that has a direct effect on the member parties. It is in this way that a core membership of the 'European party' can be permanently put in place.

Equally, the involvement of people representing a particular category or a particular interest group, enliven and enrich party work. The contributions from the associations, generally concentrating on the specific interests of their supporters, link the consensus towards which the party is always striving to the real world. Those who know and care about the subject under discussion are making an input into EPP proposals. This is of great importance for a people's party whose force is derived from being able to unite divergent interests.

All this also justifies the EPP's active encouragement of officially recognised associations. The statutes (Article 16) state the condition, that:

> national sections, which are generally connected with an EPP member party, exist in at least half the Member States; the activity of the associations is carried out on the basis of a constitution laying down its responsibilities and whom it has the right to represent; activities and positions taken are based on the EPP's programme and its political principles.

Recognition gives associations not only the right to participate in the party bodies, but also access to considerable grants from the party budget. Yet, provided they operate in accordance with what has been agreed in the constitution and the party programme, the associations remain largely autonomous as far as their internal affairs and activities are concerned.

With the exception of the EPP Independent Business and Economic Foundation (IBEF), as it was renamed in 1996, all EPP associations are also EUCD associations. This was not always the case. Originally the Women's and Youth Organisations had separate organisations for their activities in the EUCD and EPP. In time the existence of two organisations proved not to make sense. As the European Community gradually expanded it also proved downright superfluous, simply because enlargement tended make to the EPP's and the EUCD's sphere of operation one and the same.

It must also be borne in mind that – unlike the party – the associations have no political function in the 'government' of the European Union. Their *raison d'être* is not taking part in parliamentary elections or in the exercise of power, but in bringing together people from the same background and of the same mind. What they want is to build consensus, to spread understanding, and to exercise influence – to make a difference to public opinion and especially the thinking of the parties they belong to, evidently along the lines of their particular interests and perceptions. All this can also be done, perhaps more effectively, in a wider framework. The examples of the EUCDW and the EYCD have shown this very clearly.

EUROPEAN YOUNG CHRISTIAN DEMOCRATS

Associations which the EPP has recognised have each contributed in a very different way to the development, growth, and vitality of the party. Taken all in all, the European Union of Young Christian Democrats (EYCD) – recognised by both the EPP and EUCD – can surely lay claim to having achieved what must be expected of an association of this sort.[1] One important indication of the EYCD's influence – an influence it had its own way of achieving – was that in 1994, for the first time, an EYCD representative, Secretary-General Marc Bertrand, was elected an EPP Vice-President.

Every youth organisation is subject to changes and discontinuity in terms of personnel, and this was certainly one of the reasons for the EYCD's phases of minimal or inadequate activity. But the EPP's young people were always dynamic, and made a considerable contribution to spreading an EPP consciousness to the member parties' youth organisations. A large number of young people who had their first European experiences in the EYCD remained active in European politics when they were older, some of them becoming involved in the EPP's structures, or in areas close to the party.

The bi-annual Congress, the regular summer university, and the seminars and regular meetings of the Executive all offer numerous opportunities for people to meet. Occasional publications, principally the bi-monthly Newsletter/Lettre d'Information (in English and French), serve as channels of communication between the EPP associations or their leaders.

The EYCD is evidently not a rich organisation. It has little access to funds, since its members are not usually earning their own living; that is also the reason why the contributions they pay over to member associations can only be extremely limited. National organisations are dependant on the mother parties for their funds, and can therefore contribute little to the finances of the European organisation. It is true that in some countries the possibility exists of obtaining public funds dedicated to youth work for holding events which serve political education or networking. However, such funds are available only to a very limited extent for European and international activities.

So young people are dependant on contributions by the EPP and other sponsors to finance their organisation and its activities. However, those in charge of the EYCD have always known how to use such possibilities as exist.[2] With the help of the EPP Group in the European Parliament, the general secretariat of NATO, the Catalan government, and other sponsors, they were able to organise many interesting events and encounters for their members.

Given the difficult conditions and limited resources of the EYCD, they have done consistently good work over the years This is especially remarkable because there were fierce, constantly recurring, battles inside the organisation ignited by problems which were also to be found in the EPP, and led to controversies there. But in the EYCD youthful rigour led to these issues being brought to an ideological head. There were three main areas of argument: namely the double membership issue, the inclusion of the conservative associations, and who had the right to be represented in party bodies. These questions were either objectively or formally interlinked, which meant that the front lines in these battles are almost always intertwined, too.

The issue of double, overlapping membership resulted from the fact that some member associations, above all the German CDU's youth wing, the Junge Union, also belonged to the Democratic Youth Council (DEMYC). This contained both Christian Democratically-inclined and Conservative groups.[3] The motto of those opposed to joining forces with the conservatives was: you have to choose between the EYCD and DEMYC. And if it was no longer possible to force the German Junge Union or the Austrian Young ÖVP and other founder members to renounce their DEMYC membership, at least it should be made a condition that any new members could only join if they gave up the right to dual membership.

Long before the EYCD existed in its present form, there had been quarrels among the Young Christian Democrats about bringing in the conservatives. Founding DEMYC was in a certain sense the result of a compromise. In the 1970s it had become clear that there was a stalemate. Several powerful groups (for example, the Italian Movimento Giovanile, the Belgian CVP-Jongeren, and the Dutch CDA-Jongeren) were against bringing the conservatives on board; it was impossible to integrate the conservatives into the European federation of young Christian Democrats. And it was just as impossible to dissuade proponents of integration (notably the German Junge Union and the Junge ÖVP) to abandon closer co-operation with the conservatives.

The third problem arose because of an all too obvious under-representation of the Junge Union, which they felt to be unfair. It was by far the largest and politically most powerful member association, and as a result felt constantly outnumbered by a series of smaller associations taking a particularly radical position on the problems mentioned above.

In so far as the EPP had, from the beginning of the 1990s onwards, supplied a solution to the 'conservative question', the EYCD could gradually get back on an even keel. This might possibly even lead to:

the creation of a new EPP Youth Organisation, open to all EPP/EUCD member party youth organisations [and to] acceptance of a statute for the new EPP youth organisation in which it would be stipulated that members were not allowed dual membership of any other youth organisation (specifically not the DEMYC). The voting strength of member organisations would be laid down (this being based on the political importance of the mother party, and the country's population, as well as the organisation's activity, along with recognition of the basic programme and the [EPP] statutes.[4]

EUROPEAN UNION OF CHRISTIAN DEMOCRATIC WORKERS

Given the large national memberships, the association of Christian Democratic workers ought to have fairly large possibilities. In practice, it has been less successful than the EYCD. Founded in the turbulent year 1980, and despite being led by such influential figures as Alfred Bertrand and Hans Katzer, the EUCDW found it too hard, for too long, to show the kind of results which were expected of it. The organisation suffered above all from leadership problems which arose from unfortunate coalitions; these in turn could be traced to a lack of consensus about what the association was for.

The problems of the youth organisation, notably the 'conservative question', did not afflict the EUCDW, which was always solid on the issue. Moreover, there were no worker organisations in the conservative camp seeking to join the European federation of Christian Democratic workers.

The problems of Christian Democratically-inclined trade union activists belonging to EPP parties are to be found elsewhere. Their national associations, and their members, see a permanent conflict of solidarity between trade union and party. Indeed it is the flip-side of the conflict faced by the EPP employers' federation. Ideally, the organisation should represent the party in the unions, and the unions in the party. But what happens in practice in each country depends on national structures, and is very different in each case. The alliances in the EUCDW arise, after all, from the different identities and priorities of national associations, and their closeness or otherwise to their union organisations and their parties.

However, these difficulties were overcome during the last few years thanks to the efforts of Heribert Scharrenbroich, Jean-Claude Juncker, and Miet Smet.[5]

The EUCDW way of working largely corresponds to that of the EYCD. The leading bodies meet regularly to deal with practical co-operation and organisation, and to discuss and decide on current political issues and policy directions; and the EUCDW also holds seminars. There are congresses every two years to hammer out the political emphases. The issues which especially interest Christian Democratic employees are in the field of community and social policy. However, they are traditionally interested in politics altogether, and especially committed in terms of European policy.

The organisation and finance of educational work – which mainly consists of running seminars for members and others involved with companies and trade unions – is done by the European Centre for Training Employees, set up for this purpose by the EUCDW.

EUROPEAN CHRISTIAN DEMOCRATIC WOMEN

Staying fairly low-profile, the EPP Women's Section has maintained continuous contact and co-operation between women in the member parties. They did not form a distinct organisation. In contrast to the EYCD and the EUCDW, the Women's Section has no secretariat. The necessary connections and preparation for occasional meetings are, so to speak, dealt with as 'homework'. It also has no funds to speak of, apart from regular contributions from the EPP. The national or regional women's associations contribute nothing to their European association, since they themselves receive no membership dues – each being dependent on its respective party. All this means that the EPP Women's Section, *qua* association, is rarely in the public eye, or in the forefront of EPP affairs.

However, its leading figures were always prominent on the party stage. The chairman, Marlene Lenz, was elected an EPP vice-president in 1994. The secretary-general, Monique Badenès, has for many years been the most active member of the EPP Executive. Her steady participation in various working groups, and her presence in many delegations (in particular, since 1989, those to the countries of central and eastern Europe) have given the Women's Section a strong, direct influence on the policies and self-image of the party.

It was not until very late in the day that the two indepedent women's associations, the EUCD's and the EPP's, were merged.[6] In 1992 they formalised this fusion at a Congress of both organisations, which had largely taken place in practice by this time anyway. The necessity of fusion was clearly underlined by the impending expansion of the European Community, a real, concrete prospect from 1989 onwards. It meant that the apprehensions of the women whose countries did not (or did not yet) belong to the EC became less important. Rivalry between the associations, evidently mixed up with rivalries between certain leading figures, also fell away to a great extent.

THE EPP ASSOCIATION OF LOCAL AND REGIONAL POLITICIANS

Local politicians have always been among the staunchest defenders of European union. The network of twinned cities and community partnerships has done a great deal to breath life into the European idea, as well as to include Europe's citizens in the integration process. The Council of European Regions, part of the International European Movement, co-ordinated these efforts and also gave them a political conduit. So it was natural enough that Christian Democratically-inclined local politicians working together in the Council of European Regions felt the need to institutionalise things in an EPP association. This came about at the beginning of the 1980s with the foundation of the European Federation of Local Politicians (EFLP). No doubt it was hoped or assumed that by establishing an EPP Group in the Council of European Regions this would strengthen their position *vis-à-vis* the Socialists, who were especially strong in this institution.

The EFLP tried, initially with some success, to develop a network of local politicians from various member parties who were involved in European politics. However, in practice, the mainstream European issues were being debated and decided in the usual EPP bodies. Finding a clear area of activity at European level which local politicians could make their own was not easy. Given the subsidiarity principle – held especially dear by local politicians – to formulate a regional policy for Europe was hardly in their interests. And European policy from a local political perspective could be nothing other than a general European policy – which it is not up to local or city councils to formulate.

So the work of the European Federation of Local Politicians could not really develop beyond useful contacts and agreements. It was the local political conscience of the EPP: in that respect, the EFLP was thoroughly effective. It channelled the local political point of view into the process of elaborating party programmes, and it also spread the EPP's message at the local political level. But that was evidently not enough as a basis for an association of active politicians with actual work to do at home.

The absence of any definite project relevant to their actual problems necessarily meant that local politicians never became genuinely interested in the association. Then, partly because of this, there were radical problems about the leadership. Both the President, Leoluca Orlando, then mayor of Palermo – who had been elected in 1985 – and Secretary General Peter Daners completely neglected the organisation. The member associations were inert, in effect leading to the *de facto* extinction of the EFLP.

It came back to life after 1991, and the reason for that was the process which was leading to the further development of the European Union and expressed the Maastricht Treaty. Subsidiarity was recognised as the key principle of the European Union, a fact which for the first time gave constitutional recognition to the role of regional and local politics in shaping the European Union. It had the effect of mobilising people, and made it possible, after detailed preparations during the spring of 1993, to set up the successor organisation to the EFLP. This was the European Union of Local and Regional Politicians (EULRP). Adolf Herkenrath, who had already been a driving force in the EFLP, and who had taken the initiative of reforming the association, was elected president. François Biltgen, who had done most of the practical work in the run-up to refounding the association, became Secretary General.

As its name implies, the EULRP aims to include politicians who are active in the regions as well. This new organisation is more promising than its predecessor because the Maastricht Treaty has raised the profile of communes and regions as necessary elements in European construction. The debate provoked by the Treaty in the member states has had a similar effect. The Committee of the Regions (CoR), set up in March 1994 as a new European institution to involve the communes and regions in forming political will, will also become an important arena for the EPP's European Union of Local and Regional Politicians.

On the very day the Committee of the Regions was officially founded, 8 March 1994, an EPP Group in the Committee of the Regions was established, on the initiative, and under the chairmanship of, EPP President Wilfried Martens. Since then, under the chairmanship of Jos Chabert, this Group has grown to about 85 members, and the largest of the four groups in the CoR.[7]

THE EUROPEAN SMALL AND MEDIUM-SIZED BUSINESSES ASSOCIATION

The European Small and Medium-sized Businesses Association (ESMBA), as it was known when it was founded in 1980, always confined itself to being a forum for discussion. The executive president, Lieven Lenaerts, has for many years been the motor, animator, and organiser of the association. His main concern has been to ensure that the views and interests of politicians representing small to medium-sized enterprises are included in EPP discussions. And he at the same time has sought to offer a service to the members – by holding further education seminars and by supplying contacts and information.

The politically neutral Information Office for Small and Medium-sized Businesses in Brussels, largely financed by the European Commission, for example, started life as an ESMBA initiative.

One of the problems of this association is that there are too few member parties in the EPP with comparable organisations of their own. The result of this is a lack of branch organisations, and therefore an active base. If the ESMBA appears to be becalmed, it is hoped that a fusion with the European Union of Medium-sized Enterprises (EMSU) will overcome the problem. This was founded at the same time as the ESMBA in 1979 to represent the political interests of small and medium-sized entrepreneurs, the self-employed, artisans, and skilled employees.[8] The EMSU's political direction was always Christian Democratic and conservative. However it wanted to avoid, at least during its first year of existence, and certainly officially, being a party association. It recruited members from the non-party or principally apolitical professional associations of small to medium-sized business. Despite this, not least because of the figures who headed the EMSU, there were always close links with the EPP, and in particular with the EDU, which has for some years regarded the EMSU as *de facto* an EDU association.[9]

THE EPP PENSIONERS' ASSOCIATION

Since 1992 there have been efforts to form a European Pensioners Union (EPU) as an EPP association. The rediscovery of the 'Third Age' has meant that some member parties offer old people the opportunity of party work within special associations. The success of these initiatives, and the increasing need for a new policy to help older people, eventually led to these national associations being brought together at European level. The foundations of a European Union of Pensioners were laid during a pensioners' conference in May 1993, organised by the EPP Group in the European Parliament with the co-operation of the Konrad Adenauer Foundation.

After many false starts, a 'European Pensioners Union Workshop' was founded in Aachen on 5 May 1995. This had the job of preparing the foundation of an association in the framework of a Congress.[10] The very small number of people in this workshop, coming from Belgium, Germany, Finland, Luxembourg, Austria, and Spain, indicates a particular difficulty with the pensioners. If there is a lack of national structures embracing small to medium-sized businesses, local politicians, or employees, this obstacle is far more pronounced in the case of pensioners.

Will it be possible to persuade parties in other countries to organise their pensioners? Will enough parties recognise the value of an initiative which tries to bring together Christian Democratic and conservative pensioners in one organisation? And will everyone in the EPP be prepared to recognise and support an association if only a minority of member parties are interested in it?

16 The EUCD and the New Parties in Central and Eastern Europe

In spring 1989 it was decided to abandon the idea of merging the EPP and EUCD.[1] This decision was taken against the background of the revolutionary events in Moscow and the capitals of Central and Eastern Europe, and the vast upheavals in the political landscape which were now coming into focus. The hope was that Christian Democrats would play an important, autonomous role in rebuilding democracy, and in bringing together Christian Democratic forces and their allies in the countries liberated from Communism.

At the XXIII EUCD Congress in Malta in November 1989, Christian Democrats from Poland, Hungary, and Estonia could take part for the very first time. And they were not representing exile organisations but parties or groups which were active in their own countries.

The EUCD's Political Bureau, Presidency, and General Secretariat were from now on focused on one goal, which was the transition from a western European organisation to one which embraced the whole continent. This work involved several different areas.

THE NEW PARTIES

Since the great upheaval of 1989, all EUCD activities have been bound up with the process of including the re-established or newly-founded parties of Christian Democratic inspiration from the countries of central, eastern, and south-eastern Europe.

The collapse of the Communist regimes, and the exposure of the socialist illusion, heralded the 'end of ideologies' and resulted in renewed interest in Christian Democracy.[2] This mirrored the situation immediately after the Second World War. To the populations of western Europe in the aftermath of a catastrophe, the message of Christian Democracy was peculiarly attractive. The peoples of Central and Eastern Europe, who had seen the collapse of societies and governments warped by Communism, gladly accepted what Christian Democracy had to offer, and willingly trusted its policies.

It meant that many of the new people's parties based themselves on the ideas and policies of the successful Christian Democrats in western Europe. They could either pick up the reins of Christian Democratic parties that had existed in their countries before,[3] or turn instead to the traditions of the peasant parties.[4] In many of these countries, such parties had been politically dominant until the Communists seized power. Alongside these 'historical' parties there were other parties which emerged in the struggle with the Communists in the mid 1980s. These had grown out of democracy movements or national emancipation movements, and some recognised in Christian Democracy their political family.[5]

Progressively these parties played a more important role in restoring democracy and the rule of law. They enjoyed varying success in elections, and in some cases also took on government responsibility.

THE CHRISTIAN DEMOCRATIC UNIONS OF CENTRAL EUROPE

A conference of representatives from central and eastern European parties with a Christian Democratic direction took place in Budapest at the beginning of March 1990. It was convened by the Christian Democratic Union of Central European (CDUCE), and was organised in conjunction with the Christian Democrat International (CDI) and the EUCD and EPP Group in the European Parliament. The parties which were represented took the opportunity to express the hope that they would soon be accepted as members of the EUCD. But they also decided to revive the CDUCE in order to promote their parties, particularly in the transition period.

The CDUCE had come into being during the 1950s.[6] It incorporated the Christian Democrats of central Europe, who had been in exile in America or Europe and represented the legitimacy and historical continuity of the parties in their home countries, which had been forced to retreat by Communist repression. During the fifties and sixties, the CDUCE, which was also recognised as a regional organisation of the CDI, became very active. It cultivated contacts with democratic opposition active in the underground (or condemned to inactivity) in the eastern bloc countries. And in the west, it tried to ensure that the destiny of the people living under Soviet or Communist rule was not forgotten.

Several factors led, after the seventies, to the progressive decline in the importance of the CDUCE, even within the international Christian Democratic movement. The politics of détente made the relevant political forces more indifferent, and the fact that the leading figures[7] in the organisation were getting old was also relevant. Despite the best intentions of its protagonists, the CDUCE entered the new situation of a liberated Central Europe without the means to play a decisive role. It lacked the necessary organisation, people, and ideas. Further, those who had been responsible for the re-establishment and development of parties following the great political change, were not interested in having their own 'central European' party federation. They wanted to belong to an organisation which included all of Europe, namely the EUCD, which could guarantee direct co-operation with the western European parties and the EPP in particular. And they did not want to take orders from the 'old men' (even if they were highly respected) who had returned from exile.

So in the course of the XXIV congress of the EUCD in Warsaw (21–23 June 1992), the representatives of the new central European parties resolved to disband the CDUCE. That step also cut them free from the claims of their compatriots in exile to speak for them.

WHAT THE EUCD TRIED TO DO

From the outset, the European Union of Christian Democrats had worked hard to establish contacts and co-operation with, and to support, the central and eastern European Christian Democratic parties as they gradually came back to life. And progressively their party representatives were included in the work of the EUCD.

The starting point was a conviction about western efforts generally, and in particular European Community policy, towards the countries of central and eastern Europe. This conviction was that, in the short term, efforts must be concentrated on establishing democracy and a social market economy. In the medium term, the goal must be economic upturn, social justice, and social and cultural recovery. And the long-term aim is membership of the European Community.

From autumn 1989 onwards, a special EUCD and EPP working group more or less systematically compiled information, and co-ordinated projects and activities. It was chaired by Josef K. Hahn, and from 1990 onwards by Wim Van Velzen.

At the end of June 1990, in Budapest, the Christian Democrat International put on a conference of party leaders. Numerous government leaders and ministers from all over the world attended. The focus, naturally enough, was what had happened in central and eastern Europe, and parties from the region were present in force.

Two other conferences in the summer of 1990 and 1991, organised by the EPP Group under the banner 'Europe 2000', were key elements in forging a spirit of co-operation and solidarity. It was especially important that many of those who had now been elected members of parliament in different countries of central and eastern Europe took part in the meeting. It was an opportunity to have a dialogue with deputies from the European Parliament and with national members of parliament from western Europe.

Over the years, quite a number of EUCD member parties arranged in this context opportunities for further meetings and exchange. It is also worth noting the keen efforts of the foundations and institutes connected with the Christian Democratic movement; they arranged chances for like-minded people from both parts of Europe to meet and to debate in the course of seminars they organised. The ÖVP Political Academy, the German Foundations (Konrad Adenauer and Hanns Seidel), the Dutch Edoardo Frei Foundation, the Belgian CESPES Institute, the Italian Fondazione Alcide De Gasperi, and the French Fondation Robert Schuman – all did extremely important work in this regard.

Thanks to the support of the foundations and institutes, it became possible in October 1991 to establish the Academy for Central and Eastern Europe based in Budapest. Founded by the EUCD, it is supported by the EPP. Its task is to offer systematic education and training seminars to actual, and future, party workers in the Christian Democratic parties and those politically allied to them. Those responsible for this project were above all determined to pass on democratic, political, and parliamentary know-how to the new parties.

The EUCD itself organised a number of seminars and colloquia for representatives of central and eastern European parties. Those that stand out are the conference on Issues Relating to the Organisation of Political Work in Stirin/Prague (July 1991, in conjunction with the American National Democratic Institute); the conferences on the problems of national minorities in Bratislava (November 1991 and June 1993); and that on 'Civil Society' in Bucharest (November 1993).

Finally there were a large number of visits to central and eastern Europe by all sorts of delegations. These took place under the auspices of the EUCD, the CDI, the EPP Group, or individual member parties and their parliamentary groups. All wanted to inform themselves about political developments, and also about the problems faced by politically friendly parties. All this intensive travel, which included attending party congresses held by the new parties, and participating in their election campaigns, had two essential aims. One was for western parties to make themselves a familiar part of the landscape, the other to demonstrate the solidarity of the western European Christian Democrats.

THE EUCD'S NEW CONSTITUTION

The EUCD's structures needed to be adapted to the new situation. The constitutions had to be reformed anyway, and those reforms needed to include new rules for according membership. Moreover, voting rights and other matters relating to membership had to be re-ordered in the light of the likely huge increase in the number of members. The EUCD's organisation altogether needed modernisation and to be adapted to the challenges of the present and future, taking into account the EUCD's experiences since it was founded in 1965. The EUCD had to redefine its own value in relation to the EPP, and to decide anew on how to divide the work.

After long discussions in a commission chaired by the secretary-general, the Political Bureau finalised the new EUCD statute in autumn 1991. It came into effect at the same time as the Warsaw Congress in June the following year.[8] On the basis of this new statute, the EUCD Council (representing member parties) met in January 1993, elected a new president, and laid down the general direction of forthcoming work. Emilio Colombo, President since 1985, was succeeded by Wilfried Martens, who was now President both of the EUCD and the EPP. For the first time representatives of central European parties were elected to the Presidency in the person of the Slovene Lojze Peterle and the Hungarian Laszlo Surjan.[9]

The Warsaw Congress clearly marked a break in the history of the European Union of Christian Democrats, which at this time united 28 member parties and 11 further parties with observer status.

It was the first time that an EUCD Congress had taken part at the heart of central Europe. For the first time representatives of Christian Democratic parties from the whole of Europe were represented. And it was the last time that a Congress took place on the basis of the constitution agreed in 1965, when the EUCD was founded. It had developed from the Nouvelles Equipes Internationales which had been founded in 1948. Until the peaceful revolution in central and eastern Europe, it had remained a purely western European affair. Now, at last, the EUCD had become what its name claims it to be: the European Union of Christian Democrats.

NEW PARTIES JOIN

In deciding on membership applications, the relevant EUCD bodies always sought detailed information, and made sure there was consensus among member parties about whether or not to admit a new member.

The EPP Congress in Dublin (14–16 November 1990) supported the urgent plea for coordinated action, voting for a resolution which, *inter alia*, called for:

> dialogue and systematic expansion of contacts with the parties of central and eastern Europe as a first priority. A coherent EPP/EUCD policy to central and eastern Europe is of great importance. Bilateral relations must contribute to this. Giving support to developing an infrastructure of Christian Democratic parties, and Christian Democratic thought, is a priority. The EPP/EUCD working group is tasked with making the necessary initiatives.[10]

It was clearly of the essence to have a basis for deciding on the admissibility or otherwise of a party, and it had to be as unambiguous as possible. Not only did many parties want to join, but there was considerable political pressure from different directions. There were constantly real and pressing reasons for this or that (western European) party as to why certain (central or eastern European) parties should immediately be admitted, or receive precedence over other parties. Often several motives were in play at the same time: party-political, governmental, national-sentimental, ideological, personal, and tactical. But given what they were, such considerations were not in general likely to find general agreement, which was why the central and eastern Europe working group defined criteria for admitting members which were later enshrined in the EUCD constitution.

The EUCD is open to all European parties with a Christian Democratic orientation, and fulfilling these conditions:

> they operate in countries which have a system based on liberty, democracy, and the rule of law; they have taken part in free elections and are represented in parliament; they accept the 'Manifesto of European Christian Democrats', the 'Political Manifesto of the World Union of Christian Democrats', and this constitution. (Article 3c)

> If there are applications from several competing parties in one country, then the Council can make membership conditional on the formation of a national Equipe. In such cases, those applying for membership are required to develop an appropriate co-operation and consultation structure, ensuring they can have common representatives, and take a common position in the framework of the EUCD. (Article 3d)

> An application for observer status can be made by democratic political associations and like-minded European parties which accept the

political principles and main intellectual directions of the EUCD. (Article 4)

Members all have the right to play a part in the EUCD's work and to participate in decision-making. They accordingly have equal rights in all EUCD bodies. The constitution places on them the obligation to be loyal to the EUCD and to its member parties, and to EUCD decisions about policy and its programme.

Recognition as an observer is granted to parties which have not (yet) fulfilled the requirements for acceptance as members, or where there are doubts about their identity, development, role or politics. Observer status is above all justified by the extent to which it serves the political or operational interests of the EUCD, which must above all strive to make sure its message is heard in as many countries as possible, and to develop appropriate political structures.

This also involves a pedagogical responsibility on the part of the EUCD toward parties which want to join. Such parties should be given the chance to learn by taking part in events. Active observation will also teach them how to develop their political programmes, their instruments of power, and their whole *modus operandi*, all with the eventual object of becoming members. Observer status implies a right to political support. Opening up these possibilities is, eventually, a natural element – even an obligation – of showing solidarity. It is solidarity with parties which are, for their part, also showing solidarity – by committing themselves to Christian Democracy and putting their hopes in the EUCD. There are no institutional links between the EUCD and the observer members; the only obligation the EUCD accepts towards them is to invite their representatives (without the right either to speak or to vote) to EUCD events.

All decisions which subsequently had to be made about admitting new members[11] or recognising them as observers[12] were based on these criteria. In each case thorough investigations took place on the spot, carried out by specially commissioned delegations, and there were detailed discussions in the working group and in the EUCD Council. But not every decision reached turned out to be tenable. The party landscape during those first years of democratisation was shifting very quickly; a few changes became necessary. The Hungarian Small Landowners Party lost its membership, and the Polish Christian Democratic Congress, made up of a number of parties and groups, had its observer status withdrawn. The status of several other parties proved to need re-examination because of developments either in domestic politics or in the parties themselves.

There was, moreover, no active political recruitment drive by the EUCD among potential member parties. The formal criteria for a membership application were one thing. But the most important sign of belonging to the Christian Democratic family must be the party's self-image and that it itself is ready to take the initiative.[13] In the light of European Union expansion to take in the countries of central and eastern Europe, all EUCD members would of course be candidates for membership of the European People's Party. The EPP constitution allows for associate membership for those parties whose EU membership is being negotiated, and several EUCD member parties from Central and Eastern Europe have already made such applications.

17 The Protagonists

Those who played a role in making the European People's Party are essentially 'those who were always there', or delegated representatives of member parties sitting in EPP bodies. They were, for the most part, heads of party and government, and members of the Presidency or Executive. Among their number are also found the Secretaries General and the 'International Secretaries' who, alongside leading figures in the European parliamentary Group, play such a prominent part when it comes to decisions and to party activities. However, the most important role is that of EPP President. He is the key decision-maker.

THE PRESIDENTS

Since 1976, when the party was founded, the office of EPP President has been held by four people: Leo Tindemans, Piet Bukman, Jacques Santer, and Wilfried Martens. It is no coincidence that all four come from Benelux countries, Leo Tindemans and Wilfried Martens from Belgium, Piet Bukman from Holland, and Jacques Santer from Luxembourg. These countries, which lie at the heart of Europe, on the fault line between the dominant European cultures, are destined to play the part of balancing the interests of their larger neighbours. Politicians from the Benelux are evidently thought to have the greatest talents in directing such a multi-voiced choir. Moreover, this is no mere Christian Democratic prejudice; the Socialists and Liberals have also preferred to recruit their party chairmen from the Benelux countries.

There are practical reasons for this. Politicians from these countries master a number of languages, and beyond these linguistic skills have a great capacity for appreciating different cultural sensibilities. And apart from all that: a president who lives in Brussels itself, or in Luxembourg, or the Hague, is better able to follow events centred on Brussels, and to take part regularly in the necessary meetings and discussions.

Three of the four EPP Presidents were prime ministers of their countries at the time of their election. Only Piet Bukman held no government office, being 'only' a party chairman when he became President of the EPP. Choosing personalities who had already made a name for themselves in Europe as prime ministers reflected the EPP's need to make itself known. Right from the start it had to secure a political profile. It is an obvious advantage for the party to have a President who can count on the kind of public attention which a recognised figure in high office will attract.

But this tactic also has built-in disadvantages as well as advantages. The priorities of a national government leader are determined by his government's political agenda. If he is at the same time head of a European party, he will constantly face the temptation to use this position in the service of his work as a head of government. And even if he has no intention of using the European party he leads as an instrument of national government, he still cannot let his hands be tied by his party position.

This dilemma never threw up really serious problems or conflicts, but it was ever-present. One way it made itself felt was the priority given to government activities and appointments. The expectations of EPP bodies, and the policy outlines they laid down, were out of sync with the reserved, cautious, diplomatic way of speaking that characterised all EPP Presidents who were simultaneously either prime ministers or members of a government. Evidently there were also differences between them resulting from their different temperaments.

LEO TINDEMANS, 1976–85

Leo Tindemans was the EPP's first President. He had been known as 'Mister Europe' ever since writing the now famous 1975 report commissioned by heads of EC states and government, entitled 'Report on European Union'.[1] He was extremely popular everywhere in Europe. This was not just thanks to his political position or role on the national and international stage. It was also because of his charismatic, communicative nature. He was able to express himself in many languages, and was a highly effective communicator via the media. Tindemans already had a long career of distinguished government service behind him. He was essential to his party, the Flemish-Belgian Christian People's Party (CVP), as an electoral campaigner. He was just as important as a linchpin in the great debate between the Flemish and the Walloons about a new order in Belgium, a dispute which threatened to rip the country apart. But his character and inclination also made him indispensable to the party's international relations. From 1965 until 1972 he played an important role in multinational party co-operation as Secretary General of the European Union of Christian Democrats, and collected pertinent experiences and knowledge.

Tindemans had not been involved in founding the EPP because of his duties as Prime Minister. But because of his past history and political profile he was identified with this initiative; the proposal to elect him the first President met with spontaneous general agreement.

When in 1978 Leo Tindemans had to give up his position as Prime Minister, he became chairman of his party, the CVP. The following June, the first direct elections to the European Parliament saw him elected in Flanders. The size of his victory broke all records, and has not been surpassed since: he gained some 1 million preferential votes (out of a total poll of around 3million) But in 1982 his hopes of succeeding Simone Weil as President of the European Parliament were dashed when the chairman of the EPP Group, Egon Klepsch, threw his hat into the ring as well, after getting the nomination from the EPP Group in autumn 1981. Eventually the Dutch socialist Piet Danckert was elected.

Before the end of the year, Tindemans had left the European Parliament to become Foreign Minister of Belgium in Prime Minister Wilfried Martens's government. During the last phase of his EPP Presidency, up to April 1985, Tindemans was simultaneously Foreign Minister, a post he held until mid-1989. It became clear that being Foreign Minister was not a satisfactory 'moonlighting' job for the President of a European party. The hands of a Foreign Minister are bound by the exigencies of diplomacy, far more than those of a Prime Minister. If he wishes to be successful in terms of the government of his country, he cannot – as the party bodies expect – publicly make critical demands or launch radical initiatives. Members of the Political Bureau, and Congress delegates, hoped the party President would lead them in the European federal direction set out in the EPP programme. But Foreign Minister Tindemans regularly felt compelled to tell them only what they already knew from public communiqués. The conflict of interest became too much, and after the second direct elections to the European Parliament Tindemans gave up his position as EPP President.

PIET BUKMAN, 1985–87

Piet Bukman was elected Tindemans's successor in March 1985. His background was in farmers' associations, and had been Secretary General and President of the Dutch Evangelical Farmers and Gardeners Association. His political career had begun in the Evangelical Anti-Revolutionary Party (ARP); he had belonged to its executive and involved itself in its management during the 1970s.

When he was elected President of the EPP, Bukman was party chairman of the Dutch CDA, which he had led since 1980. Indeed he was the first chairman of the party, which had been created by merging three Christian confessional parties – KVP, CHU, and ARP – which had previously existed side by side. He proved himself a capable and important figure in guiding the integration process. But Piet Bukman already had a good name in the EPP as well. He had been a member of the Presidency since 1982, and was, though this was never formalised, the party's first Vice-President. In the absence of Leo Tindemans, when he was unable to attend because of his commitments as Foreign Minister, Bukman always chaired Political Bureau meetings. His style was characterised by a certain discipline and determination to get results.

His experience as chairman of a party that had grown out of a number of different components made Bukman very aware of the integration problems which the EPP had to solve. He showed great understanding, and took an active interest in the practical and organisational questions of transnational co-operation. He was always there, and his door was always open.

Bukman faced the disadvantage of not being well-known internationally: he had never held high government office. He counteracted that by always being there, making time to travel for the EPP, and speaking throughout Europe. Bukman's successful Presidency came to an end after the two-year mandate when he was made minister of development aid in Ruud Lubbers's government after the autumn 1986 election. The political conventions in Holland prevented him from holding both government office and a party position. It needed a special dispensation from the Prime Minister, confirmed by the cabinet, for Bukman, the new government minister, to complete the last few months of his mandate as EPP President.

JACQUES SANTER, 1987–90

After Belgian and Dutch Presidents, it was obvious to those looking for a successor to Piet Bukman that it must be a Luxembourger. Jacques Santer was an obvious candidate. He had been the Prime Minister of the Grand Duchy of Luxembourg since 1984. Prior to that he had led the Christian-Social People's Party. Both as Secretary General (1972–74) and as President (1974–82), he had been party to all the important decisions relating to the European Union of Christian Democrats forum, and to the foundation of the EPP. For a few years, from 1975 to 1979, he had been a deputy in the European Parliament, for a time even a Vice-President of the EP. He was familiar with party work at all levels, knew the European scene from the perspective of an experienced parliamentarian, and had served in a number of governments.

Santer's Presidency lasted from 1987 until 1990. Prolonging his mandate from two to three years anticipated a constitutional change made in autumn 1990. The practical political reason for prolonging the mandate was that, when elections for a new EPP Presidency were due that spring, the European election campaign was already in full swing, and it was therefore decided to postpone the election of the Presidency until the line-up in the next parliament was known – in particular who was in the EPP Group.

As President, Jacques Santer combined many of the qualities valued in Bukman. He was always there, he was willing to engage himself, he was interested in solving practical problems, and he was aware of (sometimes contradictory) expectations. And he had certain advantages over his predecessor arising from his position as a head of government. Doors were always open to him, and there was no obstacle to his moving in the highest political circles. And membership of the European Council of Ministers, becoming increasingly important for the development of the European Community, was an incalculable advantage for the EPP presidency; Santer knew how to use that advantage and to develop it.[2]

A high point of Santer's presidency was the VII Congress in Luxembourg, 7–8 November 1988; it had a multi-faceted importance for the party's development. The 1989–94 action programme – 'On the Side of the Citizen' – was voted through. And for the first time in the history of a European Party it was agreed by a majority after open debates. It was a reflection of spirit of the Santer presidency, of his character and inclinations, that the President's Congress speech based much of its vision of the future on the EPP's political inheritance:

We are indebted to a great tradition. From Konrad Adenauer to Robert Schuman, Alcide De Gasperi to Joseph Bech, we Christian Democrats have, ever since the Second World War, continuously stood up for the further democratic development of the Community. We Christian Democrats in the European People's Party want the European Community to become the United States of Europe.

We want to create the United States of Europe together, to ensure peace for our peoples, and to ensure the democracy of our states on a lasting basis; to guarantee peace and the security needed to do that; to make social justice and prosperity possible; to revive the rich and diverse culture of Europe's countries, regions, and local communities, and see them blossom anew.

There are a thousand other reasons. Christian Democrats have always known them and celebrated them. Europe is our political future.[3]

WILFRIED MARTENS, SINCE 1990

In March 1990 Jacques Santer passed the baton to Wilfried Martens, his colleague in the Council of Ministers, who had been Prime Minister of Belgium since 1979. Martens, above all, seemed pre-destined to be President of the EPP. He had been one of the EPP's founding fathers – along with Hans August Lücker he had proposed the first constitution and the first political programme. At the time he was chairman of his national party, the Flemish CVP. As a head of government and member of the Council of Ministers for the past ten years, he had gained a deep understanding of European politics.

His period of office falls into three phases: the first running up to the moment he resigned as Prime Minister of Belgium (from March 1990 to February 1992); the second runs up to his election as chairman of the EPP Group in the European Parliament in July 1994; and the third spans the period when he was President both of the party and the Group.

The same observation, roughly, can be made about Martens's time as both Prime Minister and head of the party, as could be made about President Santer's presidency. But the political earthquake of 1989, and the period leading up to the Maastricht Treaty, put the President of the EPP – and the EPP altogether – under much greater pressure. Martens took the resulting need to be active in the countries of Central and Eastern Europe very seriously. Above all, there was a great deal more need for discussion between member parties and especially between EPP heads of government. And in this connection, too, Martens's double function was very useful.[4]

The second phase of Wilfried Martens's presidency was characterised by the fact that he was now free of the burden of government office, and could devote himself entirely to his job as EPP President. It was especially fortunate that Martens was available for the EPP full-time between February 1992 and July 1994, a period which was decisive both for the party's development and that of the European Union in general. It was true that he was no longer Prime Minister, but he had held the position for 12 years, and brought to his work as head of the EPP the experience of office, along with the elaborate network he had cultivated. And in the job of party leader, he had over the last two years become familiar with all the relevant problems and the EPP's structures. His very concrete engagement was unsurprisingly linked with his ambition as a top-rank politician to look for more and more important tasks. His only public platform, during this period, was as President of the EPP; he had nothing else apart from his membership of the Belgian Senate. Martens's path to new and more important positions led through the success of the EPP, and was also to the party's benefit. The development of the EPP benefited greatly from this.

The third phase of Wilfried Martens's presidency is characterised by his leading of both the party and the Group. It includes the possibility of breaking down or getting rid of the contradictions and tensions which inevitably exist between the party and the parliamentary group. It offered the chance, as well, of improving co-ordination between the two organisations, their bodies and secretariats. Indeed the dual leadership was bound up with the hope that it would enable the party and parliamentary Group to harmonise their communication and co-operation structures. The resultant synergies, it was hoped, would improve the effectiveness of the European People's Party altogether, and lend it more weight in the political struggle.

THE HEADS OF GOVERNMENT

Until the tradition of joint conferences with leaders of parties established itself, member party leaders who were Prime Ministers limited themselves to making an appearance at the EPP conference. This amounted as a rule to no more than an '*acte de présence*', an opening few words, a speech. The role of party and government leaders has markedly changed since they began meeting regularly, to discuss not only general political questions, but also the development of the party. As members of a party body, they are directly involved in laying down the general directions the EPP takes, and directly influence the process of building political will and strategic decisions.

The following government leaders have taken part in EPP 'Summits' since 1983: the German Federal Chancellor Helmut Kohl; the Prime Minister of Holland, Ruud Lubbers; of Belgium, Wilfried Martens and Jean-Luc Dehaene; of Italy, Giulio Andreotti; of Luxembourg, Jacques Santer and Jean-Claude Juncker; of Ireland, Garret FitzGerald and John Bruton; of Greece, Konstantin Mitsotakis; of Malta, Edward Fenech Adami. Of this group, Kohl, Mitsotakis, FitzGerald, Bruton, and Fenech Adami were also the heads of member parties. It gave what they had to say particular weight on all issues concerning the development of the party.

Helmut Kohl is the only person taking part at these meetings who was there from the start in his capacity of both head of party and government. He was also, from that moment onwards, the most influential participant. This was no doubt because the CDU was the most powerful party to belong to the EPP. But Kohl always had more to offer the EPP than the weight of his party. He always knew what he wanted. It was on his insistence that the first meeting of this sort took place in 1983. He was almost always there, and rarely allowed himself to be represented by a substitute because he had to be somewhere else. Given his exceptionally long experience as a party leader, and his national and international prestige, as time passed he increasingly became the opinion leader in the EPP. Normally he was the first to speak, or was asked to speak first. His contribution set the tone.

It can also be said of the other government leaders that they took a particular interest in the EPP's development, and made specific contributions to it, and were prepared to carry out special tasks. A clear sign of this is the commitment that most of them occasionally show in the European Christian Democrats' co-operative structures: Santer and Martens as Presidents of the EPP, Andreotti as EUCD President, FitzGerald as EPP Vice-president, Fenech Adami as EUCD Vice-President, and Juncker as EUCDW President.

Only one Christian Democratic government leader, namely the Italian Prime Minister Ciriaco De Mita (1985–89), took no part in the work of the EPP. As 'political secretary', he was also leader of Democrazia Cristiana between 1983 and 1993. His attitude is in crass contrast to the European and international commitment of his predecessors (for instance, Mariano Rumor, Amintore Fanfani, Emilio Colombo, Arnaldo Forlani, Giulio Andreotti). This indifference is symptomatic of the rapid decline of his party during his period of office.

THE PARTY LEADERS

During the first years following the foundation of the EPP, most party leaders were happy to keep themselves informed by those in their parties responsible for European affairs, the international secretaries. The regular conferences of party and government leaders after 1983, and the increasing development of the European Community political system, meant there was a need for discussion and agreement. Their interest in the structures available to them in the EPP grew accordingly.

Apart from those political figures mentioned above who were also heads of government, between 1983 and 1994 the following party leaders took part in the EPP 'Summits': from Holland – Piet Bukman and Wim Van Velzen; Belgium – Frank Swaelen, Hermann Van Rompuy, Johan Vanhecke, and Gérard Deprez; from Luxembourg – Jean Spautz and Jean-Claude Juncker; from Bavaria – Franz-Josef Strauss; from France – Pierre Méhaignerie; from Italy – Flaminio Piccoli, Ciriaco De Mita, Arnaldo Forlani, Mino Martinazzoli, Rosa Russo Jervolini and Rocco Buttiglione; from Greece – Miltiades Evert; from Austria – Josef Riegler and Erhard Busek; from Sweden – Alf Svensson; from Ireland – Alan Dukes; from Catalonia – Concepcio Ferrer and Antoni-Josep Duran; from the Basque Country – Xavier Arzallus; from Spain – Javier Ruperez and José Maria

Aznar; from Portugal – Diogo Freitas do Amaral, Francisco Lucas Pires, and Adriano Moreira.

The chairman of the Belgian-Wallonian PSC, Deprez, who had been a Member of the European Parliament since 1984, had been continuously present throughout this period. He had closely followed the development of the EPP, and always taken a passionate interest in debates about the party's basic direction. He was almost always the one who criticised Kohl's 'conservative' positions from a 'progressive' perspective.

Méhaignerie, veteran chairman of the French CDS, was on the scene throughout this period, too; he was also a Vice-President of the EPP, though its was a function he never really fulfilled because of his obligations at home. This was especially so over the years he served as a minister in the Chirac and Balladur governments.

The following offered constant and constructive co-operation during their terms of office: the Irish party leader and EPP Vice-President Dukes, the leaders of the Belgian-Flemish CVP, Swaelen and Van Rompuy, and of the Luxembourg CSV, Spautz and Juncker, of whom the first served as Vice-President of the EPP for several years. The second – elected successor to Jacques Santer as head of government – took on the Presidency of the European Union of Christian Democratic Workers.

In particular, Van Velzen, President of the Dutch CDA (1987–94) was especially committed and prepared to get practically involved, As an EPP Vice-President he played a decisive role in shaping the party. Apart from his predecessor Piet Bukman, he was the member party leader who was most active in the EPP. Van Velzen was at the same time a Vice-President of the EUCD. And he was the guiding spirit in the working group on EPP reform; in 1990 he presented the conference of party and government leaders with a detailed report with recommendations on how to improve the EPP's image, and on invigorating the EPP's relationships and communications inside the party. Since 1990, he has also chaired the Central and Eastern Europe working group, founded the 'Christian Democratic Academy for Central and Eastern Europe', and taken over as President of the international executive.

The large number of people who resigned from the job of 'Political Secretary' of Italy's Democrazia Cristiana reflects the crisis-ridden history of this party. Initially, following its dissolution in early 1994, the successor party was the Partito Popolare Italiano.[5] The effect of the gradual collapse of a once powerful party – one which had been an important force in the European and international Christian Democratic party family – was to sap the confidence of its representatives. From 1989/90 onwards they were less and less in a position to take part in decisions made by the conference of party and government leaders.

Only once, in 1985, did a CSU leader, Franz-Josef Strauss, take part in a meeting of EPP party leaders. Otherwise he, and later his successor Theo Waigel, always sent a substitute: Gerold Tandler, deputy party chairman, who had links over many years with the EPP as a veteran party Vice-President.

But two other regional parties showed a strong presence. These were the Basque PNV and the Catalan UDC, both of which joined the EPP when Spain became a member of the Community. Concepcio Ferrer, in particular, for many years chairman of the Union of Christian Democratic Women, and Antoni-Josep Duran, vice-chairman of the Christian Democrat International, used the opportunities which the EPP could offer. This also applied to Alf Svensson, chairman of the Swedish KDS and EUCD Vice-President.

Austrian Vice-Chancellor and ÖVP leaders Riegler and Busek held office for too short a time (and the situation inside the party was too turbulent) for them to be able to play a significant role. And that was also true for Ruperez, chairman of the Spanish Democracia Cristiana, and for the Portuguese party leaders Lucas Pires, Moreira, and Freitas do Amaral.

Once the Spanish Partido Popular was admitted as a full member, its leader José Maria Aznar began playing an increasingly active role in the EPP. In spring 1993 he was elected Vice-President. With the rapid improvement in his party's position in the battle with Felipe Gonzales's Socialist Workers Party (PSOE), his own position grew stronger too. After the PP's great victory in the 1994 European elections, the party eventually took on the mantle of – previously – the Italian Democrazia Cristiana. Along with the German CDU, the PP was a major people's party from a large country. Aznar exploited the responsibilities and the influence this involved. He has become one of the key member party leaders in shaping the EPP's future.

EPP GROUP CHAIRMEN

Due to his place in the institution, and his practical importance, the chairman of the EPP Group, along with the EPP's President, is the most visible and influential figure in the EPP. He is of course a member of the conference of party and government leaders, and is automatically a member of the EPP Presidency.

Egon Klepsch (1979–81, and 1984–91), Paolo Barbi (1982–84), Leo Tindemans (1992–94), and Wilfried Martens (from 1994) have all been EPP Group chairmen. They were all in different ways linked to the EPP, all making their own contributions to the party's development and the fairly successful efforts to forge a European party out of this association of national and regional parties.

There was already discussion about making Martens party and Group chairman. As Group chairman, Tindemans, who had played a decisive role as founding President of the EPP, proved notably receptive and sensitive to the particular concerns and problems of the party.

The exceptional commitment of the Italian Paolo Barbi was marked by close co-operation with the EPP. Indeed Barbi did not differentiate between the two. For him, both the party and the Group were there to serve the end of one Christian Democratic and European federalist project. As far as he was concerned, it was reasonable to use all available means to bring it about. Barbi was not rewarded for his stand in support of the EPP. After his successful work in Brussels and Strasbourg, it emerged that the Democrazia Cristiana (or the then powerful DC figure De Mita) had neglected to ensure he had the necessary support for re-election to the European Parliament.[6]

Egon Klepsch has had a longer period in office than anyone else in the European Parliament. He immediately succeeded Alfred Bertrand (1976–77) as leader of the Christian Democratic Group, and in 1979 became the first chairman of the EPP Group in the directly-elected European Parliament. After failing to get elected as President of Parliament, he was Vice-President of Parliament between 1982 and 1984. After that he again took the helm of the EPP Group until he was finally elected EP President.

His repeated election as leader over such a long period reflects the prevailing feeling in the group that he was irreplaceable. Although his way of running the group was not uncontroversial, he never had to face a rival candidate. His strengths were the incredible degree to which he was always there, both in parliament and in the group. He also had a detailed knowledge, down to the technical details, of every procedure or combination of procedures, and the political problems connected with all of them. He relied on the two strongest national groups in the group, the Germans and the Italians. The majority of the German delegation were loyal to him, not just out of national camaraderie, but on the basis of friendly relations, which he was careful to cultivate. In the 1960s he had systematically done much the same to win the support and endorsement of the Italians during his time as federal chairman of the CDU's youth wing, the Junge Union, and as President of the European Union of Christian Democrats.

Klepsch's style of leadership in turn dominated the group's style: he always tried to head off potential controversies which might harm group unity. He was generally able to avoid conflict by bringing the relevant individuals and groups together, and reaching agreement by establishing a balance of interests. It was how he held tactical control. At the same time, he pursued the aims of the vast majority of the group – and he was consistent and clear-eyed about his strategy. Those aims were the federal organisation of the European Community, the reinforcement of its democratic and parliamentary components, and finally the consolidation of the EPP Group's central position. The goal was to ensure that all decision-making in the European Parliament depended on the EPP Group's agreement or participation.

POLITICAL FRIENDS AND COMMITTED COLLEAGUES

It was not only those holding high office who influenced the EPP's development. Above all, members of the Political Bureau (or Executive), and members of the EPP Group deserve mention in this context. Of these, quite a number actively participated in the work of party bodies alongside their parliamentary activity, either as representatives of the Group, or on their own initiative.

The 'International Secretaries' who are responsible for the external, international, or European relations of their countries, should also be mentioned. They concern themselves with, and co-ordinate, their compatriots' activities in the EPP. Both on a practical and political level they are important discussion partners for the EPP leadership. Their role is determined by their position in the individual parties. In some parties they will have a political mandate, in others they are simply functionaries (in the case of the CDU, they are traditionally civil servants given special leave from the foreign service). Irrespective of their status, they are an important element in making the internal communications and co-operations system work – a system on which a European Party depends if it is to be effective.

Nor can any overview of the *'dramatis personae'* ignore those working in the background, committed colleagues in the party secretariats who do the routine work, and make sure decisions are translated into action. They are frequently the ones who ensure that the pre-conditions for such decisions are in place.

European deputies, representatives of member parties, International Secretaries, political aides and party workers: we are dealing with a fairly large circle of personnel, and it would be beyond the scope of this study to try to describe the commitment of all, or even the key people. But it must be said that quite a few of them, by being there, because of their special tasks or their strong personal commitment, made powerful contributions both in conceptual and in practical terms. In some cases, what I have in mind goes far beyond the contributions of this or that party leader.

18 Relationships with Member Parties and the EPP Parliamentary Group

What state a party is in, and its development, are essentially dependent on the ability and willingness of its members to articulate a common will. Members of the European People's Party are – in accordance with Article 4 of the statute – the 'Christian Democratic parties' (and the 'parties with a Christian Democratic direction, who share fundamental political principles') from European Union Member States.

THE EPP IS WHAT ITS MEMBERS MAKE OUT OF IT

A European party can be neither better nor worse than what its members make of it. We can examine what EPP member parties have made of the party. It is evidently not exactly what they wanted to create. It is the product of compromises and pressures arising from the fact that not everyone involved shared the same idea at the same time – ideas, after all, diverge about what the EPP was to be, and should achieve. Generally, everyone bases his perspective on what is around in his party (or country) in the way of models, and European and transnational consciousness.

There are different interpretations of what a political party is. The internal organisation of the member parties reflects their respective histories, and also the constitution of the state in which they are operating. For instance, it is highly relevant for those representing a member party, and adjusting themselves to a European party, whether they have a federal culture and tradition. It is just as relevant if they come from a system operating under the rules of 'democratic centralism.' There is a broad spectrum of ways in which the party leader can choose to operate: he can play the manager, mediator, leading light, president or party leader. The role of the secretary-general is also open to different interpretations. In some parties he is an administrator or organiser, in others he is a political leader.

All this may explain why 'real existing' European parties cannot correspond to the picture which different people suppose, or supposed, they should be. They develop in an open forcefield, under the influence of very different impulses. Always to look only for the image one has of a national party from home is to miss the point. It is true that there are elements of these in European parties. But what characterises European parties must be something different.

There was, and still is, a more or less palpable tendency among member parties to expect the EPP to be based on national preconceptions. The logic is to judge its performance by national criteria, too. And from that follows another tendency, which is to use the EPP as a means of advancing current national party interests. These can be those of the government or of the opposition. Alternatively, the value of the EPP (along with the member party's own commitment) is measured according to how immediately useful the party promises to be. These are all reflexes which are understandable during a period of transition to a new political system in which people are not yet used to the new ways of operating, and the reference point is still the past.

THE COMMUNICATION PROBLEM

One of the main problems European parties face is the lack of communication between the European and national levels, and in the difficulties of organising this communication. This applies both to their efforts to assert themselves, and to play their role, as in developing their structures.

Member parties – not only the EPP's, but also those belonging to the Social Democratic Party of Europe (PSE) and the European Liberals and Democratic Reform Party (ELDR) – often complain that nothing much is heard or seen of the European party. Such complaints make no distinction between the party and the parliamentary group. It is true that what can be seen of European parties in terms of political activity, visible influence, or media coverage, is nothing very much compared to what people are used to from parties at home. This is because there are relatively few people working at European level, and their activities are scantily reported. The headquarters of national parties have a multiple of the staff, the mechanisms and the money available to European party secretariats. There is a similar relationship between the set-up for television, radio, and press correspondents in national capitals and the European capitals (Brussels and Strasbourg).

What happens on the political stage of the European Union is very complex indeed – without even going into what is going on behind the scenes. To understand, to gain real insight, requires knowledge and experience which the average national politician does not have. And *vice versa*.

Those engaged at European level have to show a sense of European responsibility, and to take account of the situation in several countries at the same time. And that necessarily means taking positions which are, or seem to be, at odds with those of their friends in the party back home. Even the readiness to compromise which is essential to serious or successful European policy often meets, at domestic level, with blank incomprehension. Only gradually is it becoming a matter of course – as national and European politics become more and more intertwined – for national parliamentarians, and party politicians, to take the European dimension into account in their activities and their decisions.

Then again, European party bodies often feel they have been let down by member parties. The virtual indifference of national media means that the contribution of 'the Europeans' is not recognised in the national context – so it is not recognised at all. This encourages the tendency of some national politicians to see European activities, even those of their own party, as a form of luxury item, and the European party structures as essentially decorative.

PROPOSALS FOR REFORM

The problems of how the European party relates to its national member parties have, over time, been subjected to more or less systematic attempts to reform the EPP's structures and *modus operandi*. The project of merging the European Union of Christian Democrats with the EPP, pursued over many years, and the major constitutional revision decided in 1990, both belong in this chapter.[1]

Recognising that revising clauses in a statute cannot solve everything, the working group on reform worked out a list of suggestions which clarified the direction the EPP was to take, and in particular what role the member parties were to play.[2]

> The member parties' relationship to the EPP is (in accordance with the assumption articulated in the constitution) like that of Land or regional associations. The sense of solidarity and belonging has to be more strongly developed….The cohesion of the Christian Democratic family in the European Community urgently requires that a tightly-knit, interconnected, multi-faceted nexus of contacts, meetings, connections, and co-operation be forged…. It would be critically important for strengthening EPP consciousness if national member parties identified with the EPP not just in political declarations, but also symbolically, in the way

they presented themselves, and possibly even in what they called themselves. For instance, consistently using the EPP logo alongside the party logo.... However, in order to strengthen the identification of the member parties with the EPP, and to cement relations between member parties, individual parties need better information about work going on at EPP level, as well as constant communication among themselves, which again takes for granted that they know about each other.

Member party chairmen (alternatively the party leaders) absolutely must be won over to the idea of taking an active part in co-operation, both within the EPP and between the EPP parties. It is not enough just to turn up for the occasional party leaders' meetings. The party leader himself, or someone he has directly authorised as his representative, should be available to take part in the EPP Presidency, and so take part in running the EPP. In this way the EPP has both the natural and formal authority it needs to be effective and to assert its authority: to the public, but also to the member parties and the EPP Group.... Participation and co-operation in EPP bodies by national party representatives should at the same time be institutionalised to ensure that the EPP's development and party decisions are regularly reported on, and that positions taken by the EPP are also translated into action in member parties.[3]

The clauses quoted above were all followed by concrete suggestions about how to realise the demands being made. Beyond these, measures were suggested which were designed to include in EPP co-operation not only national parliamentary groups, but those 'with government level responsibilities', meaning the head of government as well as individual ministers.

But such projects were perhaps too *avant-garde*. Although the conference of party and government leaders had agreed to these proposals, the member parties did not move when it came to putting them into practice.

PARTY AND PARLIAMENTARY GROUP: A BUILT-IN FRICTION

In every parliamentary democracy involving parties and party activity, there will be antagonism between the parties and their parliamentary groups. It creates a degree of tension, whose intensity will depend on many coincidental factors. Personalities will play a big part, along with the position of the group, whether it is in opposition or in government. Eventually the institutional situation and that of the political culture will also be relevant. Normally every strong parliamentary group has an equally strong party behind it, since the group is an expression of the party, and the group will in turn have a strong influence on the character of the party.

The extent to which the group is independent of the party, and can play a role of its own, either in parallel or at an angle to the party, flows from the results of parliamentary elections – the mandates gained in general elections, and the deputies' function in the legislative process. The party's possibilities of influencing the parliamentary group's actions or decisions are informal, and are almost entirely based on the power it derives from the selection of candidates and from the election campaign.

There is tension, too, between the party and the group at European level. However, the balance is clearly tipped in the group's favour. European parties still play no part either in selecting candidates or in European parliamentary elections. Since the right to vote in European elections is based on nationality, it is the parties in member states who are responsible for putting up candidates and organising the campaign. The organisational weakness of the European parties is another factor. Until their legal situation in the European political system is unresolved, they remain financially dependent on their (national) member parties.

This dependency is in itself unproblematic, since the European parties are eventually the sum of the national parties. But member parties are unwilling to provide European parties with the financial means necessary to do their work properly. And they are therefore forced to stick with their groups in the European Parliament, who are both more understanding and more accommodating.

THE POSITION OF THE EUROPEAN PARLIAMENTARY GROUP

The strong position of the parliamentary groups in, and in relation to, the European parties is eventually a product of history. People with the necessary knowledge of the European context combined in the groups early on. It was they who convinced their party leaders at home of the importance of closer co-operation with partners in neighbouring countries.

From the start – when national parties were still far less willing about such matters than they are now – it was the groups who provided the means and structures which enabled the first steps towards organisational co-operation to be made. Even today their contribution in terms of finance and held in kind are relatively a great deal larger than the support of individual member parties. Indeed it was the parliamentary groups who had the impulse to create European parties in the first place.

The EPP, too, was a child of the Christian Democratic Group, which in turn shares a parent in the European Union of Christian Democrats. The group's role as a progenitor has, from the beginning, given it a strong influence on the development of the party, and that remains the case to this day. As a founding member it has always been, along with the member parties, a constituent member of the EPP. This is also set out in the 1990 constitution, which says:

> The European People's party is made up of the Christian Democratic parties of the Member States of the European Community and their group in the European Parliament. (Article 1)

In the course of the discussion about constitutional reforms, this clause, which accorded the group the role of a constituent component of EPP, was questioned by various parties. Their argument was that the group was made up of representatives of member parties. It was therefore a party body articulating the political will of the EPP fighting the parliamentary fight in the name of the party. So the group could not be a constituent element of the EPP.

Finally it was agreed that the assertion contained in this statute should be read as a historical statement: since the party had been co-founded by the group, it was to that extent a constituent element of the EPP. But the group was not a member on the same level as the member parties, for which reason Article 4 of the statutes did not include the group under the 'members'. The group's function as the EPP's parliamentary wing is not in question.

However, the group's status as a constituent element of the party has substantial formal implications which in turn lend legitimacy to its political influence. Its rights of representation are especially generous. The chairman of the group is invariably a party Vice-President, too; the members of the group Presidency and the chairmen of the national delegations inside the group are members of the Executive. And all members of the group are delegates (in so far as they are in member parties) at the Congress. Apart from that, the group pays a membership fee equivalent to that paid by the strongest member party (the German CDU).

THE PARLIAMENTARY GROUP'S SUPPORT

The relevance of this formal side of the party-group relationship is that it underpins and justifies the *de facto* relations. These include the fact that the party bodies, notably the Executive, Presidency, and general secretariat, substantially depend on the EPP Group's material and political support for any projects they undertake.

For example, the EPP Group provides the party with the infrastructure it needs for meetings and discussions: its offices and also the interpreters whose help is indispensable in international co-operation. The costs of this infrastructure are extremely high for those who have to pay for them. But the party has neither the infrastructure nor the financial means to rent them when it needs them.

The group also gives the party material help by providing staff. In fact some of the people working in the general secretariat are employed by the EPP group. And in special cases, for instance during congresses, the group provides additional staff to help in various capacities.

Such support is made possible by the fact that the group itself is exceptionally well provided for. It has a large secretariat of circa 130 people.[4] This secretariat, which has all the necessary technical equipment, also has free use of the numerous possibilities available from the European Parliament's service, among them, for instance, the interpretation and translation services.

The party is dependent on the group because of what the group does for the party, and this has a further consequence. Problems and tensions surface, notably when priorities or interests do not coincide. This happens again and again, and will continue to do so: the party and group have different functions, and are different in character. The dependence of European parties on their parliamentary groups can be problematic when – as can of course happen – the party becomes an instrument of parliamentary or group requirements.

THE EUROPEAN PARLIAMENT ROUTINE

The group has its own routine. It follows a very strict calendar determined by the parliamentary timetable. Its members work together almost all the time. In the first week of the month, the group committees meet (in Brussels, or occasionally somewhere else): the group Presidency, the group Executive, the group in its entirety, and the group's working groups, which debate various specialised matters. The focus of all this is preparing for the following week, when the plenary session is held (in Strasbourg). During the second week, too, group meetings take place on the margins of the plenary session. These are to do the groundwork ahead of votes, or they can relate to negotiations with other groups about how to deal with reports, resolutions, and so on. which have been presented to parliament. During the two remaining weeks there are generally meetings of parliamentary committees (again in Brussels, but on rare occasions somewhere else).

The group's work is structured and constrained by this timetable. The role of individual deputies is dictated by membership of at least one parliamentary committee, and by his or her function in the parliamentary or group pecking order. The parliamentary pecking order is: the President of Parliament; Vice-Presidents; Quaestors; chairmen or deputy chairmen of committees. The group hierarchy goes: chairman of the group, deputy chairman, chairman or deputy chairman of workshops or working groups, group spokesmen in the committees.

Both of these hierarchies are overlapped by a third, namely that of the national delegations, which means chairman and members of the Executive. These national delegations within the group which unite deputies of the same nationality, have gained in importance over the years. The European Parliament can make its mark as a supranational institution, and the supranational groups are an important part of this. However, within the groups the national structures are intermediaries – they are an essential part of opinion-forming and decision-making. The national groups are above all involved in the personnel policy of the group, making deals with each other about posts, and deciding which national delegation gets what. At the same time they fill from their own ranks the positions accorded to them.

Furthermore, Members of the European Parliament, seeing themselves as directly-elected representatives of their electorates, are able to enforce their claim to autonomy. They fit in only because it is the only way they have of achieving any part of their project, or their ambition.

A DIFFICULT RELATIONSHIP

All of this produced an extremely sensitive and difficult body, one that is not easy to lead or to handle. However, the influence of the group on the party is not just dictated by its political interests, which are in turn an expression of its standing in the European Parliament battlefield. That influence is above all determined by relationships and by leaders.

For most of the EPP's existence, the leaders of the group and of the party were two different people. Only after July 1994 were these two offices for the first time taken on by one person. Wilfried Martens, who had been party President since 1990, was elected Chairman of the EPP Group. It is significant in view of the relationship between the party and group that it was the party President who became Chairman of the group, not the other way round.

The likelihood is, however, that the future will see these two positions being divided again, and this will probably be the general rule. It is an arrangement which of course tends to lead to antagonisms between the party and group. Depending on their temperament, their idea of what their position means, and personal ambition, one of the two will either accept the leadership of the other, or claim it for himself. And even if such conflict remains latent, serious tensions can arise from it. These manifest themselves in wasted time when friction gets in the way of co-operation or common action. Such tensions between the leading figures automatically spreads to those around them, especially to those colleagues working most closely with them in the leadership bodies, and obviously to officials and aides most of all.

Such situations have arisen from time to time with different Chairmen. However, they could always be got through with decorum and without incidents because there were always balancing and mediating elements in play, too. It is clear that, in such situations, the President of the EPP is in a weaker position than the Chairman of the group, the party being weaker because it is materially dependent. However, this material dependency can also be balanced out where the group is politically dependent on the party; an example of this was the debate about admitting conservative deputies to the group.

PROSPECTS

The process of Europeanising political life, especially in the national and indeed regional structures, will certainly have one effect. That is: to reduce the clear tendency to under-estimate the potential of European parties. This is a misunderstanding to be found in the member parties as much as in the parliamentary groups. There are more and more expectations of European solutions to the weighty, difficult problems affecting internal and social policy in the member states. That in turn evidently changes the way Union institutions are judged in terms of their role and importance. And above all it transforms the way the European Parliament is seen, the institution which directly articulates the citizens' concerns. That is not all. The EP is also able, since it decides by a majority vote, to speak clearly and – beyond diplomacy – reach agreement on concrete measures to take. The political class in member states, above all in national parliaments and parties, is finally coming to understand the real point of the European Parliament. So, finally, is public opinion. There is a growing awareness that the system can only deliver answers to the key issues of our time if nations act together, using the European Union's political machinery. Examples which spring to mind are immigration pressures resulting from mass migration from the south and east, the environment, or the challenges posed by organised crime and international drug trafficking.

That puts in place what is needed for a normal relationship of European parties to their parliamentary groups. The imbalance in their relationship creates an obvious danger. This is that the groups, by monopolising the European parties, will prevent their development into sturdily independent organisations which express the will of their member parties and translate it into action. This is of course not to criticise the parliamentary groups. Without their commitment to European parties they would be much worse off. National parties must take responsibility if they want to influence events at European level, and not leave everything to governments and administrations. Either in the short or medium term, they must make serious efforts, and a lot of noise, about investing in their supranational organisations in terms of personnel, resources, and finance.

A Personal Postscript

In October 1994 I resigned as secretary-general of the EPP. July the previous year had seen my re-election for a fourth term, on President Martens's recommendation. Eleven years in that sort of position is long enough. But I have to say that it wasn't until the day I cleared my desk that I felt I had accumulated enough experience to carry out the job effectively. Animating and organising the development of a multinational, federative party is an extraordinarily complex undertaking. There were no models or blueprints when, in April 1983, I was elected secretary-general on the recommendation of the then President, Leo Tindemans, acting on Helmut Kohl's suggestion.

I was then under the impression that it would be possible, if I took the right initiatives, to turn this EPP into a European Party worthy of the name, and that it could be achieved in a relatively short time. EPP member parties in the different Community countries had portrayed themselves as 'European parties'. The EPP itself demanded that governments press forward on the road to a federal organisation. The measures that would lead to this supranational Europe were set out in the EPP's programme, and the programmes of its national and regional structures. Governments were clearly not in a position to unite their countries around the Christian Democratic federal model. But for the time being at least the EPP should unite its member parties along federal lines, in anticipation of what was being strived for. The EPP, as I saw it, would then be in a better position to contribute to its great goal.

Even if this idea proved illusory, I am now more convinced than ever that the European Union can only successfully develop in the interests of the peoples of the member states if it is made politically vibrant. How? Through public debate. Through the open struggle for power in the Union's institutions. Through interest groups' open attempts to impose their will. So the Union's political forces – meaning the political parties – have to organise themselves so that they can articulate across Europe the will of that section of the Union's population which they seek to represent.

MUCH REMAINS TO BE DONE

Further work on building up European party structures is, then, of the utmost importance for the further development of the European unification process. Article 138a of the Maastricht Treaty gives a constitutional basis for further efforts. The necessary initiatives must now be made if this opportunity is to be exploited. A vital first priority is to press for a statute governing the transnational party federations. This would give them a legal framework for their work, and at the same time provide the possibility of financing themselves properly.

Future work in this area, made possible by Article 138a and by a statute on European parties, must initially involve making good the shortcomings of what has gone before. Inside the EPP, more attention has, crucially, to be paid to a properly institutionalised, better-organised system of establishing consensus. This should be based on efficient communication with, and between, national and regional parties alike. And it must involve elected politicians at different levels, with a maximum possible participation by members.

All this, however, depends on the willing participation of those at the head of member parties. All this will in any event command respect. Time must not be frittered away. Europeanising the member parties is a precondition of Europeanising the EPP. Those in charge must not block overdue reforms, whether out of narrow-mindedness, national egoism, or fear of losing some part of their own organisational empires. The wasted time could just mean that the EPP is too late in the competition for power and influence – which it must have, if the party is to shape the Union in the way it wishes.

The job of Secretary General of the EPP was, in 1983–94, *avant-garde*. No doubt it still is. However, I could not amaze the public with spectacular actions. The means were not there to do this. I finally accepted that parties could not behave as if constitutional change had already happened; they had to follow it. So instead, using up most of what little there was in terms of political and material capital, I tried gradually to develop co-operative structures and communications, as well as systematically establishing consensus between the member parties.

GROWING CONSENSUS

During my years as Secretary General, further co-operation in the EPP was marked by a constantly growing consensus on the political programme, on practical European political issues, on international relations, and on economic and social issues too. At the same time there was more and more contact between the member parties and their leading representatives in parliament and government. The EPP grew enormously as new members joined. The number of parties connected with the EPP, either as full members, associate members or as permanent observers, doubled between

1983 and 1994 from 13 to 26. As a result, the EPP also grew considerably as a political influence.

The EPP is without question further down the path to becoming a trans- or supranational party than the Socialists, the Greens, or the Liberals. However, there is still a long way to go, because there is insufficient consciousness in the party's own ranks. For instance, it is not enough that the Executive and experts in the member parties know what is being discussed in the EPP, or that the Members of the European Parliament and their aides proselytise for the EPP. The EPP is right at the beginning of the long haul of winning over the local and regional sections of member parties, and eventually individual members. They are the ones who must support the EPP as a cohesive political unit in the European Union, inspire the party, and fill it with life.

The European People's Party's destiny, as I see it, is a double one. It must contribute to the unification of Europe by bringing together like-minded political forces. On the other hand, its job is to help bring about the cultural and political breakthrough of 'Christian Democracy'. The Athens Basic Programme (1992) explains exactly what these two tasks involve. It is also important to keep these in mind in future. The EPP can in no circumstances abandon either its European federalist goal, nor its ambition to be Christian Democratic.

Those responsible for the EPP's development owe allegiance to tradition, and to the political programme. That is not just a personal obligation, and one to those whose work they are building on; it is also a duty to those who have joined the EPP from other traditions. If the EPP's identity as a European federalist and Christian Democratic-oriented party were lost, its cohesion would be in danger. And that in turn would mean a loss both of political strength and attractiveness.

Protecting the EPP's identity does not, evidently, mean insisting that nothing changes. On the contrary: further development of tradition and of the heritage is a pre-condition of protecting the party's identity, while taking new understandings and new situations into account. The EPP's identity must come out in its programme, in its capacity to develop projects and to make proposals, and also in the way it behaves and the actions it takes. Elected politicians, deputies, officials, and EPP members must practice what they demand of others.

AN OBLIGATION

It seemed to me an obligation to describe how the EPP was born and grew up, to sketch the making not only of a political party but the gradual development of a European party system. The decision to write this book coincided with the realisation that the time had come to hand on the baton as Secretary General. The sense of obligation came from the fact that the job had given me an overview of events during several decisive years. I was in a position to share much that someone else could only learn from wearisome study in the archives, and through extensive questioning of those who were there.

Of course I wanted to write a book which strives for an objective, even scholarly character. I was always aware of the methodological problems of my bold undertaking. There was the risk that my bias about the subject – one I care about – would distort my judgment. I have therefore studied the sources and kept to a systematic way of presenting the material in order to maintain as large a distance as possible from the facts and events described here. On the other hand, sympathy and commitment are part of the way I have approached this subject, for all my scholarly ambitions. And I would argue that those qualities have helped me to reach a better comprehension of the events and phenomena I have depicted and analysed here.

Annex 1
List of EPP Member Parties

(* Denotes Associated Members)

Austria
Österreichische Volkspartei (ÖVP)

Belgium
Christelijke Volkspartij (CVP)
Parti Social Chrétien (PSC)

Cyprus
Democratic Rally (DR)*

Denmark
Det Konservative Folkeparti

Finland
Kansallinen Kokoomus

France
Force Démocrate (FD)

Germany
Christlich Demokratische Union (CDU)
Christlich Soziale Union (CSU)

Greece
Nea Demokratia (ND)

Ireland
Fine Gael (FG)

Italy
Partito Popolare Italiano (PPI)
Centro Cristiano Democratico (CCD)
Cristiani Democratici Uniti (CDU)
Südtiroler Volkspartei (SVP)

Luxemburg
Chrëschtlech Sozial Volkspartei (CSV)

Malta
Partit Nazzjonalista (PN)*

Norway
Hoyre*

Netherlands
Christen Democratisch Appèl (CDA)

Portugal
Partido Social Democratido (PSD)

Spain
Partido Popular (PP)
Unió Democrática de Catalunya (UDC)
Partido Nacionalista Vasco (PNV)

Sweden
Kristdemokraterna (Kds)
Moderaterna (MS)

Switzerland
Christlichdemokratische Volkspartei (CVP)*

Annex 2   The Author – Biographical Note

Thomas Jansen, born 1939; studied Political Science, Sociology and History 1962–7 at the Universities in Bonn and Munich, concluding with a PhD degree; academic assistant and lecturer, 1967–9 at the Institute of Political Science, University of Mainz; assistant to Walter Hallstein MP and adviser on European policy of the CDU/CSU Parliamentary Group in the German Bundestag, 1970–1; personal adviser to the Chairman, Rainer Barzel MP, 1971–5; Deputy Secretary General and Secretary General of the European Union Deutschland (European federalist movement), 1975–80; Editor-in-chief of 'Dokumente. Zeitschrift für den deutsch-französischen Dialog', 1978–81; Director of the Konrad Adenauer Foundation in Rome/Italy, 1981–3; at the same time Secretary General of the International European Movement; Secretary General of the European People's Party (EPP) and of the European Union of Christian Democrats (EUCD), 1983–94; since 1995 Member of the Forward Studies Unit of the European Commission. Publications include several books and numerous essays and articles on the problems of international relations and European unification.

References

1 THE EMERGENCE OF EUROPEAN PARTIES

1. Cf. Eberhard Grabitz and Thomas Läufer, *Das Europäische Parlament*, Bonn 1980, see p. 295 *et seq.*
2. See *inter alia, Zusammenarbeit der Parteien in Westeuropa, Auf dem Wege zu einer neuen politischen Infrastruktur?*, Bonn (Institut für Europäische Politik) 1976; Theo Stammen, *Parteien in Europa. Nationale Parteiensysteme. Transnationale Parteienbeziehungen. Konturen eines Europäischen Parteiensystems*, Munich 1977.
3. Cf. Norbert Gresch, *Transnationale Parteienarbeit in der EG*, Baden-Baden 1978, see p. 23 *et seq.*
4. Cf. Martin Bangemann *inter alia, Programme für Europa. Die Programme der Europäischen Parteienenbünde zur Europawahl 1979*, Bonn 1978; Eva-Rose Karnofski, *Parteienbünde vor der Europawahl 1979, Bonn 1982*.
5. Klaus von Beyme, *Parteien in Westlichen Demokratien*, Munich 1984, p. 193.
6. Oscar Niedermayer, *Europäische Parteien? Zur grenzüberschreitenden Interaktion politischer Parteien im Rahmen der Europäischen Gemeinschaft*, Frankfurt/New York 1983, p. 13.
7. Cf. Thomas Jansen, 'Zur Entwicklung supranationaler Europäischer Parteien', in: Oscar W. Gabriel *inter alia* (eds), *Der Demokratische Verfassungsstaat. Theorie, Geschichte, Probleme. Festschrift für Hans Buchheim*, Munich 1992, p. 241 *et seq.*
8. On the development of the individual party confederations cf. the regular contributions of Rudolf Hrbek since 1980 (to 1989/90), Melanie Piepenschneider (1990/91) and Thomas R. Henschel (to 1993/4), 'Die europäischen Parteienzusammenschlüsse'; from 1994/95 Thomas Jansen, 'Die europäischen Parteien' in: Werner Weidenfeld/Wolfgang Wessels (eds), *Jahrbuch der Europäischen Integration* 1980 *et seq.*, Bonn 1981 *et seq.*
9. Alf Mintzel and Heinrich Oberreuter (eds), Parteien in der Bundesrepublik Deutschland, Bonn 1992.
10. Ibid., p. 508.
11. Cf. Klaus von Beyme, p. 22 *et seq.*; Theo Stammen, p. 52 *et seq.*; Heinrich Oberreuter, 'Politische Parteien: Stellung und Funktion im Verfassungssystem der Bundersrepublik' in: Alf Mintzel and Heinrich Oberreuter (eds), pp. 15–40 (here pp. 28 *et seq.*); see also Raph M. Goldman (ed.), Transnational Parties. Organising the World's Precincts, Lanham/New York/London 1983, who sees all the constituent elements of 'transnational political parties' in both the regional and international party confederations: 'Political parties become transnational when they develop supranational organisations that cooperate across national boundaries. Such transnationals have explicit (public) and formal (officers, headquarters, etc.) organisations whose supranational executives conduct their

activities from some central office .... Transnational parties, in their most comprehensive form, have member-affiliated national parties and/or individual party members in two or more countries .... While the European Community and the United Nations are not yet perceived as supranational governments, it will be the transnationals that will inevitably become the principal promoters of the perception as well as that reality. In this effort they will – already do – function as a kind of pre-governmental party system.' (p. 8; cf. p. 293 *et seq.*).

12. Dimitros Th. Tsatsos, 'Europäische politische Parteien? Erste Überlegungen zur Auslegung des Parteienartikels des Maastrichter Vertrages – Art. 138A EGV,' in: *Europäische Grundrechte-Zeitschrift* (EuGRZ) 1994, 21st year/vol. 3–4, pp. 45–53 (here p. 49).

13. Wolfgang Graf Vitzthum, 'Demokratie, Parteien, Parteiendemokratie Ein oft kristisierter, aber unlösbarer Zusammenhang' in *Frankfurter Allgemeine Zeitung*, 11 November 1994, pp. 9–10.

14. Letter from W. Martens, D. Spitaels, and W. De Clercq: archives of the EPP general secretariat.

15. For instance, the staff of the general secretariat of the EPP has been partly employed by the EPP Group in the European Parliament, and partly by the Belgian member parties.

16. Proposal by President Enrique Baron Crespo on uniform electoral procedure for elections to the European Parliament made during the meeting with the presidents of the ELDR, USP, and EPP on 2 October 1991. Archives of the EPP general secretariat.

17. Communiqué of 12 December 1991: archives of the EPP general secretariat.

18. The following heads of governments took part in the EPP 'summit' in The Hague and in the meeting of the European Council in Maastricht: Ruud Lubbers, Helmut Kohl, Konstantin Mitsotakis, Giulio Andreotti, Jacques Santer and Wilfried Martens.

19. Tsatsos, op. cit. p. 49, regards this as a decision 'against the pure confederation model' which he saw as the intention of party leaders' proposal. The EPP's consistent ambition has been to become a federative 'European party', an aim more recently echoed by the Socialists as well as the Liberals. The party leaders' definition indirectly refers to this. But it is not to a confederation model. Rather – and this is quite clear, as Tsatsos rightly states – it is a reference to the same model as that of Article 138A: 'one having its own European institutional subjectivity, and also permitting individual membership, either directly or indirectly through membership of a national party.'

20. See the agenda for the meeting of 18 September 1990; archives of the EPP general secretariat.

21. Communiqué of 12 December 1991: archives of the EPP general secretariat.

22. Tsatsos, op. cit., p. 52.

23. The analysis of the essential elements of a European party statute is based on the reflections of Secretaries General of the ESP, EPP, and ELDR (Axel Hanisch, Thomas Jansen, and Christian Ehlers) recorded in a working paper presented to the party leaders on 20 May 1992: archives of the EPP general secretariat.

2 THE 1994 EUROPEAN ELECTIONS – TRANSFORMING THE PARTY LANDSCAPE

1. European Social Democratic Party; activity report by Axel Hanisch, secretary-general (ESP c/o European Parliament, B-1047 Brussels.)
2. Agence Europe, 8 March 1995, p. 2 *et seq.*
3. Hanisch, op. cit.
4. Ehlers, Christian: A Successful Year for the ELDR Party, in: ELDR Newsletter no. 3/94 (ELDR c/o European Parliament, B-1047, Brussels).
5. For instance Guy Spitaels, president of the European Union of Socialist Parties, in Madrid on 10 December 1990, on the occasion of the conference of party leaders: 'I personally believe that we must closely observe what is happening in the EPP. As a result of their last congress, they have for the time being succeeded – justifiably or not – in shedding their image of being self-contained. Second, they have also shown the will to open themselves up to the Spanish conservatives; the next could be the British Conservatives and Giscard d'Estaing's friends, and in the future no doubt the brother parties in central Europe. Through this openness the traditional balance of power could be completely changed.'
6. Cf. Zur Geschichte der christlich-demokratischen Bewegung in Europa, vol. 2 of the European People's Party series '*Geistige und Historische Grundlagen christlich-demokratischer Politik*', Melle 1990.
7. Cf. Thomas Jansen, Europäische Christdemokraten überprüfen ihre Doktrin in: *Politische Meinung*, vol. 256/March 1991, p. 66 *et seq.*; Tradition und Aktualität der Bemühungen um eine 'Doktrin'. With contributions by Piet Bukman *inter alia*, vol. 1 '*Geistige und historische Grundlagen christlich-demokratischer Politik*', Melle 1988.
8. See for example Hans Jenitschek, The contemporary Socialist International, in: Ralph M. Goldman (ed.) pp. 73–97; Charles R. Dechert, Christian Democracy as International Movement, ibid. pp. 99–147; Urs Schoettli, New Horizons for International Liberalism, ibid. pp. 149–173.

3 THE INTERNATIONAL SECRETARIAT OF DEMOCRATIC PARTIES INSPIRED BY CHRISTIANITY, 1925–1939

1. See *inter alia* Jean-Marie Mayeur, *Des Partis catholiques à la démocratie chrétienne*, Paris 1980; Michael P. Fogarty, *Christian Democracy in Western Europe, 1820–1953*, London 1957; see for Germany, Austria, Belgium and the Netherlands the relevant extracts in: Winfried Becker/Rudolf Morsey (eds) *Christliche Demokratie in Europa. Grundlagen und Entwicklungen seit dem 19. Jahrhundert*, Cologne/Vienna 1988.
2. On Sturzo's contacts and his efforts to spread the idea of the 'Internazionale Popolare', and also in particular on the founding and activities of the SIPDIC, see the description of Alwin Hanschmidt, with its numerous sources and references, 'Eine christlich-demokratische "Internationale" zwischen den Weltkriegen. Das Secrétariat International des Partis Démocratiques d'Inspiration Chrétienne à Paris", in: Winfried

Becker/Rudof Morsey, pp. 158–188, and also Roberto Papini, *L'Internationale Democrate-Chretienne. La coopération entre les partis démocrates-chrétiens de 1925 à 1986*, Paris 1988, see p. 31 *et seq.*; cf. especially Robert Papini's work, II corraggio della democrazia. Luigi Sturzo e l'Internazionale Popolare tra le due guerre (Manuscript of 1995), which is very informative about the whole period dealt with in this chapter, on Don Sturzo's philosophy, and the development of co-operation between Christian Democrats in Europe.

3. Raymond Laurent, general secretary of the PDP, quoted by Hanschmidt, p. 168.

4. Ibid. p. 169 *et seq.*

5. Parties from Luxembourg (Right party), Hungary (Christian-Social Economic party) and the Netherlands (Roman Catholic State party), joined later. See list of SIPDIC member parties in Hanschimdt, p. 187 *et seq.*, which also indicates that, apart from the parties mentioned above there were also relations with kindred political figures and groups in Spain, Jugoslavia, and Rumania.

6. Alwin Hanschmidt, p. 172.

7. On the role, orientation, and contribution of the PDP, see Jean Claude Delbriel, 'Les démocrates d'inspiration chrétienne et les problèmes Européens dans l'entre-deux-guerres', in: Serge Berstein/Jean-Marie Mayeur/Pierre Milza, *Le MRP et la construction Européenne*, Brussels 1993, pp. 15–39.

8. For list of SIPDIC conferences/congresses and information about delegations taking part see Alwin Hanschmidt p. 186 *et seq.*; cf. Roberto Papini's account p. 35 *et seq.*

9. Alwin Hanschmidt, p. 179.

10. Ibid. p. 180: SI = SIPDIC; 'une force....' = a force helping to build peace and international co-operation.

11. Roberto Papini, p. 36.

12. Alwin Hanschmidt, p. 184.

13. Quoted by Roberto Papini, p. 36.

14. Text in: Zur Geschichte der christlich-demokratischen Bewegung in Europa, vol. 4 of EPP series *'Geistige und historische Grundlagen christlich-demokratischer Politik'*, Melle 1990, p. 128 *et seq.* The proposal to create a Common European Market was raised in 1923 – and variants repeated – by Konrad Adenauer (Oberbürgermeister of Cologne from 1917, and from 1921 president of the Prussian State Council).

15. See Alwin Hanschmidt, p. 184 *et seq.*; also Roberto Papini, p. 44 *et seq.*

4   THE 'NOUVELLES EQUIPES INTERNATIONALES', 1948–1965

1. Cf. Roberto Papini, 'Les débuts des Nouvelles Equipes Internationales', in: Hughes Portelli/Thomas Jansen (publ.), *La Démocratie Chrétienne. Force Internationale*, Nanterre, 1986, p. 31 *et seq.*; see also Roberto Papini, *L'Internationale Démocrate Chrétienne. La coopération internationale entre les partis démocrates-chrétiennes de 1925 à 1986*, Paris 1988, p. 47

et seq.; also Philippe Chenaux, *Une Europe Vaticane? Entre le Plan Marshall et les Traités de Rome*, Brussels 1990, p. 119 *et seq.* On the motives of the French and on the related controversy in the MRP see Jean-Claude Delbreil, 'Le MRP et la construction Européenne: résultats, interprétations, et conclusions d'une enquête écrite et orale', in: Serge Berstein/Jean-Marie Mayeur/Pierre Milza (eds), *Le MRP et la construction Européenne*, Brussels, 1993, p. 309 *et seq.*

2. Cf. Robert Bichet, *La Démocratie Chrétienne en France. Le Mouvement Républicain Populaire*, Besançon 1980, p. 27 *et seq.*

3. Only in 1960 following the resignation of De Schrijver, who had been NEI President for a decade, did the PSC (then still the joint Flemish and Walloon CD party in Belgium) become a member of the NEI. On the role of the PSC and De Schrijver, see the contribution by Philippe Chenaux, 'La contribution belge a la démocratie chrétienne internationale' (manuscript 1995).

4. Cf. Karl Josef Hahn/Friedrich Fugmann, 'Die Europäische Christlich-Demokratische Union zwischen europäischen Anspruch und nationalen Realitäten', in: *Zusammenarbeit der Parteien in Westeuropa. Auf dem Weg zu einer neuen Infrastruktur?* Institute for European Politics, Bonn 1976, p. 255 *et seq.* This text also indicates that in the 1960s, Labour members withdrew from the English Equipe because their party no longer tolerated individual party members holding dual international membership. The effect of this was to pull the rug out from under the supranational English equipe and so, in effect, to undermine all political delegations from Great Britain.

5. Text of the statute in: *Zur Geschichte der christlich-demokratischen Bewegung in Europa*. With contributions from *inter alia* Winfried Becker, vol. 4 EPP series 'Geistige und historische Grundlagen christlich-demokratischer Politik', Melle 1990, p. 121 *et seq.* Exile groups from Poland, Hungary, Czechoslovakia, the Basque country, Romania, and Bulgaria, were NEI members.

6. Bichet's successors were also PSC-B members: Auguste Edmond de Schrijver (1950–9); Theo Lefèvre (1960–5); Soyeur's successors, like him, were MRP-F members: Robert Bichet (1950–4); Alfred Coste-Floret (1954), and Jean Seitlinger (1955–62).

7. NEI constitution reproduced in: *Zur Geschichte…*, p. 121 *et seq.*

8. Cf. in this context and generally on the subject of this chapter, Nicole Bacharan-Gressel, 'Les organisations et les associations pro-Européennes', in: Serge Berstein/Jean-Marie Mayeur/Pierre Milza (eds), p. 41 *et seq.*, see also Heribert Gisch, 'Die europäischen Christdemokraten (NEI)', in: Wilfried Loth (eds), *Die Anfänge der Europäischen Integration 1945–1950*, Bonn 1990, p. 227–236; also Philippe Chenaux, 'Les Nouvelles Equipes Internationales,' in: *Fondazione Europea Luciano Bolis, I Movimenti per l'unita Europea dal 1945 al 1954. Atti del convegno internationale Pavia 19-20-21 ottobre 1989, a cura di Sergio Pistone*, Milano 1992, pp. 237–252.

9. Reproduced in: Zur Geschichte…. pp. 114–120.

10. Documentation of the congresses and decisions of international Christian Democratic organisations are to be found in: *La Démocratie Chrétienne dans le monde. Résolutions et déclarations des organisations internationales démocrates chrétiennes de 1947 à 1973*. With a foreword by Mariano Rumor and an introduction Karl J. Hahn, Rome 1973. Resolutions of the 16 NEI congresses (1947–1963) also in: *Zur Geschichte…*, p. 156

et seq. Archives of the NEI, including congress documents (reports, speeches etc) are to be found in the Christian Democracy archives of the Konrad Adenauer Foundation (ACPD/KAS), St Augustine near Bonn.

11. Cf. ibid.; see also Roberto Papini, *L'Internationale...*, p. 71 *et seq.*; also Bruno Dörpinghaus, 'Die Genfer Sitzungen–Erste Zusammenkünfte führender christlich-demokratischen Politiker im Nachkriegseuropa', in: Dieter Blumenwitz *inter alia* (eds), *Konrad Adenauer und seine Zeit. Politik und Persönlichkeit des ersten Bundeskanzlers. Beiträge von Weg- und Zeigenossen,* Stuttgart 1976, pp. 358–65; also Philippe Chenaux, Une Europe.... p. 128 *et seq.* The 'Discussions in Geneva' took place between 1947 and 1956, but only until 1952 at the level of leading politicians; once the first European Community, the Coal and Steel Community, had been established, there were numerous other opportunities for them to meet.

12. See in this context of questions concerning the Christian Democratic International above all Roberto Papini, *L'Internationale...*; as well as the pertinent contributions of Hughes Portelli, Bryan Palmer, André Louis and Jürgen Hartmann in: Hughes Portelli/Thomas Jansen (eds), *La Démocratie Chrétienne...*

13. Cf. Konrad Siniewicz, 'L'activité internationale des Démocrates-Chrétiennes de l'Europe Centrale', ibid. p. 233 *et seq.*, also Roberto Papini, *L'Internationale...*, p. 82 *et seq.*

14. Cf. Jean-Dominique Durand, 'Les rapports entre le MPR et la Démocratie Chrétienne italienne (1945–1955)', in: Serge Berstein/Jean-Marie Mayeur/Pierre Milza (eds), p. 251 *et seq.*; also Reinhard Schreiner, 'La politique Européenne de la CDU relative à la France et au MPR des années 1945–1966', ibid. p. 275 *et seq.*

15. Adenauer: 'Es musste alles neu gemacht werden.' *Protocols of the CDU federal leadership 1950–1953.* Edited by Günter Buchstab, Stuttgart 1986, p. 49.

16. Ibid. p. 66.

17. Konrad Adenauer's speech to the NEI, Bad Ems, 14 September 1951, reproduced in: Werner Weidenfeld, *Konrad Adenauer und Europa. Die geistigen Grundlagen der Westeuropäischen Integrationspolitik des ersten Bonner Bundeskanzlers,* Bonn 1976, p. 326–34, see here p. 331 *et seq.*

18. A. Coste-Floret, quoted in Jean-Claude Delbreil, p. 325.

5   THE EUROPEAN UNION OF CHRISTIAN DEMOCRATS 1965–1976

1. Emilio Colombo, 'Internationale Prässenz der Christlichen Demokraten', in: *Zur Geschichte der christlich-demokratischen Bewegung in Europa.* With contributions by Winfried Becker *inter alia* (vol. 4 of EPP series 'Geistige und historische Grundlagen christlich-demokratischer Politik'), Melle 1990, p. 80.

2. Mariano Rumor, 'Die gemeinsame Aktion der Christlichen Demokraten in Europa', in: *Zur Geschichte...*, p. 89.

3. On the development of the EUCD cf. Pierre Letamendia, L'Union Européenne Démocrate Chrétienne, in: Hughes Portelli/Thomas Jansen, *La Démocratie*

Chrétienne. Force Internationale, Nanterre 1986, pp. 55–63; also Roberto Papini, *L'internationale Démocrate Chrétienne*, Paris 1988, p. 94 *et seq.*

4. Roberto Papini, p. 98.
5. Clause in the constitution of 18 July 1971, reproduced in: *Zusammenarbeit der Parteien in Westeuropa. Auf dem Wege zu einer neuen politischen Infrastruktur?* (Schiften des Instituts für Europäische Politik), Bonn 1976, p. 332; this statute remained effective until 1992, apart from a few small changes, which did not alter the organisational structure.
6. Text of the resolution in: *Zur Geschichte...*, pp. 197–200.
7. Ibid. pp. 201–203.
8. Ibid. pp. 204–206.
9. Roberto Papini, p. 105.
10. From 1971 to 1982 Karl Josef Hahn was also deputy secretary-general of the EUCD. On the CIDCID see Roberto Papini, p. 100 *et seq.*
11. Ibid. p. 101 (footnote 169).
12. Text in: *Programm und Statut. Dokumentation 1*, published by the secretary-general of the European People's Party, 2nd edition, (Brussels) spring 1984, pp. 23–31.
13. Ibid. pp. 33–41.
14. Heinrich Böx, 'Demokratie im christlichen Europa', in: Philipp Jenninger *et alia* (eds), *Unverdrossen für Europa. Festschrift für Kai-Uwe von Hassel*, Baden-Baden 1988, pp. 139–146, see here p. 144.

6 THE CHRISTIAN DEMOCRATIC GROUP IN THE EUROPEAN PARLIAMENT 1952–1979

1. Published in the Journal Officiel of the European Coal and Steel Community, 21 July 1953.
2. Theo Stammen, *Parteien* in Europa, München 1977, p. 254 *et seq.*
3. Cf. Karl Josef Hahn/Friedrich Fugmann, *Die Europäische Christlich-Demokratische Union zwischen europäischem Anspruch und nationalen Realitäten, in: Zusamenarbeit der Parteien in Westeuropa. Auf dem Weg zu einer neuen politischen Infrastruktur?*, Institut für Europäische Politik, Bonn 1976, pp. 304–331.
4. Article 1 of the By-laws of the Political Committee of the Christian-Democratic Parties from the Member states of the European Communities, 7 April 1972; reproduced in: *Zusammenarbeit der Parteien*, p. 338 *et seq.*
5. Arnaldo Ferragni, Secretary General of the CD-Group, in a latter to Karl-Josef Hahn, Deputy Secretary General of the EUCD, 4 January 1972, ACDP IX-004-081.
6. Cf. the articles by Egon Klepsch (p. 31 *et seq.*), Arnaldo Ferragni (p. 84 *et seq.*) and Josef Müller (p. 111 *et seq.*) in: *Liber Amicorum. Erinnerungen an Hans-August Lücker zum 70. Geburtstag*, Bonn (1985).
7. Minutes of the meeting from 12 June 1974 in Strasbourg, ACDP IX-001-008/1.
8. Walter Hallstein, former President of the EEC Commission (1958–1968) had published a book about his experiences and the political philosophy

underlying his work in the Community under the significant title *Der Unvollendete Bundesstaat* ('The Unfinished Federal State') Düsseldorf 1969; English: *Europe in the Making, Allen and Unwin*, 1972.

9. Since 1967 the Dutch parties represented in the Christian Democratic Group (KVP, CHU and ARP), who were competitors at home and who normally did not follow the same political line, worked together, 'more and more', and established as a consequence of their common membership within the EUCD, a 'contact committee'; on 17 June 1972, a 'strategy paper' was presented to this committee claiming 'the formation of one party'; this project was realised in 1977 with the foundation of the Christian Democratic Appeal (CDA), cf. ACDP IX-004-100/8.

10. The text was published in different languages by the CD-Group of the European Parliament in CD-Europa on 16 July 1970; cf. ACDP IX-001-055/2.

11. Cf. Karl-Heinz Nassmacher, Demokratisierung der Europäischen Gemeinschaften, Bonn, 1972.

12. ACDP IX-004-082.

13. Josef K. Hahn/Friedrich Fugman, p. 329.

14. Dossier sur la Formation d'un parti démocrate chrétien européen, Doc 16/10.9.1975, ACDP IX-004-096.

15. Robert Houben, *La formation d'un parti européen*, ibid.

7 FOUNDING THE EUROPEAN PEOPLE'S PARTY, 1976–1978

1. The European Council later changed the election date to 7–10 June 1979.

2. ACDP IX-004-096.

3. Reproduced in: *Programm und Statut*, vol. 1 EPP series 'Dokumentation', Brussels 1984, p. 45 *et seq.*

4. Cf. documentation in *CD-Europa*, no. 2/1978, ed. by EPP Parliamentary Group, Luxembourg.

5. Reproduced in: *Programm und Statut*, p. 6 *et seq.*

6. The arguments of this position are well explained by P. H. Kooijmans, La Démocratie Chrétienne en Europe, in: *Dossier sur la formation d'un parti d.c. européen*, Doc. 16/10.9.1975, ACDP.

7. Hans August Lücker/Karl Joseph Hahn, *Christliche Demokraten bauen Europa*, Bonn 1987, p. 130.

8. Plichten en perspectiven. Aanzet voor een profielschets van het CDA, Centrum voor Staatskundije Vorming, The Hague 1975.

9. Reproduced in: *Programm und Statut*, p. 27 *et seq.*; and p. 33 *et seq.*

10. Cf. Egon Alfred Klepsch, 'Das Programm der EVP', in: Martin Bangemann *inter alia*, p. 77 *et seq.*

11. Eva-Rose Karnofski, *Parteienbünde vor der Europawahl 1979. Integration durch gemeinsame Wahlaussagen*, Bonn 1982, pp. 245 and 248.

12. ACDP IX-004-095.

13. ACDP IX-004-096.

14. Kai Uwe von Hassel in a note for the CDU Party Chairman, Helmut Kohl, ibid.

15. Christoph Brüse, official in CDU department of foreign relations, in a report on the meeting of EPP/EUCD bodies in Brussels, 20–23 October 1976.

16. Quoted in: *Die europäischen Parteien der Mitte*, ed. by Konrad Adenauer Foundation, Bonn 1978, p. 154.
17. Cf. Franz Horner, *Konservative und christdemokratische Parteien in Europa. Geschichte, Programmatik, Strukturen*, Vienna/Munich 1981; Andreas Khol, Europäische Demokratische Union (EDU). Die europäische Parteiengruppierung der fortschrittlichen Mitte, in: *Österreichische Monatshefte*, Nr. 5/1978, p. 4 *et seq.*
18. Minutes of a Joint EPP/EUCD Meeting in Berlin, 6 June 1978: ACDP IX-004-095.
19. Ibid.

8 CONGRESSES AND EUROPEAN ELECTIONS, 1979–1990

1. Text printed *inter alia* in: Eva-Rose Karnofski, *Parteienbünde vor der Europa-Wahl 1979. Integration durch gemeinsame Wahlaussagen?* Bonn 1982, p. 219 *et seq.*
2. The text of these reports is printed in CD-Europa 2/1979, ed. by the Christian Democratic Group in the European Parliament), which reports on the II EPP congress.
3. Hans August Lücker, *Christliche Demokraten bauen Europa*, Bonn 1987, p. 159.
4. Cf. Rudolf Hrbek, 'Die europäischen Parteienzusammenschlüsse', in: Werner Weidenfeld/Wolfgang Wessels (eds), *Jahrbuch der Europäischen Integration* 1980, Bonn 1981, p. 261.
5. The texts are printed in *Beiträge zur europäischen Wirtschafts und Sozialpolitik. Programme, Berichte, Resolutionen 1981–1984; Freiheit, Gerechtigkeit, Friede. Die Verantwortung der Europäer in der Welt, Programme, Berichte, Resolutionen 1981–1984*, vols 4 and 5 EPP series 'Dokumentation'; also see the report about the Paris congress in CD-Europa no. 1/1983, ed. by EPP group, European Parliament.
6. Hans August Lücker, op. cit., p. 175.
7. Cf. Paolo Barbi, *Napoli–Strasburgo e ritorno. I cinque anni al Parlamento Europeo*. Naples 1985, p. 151.
8. Text in vol. 6 of the EPP series 'Dokumentation', op. cit.
9. Cf. Paolo Barbi, op. cit. p. 281, which indicates that this disaster can be traced to an intrigue between the 'correnti' of De Mita and Andreotti.
10. Cf. reports and documentation in: EPP-Bulletin no. 5, June/July 1986 (ed. by the secretariat general).
11. Text in: *An der Seite der Bürger.(On the People's Side). Aktionsprogramm 1989–1994*, with reports by Jacques Santer, Egon A. Klepsch, Lutz Stavenhagen and Thomas Jansen, as well as other documents from the VII Congress in Luxembourg, Melle 1989.
12. Documentation of the results of the third direct election of the European Parliament from 15–18 June 1989 in: Werner Weidenfeld/Wolfgang Wessels (eds), *Jahrbuch der Europäischen Integration 1988/89*, Bonn 1989, p. 433 *et seq.*
13. The text is printed in EPP-Bulletin no. 5/6 December 1990.

9 THE CONFERENCE OF GOVERNMENT AND PARTY LEADERS, 1983–1995

1. Description of the debate on 24 February 1980 in Strasbourg: EPP general secretariat archive.
2. Ibid.
3. Recommended agenda for the meeting of party leaders and the EPP group, Brussels 3 October 1983, Chateau de Val Duchesse: EPP general secretariat archive.
4. Conferences of party and government leaders: 26 November 1983 in Brussels; 23 April 1985 in Luxembourg; 19/20 June 1985 in Rome; 9 November 1985 in Brussels; 1 March 1986 in The Hague; 30 May 1987 in Brussels; 30 May 1988 in Bonn; 19 October 1988 in Brussels; 17 February 1990 in Pisa; 25 October 1990 in Brussels; 13 April 1991 in Brussels; 21 June 1991 in Luxembourg; 6 December 1991 in The Hague; 14 February 1992 in Brussels; 5 June 1992 in Brussels; 25 September 1992 in Brussels; 13 November 1992 in Athens; 4 December 1992 in Brussels; 2 June 1993 in Brussels; 2 June 1993 in Brussels; 9 December 1993 in Brussels; 22 June 1994 in Brussels; 8 December 1994 in Brussels; 25 June 1995 in Cannes.
5. See also Chapter 12 in this context.
6. Decision of 13.4.1991: EPP general secretariat archives.
7. Decision of 14.2.1992: EPP general secretariat archives.
8. The first of these meetings took place in Brussels in September, the second on the periphery of the NATO summit meeting on the 7/8 November in Rome.
9. See note 6.
10. John Major on 19 March 1991 in Bonn; cf. text in: *The Evolution of Europe*, published by The Conservative Political Centre and the Konrad Adenauer Foundation, London 1991.
11. Press statement on the conference on 21 June 1991: EPP general secretariat archives.
12. Communiqué on the conference on 6 December 1991: EPP general secretariat archives.
13. *Note d'évaluation pour la Conférence des Chefs de gouvernements et de partis du PPE, 14 février 1992* (Pascal Fontaine, 21.01.1992): EPP general secretariat archive.
14. Ibid.
15. *Aide-mémoire* for the EPP Conference of government and party leaders on 17 February 1990: EPP general secretariat archive.
16. On co-operation of Christian Democratic parties within cf. the EPP report by the working group on 'Reform', presented by Wim Van Velzen: EPP general secretariat archives.
17. The text of the statutes agreed at the Dublin Congress and of the amended treaty at the Athens and Brussels Congresses: see appendices, document 2.
18. The ESP statutes accepted at the first party congress, in The Hague 9/10 November 1992, envisage 'meetings of party leaders, to be called at least twice a year' and to which 'Social Democratic members of the European Community and the Council of Ministers' can be invited.

10 ATTEMPTS TO MERGE THE EUCD WITH THE EPP, AND THE REVISION OF THE STATUTES, 1985

1. On the problem of the coexistence of the EDU and EUCD, and the connected problem of joint membership of some parties, see Thomas Jansen, 'Christlich-demokratisch und/oder konservativ?', in *Sonde. Neue Christlich-Demokratische Politik*, no. 1/1990, pp. 42–9.
2. Thomas Jansen, the author of this book: see A Personal Postcript.
3. From Spain: Partido Democrata Popular (PDP), Unio Democratica de Cataluna (UDC), Partido Nacionalista Vasco (PNV); from Portugal: Centro Democratico Social (CDS).
4. Christdemokratische Volkspartei of Switzerland (CVP/PDC), The Austrian Volkspartei (ÖVP), The Christian Democratic Alliance Party of Sweden (KDS), The Christian People's Party of Norway (KrF), The Christian-Democratic Party of San Marino (PDCSM), The Maltese National Party, and The Democratic Rally of Cyprus (DR).
5. Decision by the XXII EUCD Congress in Madrid (1985): EUCD general secretariat archive.
6. Decision of the JECD for the VI Congress of the EPP in The Hague, 10–12 April 1986: EPP general secretariat archive.
7. Mandate of the Statutory Commission, decision of the EUCD and EPP political bureaux on 7 June 1988: EPP general secretariat archive.
8. EPP Statute of 8 July 1976, reproduced in: *Programme und Statute*, vol. 1 of the EPP series 'Dokumentation', ed. by the general secretariat, Brussels 1984.
9. See note 7.
10. In this context see chapter 16.
11. 'Struktur und Arbeitweise der EVP-Gremien', explanation for the Political Bureau: EPP general secretariat archive.
12. Ibid.
13. Decision of the EPP Political Bureau, Strasbourg, 26.6.1984: EPP general secretariat archive.
14. EPP general secretariat archive.
15. With effect from 7 March 1991, printed in: *Handbuch der Europäischen Volkspartei (Christlich-demokratische Fraktion) des Europäischen Parlaments*, 4 ed. 1993, p. 355 *et seq.*
16. The financial rules were agreed by the EPP Executive on 9 September 1993: EPP general secretariat archive.

11 SHAPING THE PROGRAMME, 1989–1993

1. See in this context the works inspired by the European Values Study Group (EVSSG), e.g. Sheena Ashford/Noel Timms: *What Europe thinks. A Study of Western European Values*, Aldershot (Dartmouth) 1992.
2. See *Tradition und Aktualität der Bemühungen um eine 'Doktrin'*. With contributions from Piet Bukman *inter alia*, book 1 of the EPP series *Geistige und historische Grundlagen christlichdemokratischer Politik*, Melle (Knoth) 1988.

3. See also Thomas Jansen 'Europäische Christdemokraten überprüfen ihre Doktrin', in: *Politische Meinung*, book 256/36. The annual issue, March 1991, pp. 66–72. These seminars in conjunction with an 'allied' institute or foundation were prepared and put into effect, to create a 'network'. Later in 1991/1992 President Martens tried very hard, initially unsuccessfully, to get the Christian Democratic inspired economic institute (and in some cases the relevant foundations) to agree to, permanent, if possible formalised, cooperation.

4. See IPIE/CDS/PPE (ed.): *Les Démocrates Chrétiens et l'économie Sociale de Marché*, Paris (Economica) 1988.

5. See the pamphlet published by Philippe Daublin and Hughes Portelli on behalf of the Organisation Committee: *L'avenir de l'Europe et la pensée sociale de l'Eglise*. Séminaire internationale, 5–6–7 October, Chantilly, France.

6. Text in: *Europe 2000. Unity in diversity*, book 9 in the EPP documentation series, Melle (Knoth) 1994.

7. The text of the decision of the party and government leaders in appendices, document 3.

8. The Mandate also lists the texts which the Commission should strive to put into action and develop:
   – Political programme 'Together for a Europe of Free people', 1978;
   – Manifesto of the European Christian Democrats (EUCD), 1976;
   – Political manifesto of the Christian Democratic World Union, 1976;
   – Programme of action for the second legislature;
   – Programme of action 1989–1994 (On the People's Side), 1988;
   – In favour of a federal constitution for the European Union, 1990.
   Published in the preface of the documentation for the basic programme committee 'In preparation for the IX EPP Congress – 1992: basis of the programme', EPP general secretariat. The texts listed in the mandate are reproduced in the documentation.

9. See note 6.

10. The Athens Declaration, EPP general secretariat archive.

11. See in this context Chapter 8.

12. See note 6.

12   BRINGING IN THE CONSERVATIVES 1989–1995

1. See in this context Chapter 5.

2. The EDU activities, which are strongly influenced by the dynamic presence of both the leading figures, Alois Mock and Andreas Khol, who since the beginning in 1978 had been respectively President and Executive Secretary. Documentation in the EDU-Yearbooks, published by the EDU secretariat in Vienna.

3. Cf. Stefan Jost, *Die Politische Mitte Spaniens. Von der Union de Centro zum Partido Popular*, Frankfurt/M. 1994, p. 255 *et seq*.

4. Communiqué from the conference of party leaders in Luxembourg, May 1989: EPP general secretariat archives.

5. EPP general secretariat archives.

6. Ibid.
7. Key finding of the EPP/EDG working group (January 1992): EPP Group archive.
8. EPP general secretariat archives.
9. Decision of the EPP execution in February 1995: EPP general secretariat archive.
10. Text in: *Europa 2000. Einheit in Vielfalt*, vol. 9 EPP series 'Documentation', Melle 1994.

14   WORKING METHODS OF THE PARTY BODIES

1. Text in: *Programme and Statute*, vol. 1 EPP series '*Documentation*', 2nd edition, Brussels 1984.
2. Text in: *The EPP Handbook* 1993 (4th edition), p. 343 *et seq.*
3. The XI Congress in Madrid in November 1995 decided on a further change to the statutes limiting the Presidency to the President, Treasurer, Secretary-general, and only four Vice-presidents. The first election under this arrangement took place in February 1996, producing the following presidency: Wilfried Martens was confirmed as President, with the following Vice-presidents, Ottfried Hennig (CDU-D), José-Maria Aznar (PP-E), Margaretha af Ugglas (MS-S), and Jean-Claude Juncker (CSV-L); Ingo Friedrich (CSU-D) became Treasurer.
4. ELDR: Mechtild von Aleman 1984–89, Christian Ehlers from 1992; PES: Axel Hanisch 1990–95; EPP: Thomas Jansen 1984–94, Klaus Welle from the end of 1994.
5. Since loosing his seat in 1972, Josef Müller (Aachen) had, on behalf of the CDU, busied himself establishing an office in Brussels whose job – working closely with the EPP Group in the European Parliament – was to coordinate the work of the EUCD parties at Community level. This office was simultaneously the EUCD's Brussels office, the secretary-general at that time being based in Rome.
6. See 'A Personal Postscript'.

15   THE ASSOCIATIONS

1. Once the EPP had been founded, initially a so-called 'Team of the Nine' was set up as an EPP association in the framework of the European Union of Young Christian Democrats (EUYCD). (Once Greece joined the EC it became the Team of The Ten.) The EUYCD was the EUCD's association. In the early 1980s, when the EYCD was reformed, the two structures were re-integrated.
2. Worth mentioning in this context are presidents Massimo Gorla, Andrea De Guttry, Enrico Letta; secretaries-general Filippo Lombardi and Marc Bertrand, as well as managers Anke Van der Mei and Denise O'Hara.
3. Corresponding to dual membership of the CDU/CSU and other EPP member parties in the EDU.

4. Marc Bertrand interview: The Future of the European Young Christian Democrats. The Youth Organisation Faces Change of Course. In EPP News no. 24/1995. It is worth noting that the question of dual membership, mentioned in the interview, could in effect resolve itself for the EYDC with the expansion of the European Union and the admission of the 'conservative' parties into the EPP after that: DEMYC, becoming superfluous, could dissolve itself.

5. Scharrenbroich, President of the International Union of Christian Democratic Workers, took over as leader after a critical development in 1992; in 1993 Juncker took over the presidency until his election as prime minister of Luxembourg; his predecessor was from early 1995 the Belgian social affairs minister, Miet Smet.

6. European Union of Christian Democratic Women (EUCDW); the last President was Concepcio Ferrer, the last Secretary General Anamaria Cervone.

7. See EPP-News no. 8/1995: The EPP Group in the Committee of the Regions.

8. See EPP-News no. 13/1995: EMSU and ESMBA plan Fusion.

9. The EMSU Presidents have been Bundestag members Christian Schwarz-Schilling and Ingeborg Hoffmann (both CDU), and the MEPs Ingo Friedrich (CSU) and Ursula Braun-Moser (CDU).

10. See EPP News no. 14/1995: 'European Pensioners Union Workshop Founded'.

16 THE EUCD AND THE NEW PARTIES IN CENTRAL AND EASTERN EUROPE

1. See Chapter 10.

2. Even if ideologies continue to have relevance in history and politics, it is accurate to talk of the 'end of ideologies' with reference to 1989, and also 1945. For what burned itself out was not merely Socialist power, and the regimes and social systems based on it, but a 20th century phenomenon altogether. By this I mean the insane notion that it is possible to shape the world on the basis of a single ideal, and to do so without caring about the needs of human beings, or the plethora of human ideas, desires, or hopes.

3. Parties of Christian Democratic inspiration in Central Europe which already existed between the world wars, or in some cases after 1944/45, before they were either banned by the Communists once they had seized power, or brought into line, were: the Czechoslovak People's Party, the Hungarian Democratic People's Party, the Latvian Christian Peasants' Party, the Lithuanian Christian Democratic Party, the Policy Labour Party, the Slovene Christian Democratic People's Party in Yugoslavia. See: *Christian Democracy in Central Europe*, New York 1952.

4. For example: the Bulgarian National Peasants' Union, the National Romanian Peasants' Party, the Polish Peasants' Party, the Croatian Peasants' Party, the Hungarian Party of Small Farmers etc; they were at their zenith not parties representing a partisan bourgeois interest, but they were genuine people's parties: in reality, the peasants in such predominantly agricultural societies did represent the people.

5. For instance: the Hungarian Democratic Forum, the Croatian Democratic Forum.

6. Cf. Konrad Siniewicz, in Thomas Jansen/Hughes Portelli (eds): *La Démocratie Chrétienne. Force Internationale*, Paris-Nanterre 1986; and Roberto Papini: *L'Internationale Démocrate Chrétienne*, Paris 1988.

7. The leading representatives of the UCDCE, Secretary General Konrad Siniewicz (Poland) and President Bohumir Bunza (Czechoslovakia) were by 1990 over 70 years old. They were replaced by President Sandor Karczay (Hungary) and as Secretary General Ivan Carnogursky (Slovakia); all other members of the new executive were representatives of government in exile, and lived in Rome, Paris, Brussels, Geneva etc.

8. EUCD statute: EUCD general secretariat archive.

9. Further members of the presidium: as Vice-Presidents: Ottfried Henning (CDU-D), Marietta Giannakou (ND-GR),Ludovica Incisa (DC-I, until spring 1994), Wim Van Velzen (CDA-NL), Ludwig Steiner (ÖVP-A), Odilo Guntern (CVP-CH), Alf Svensson (KDS-S), Jacques Mallet (CDS-F), Edward Fenech Adami (NP-Malta); as Treasurer Rika De Bakker (CVP-B); as Secretary General Thomas Jansen (until the end of 1994), and since then Klaus Welle.

10. Resolutions of the EPP Congress, Dublin 1990: EPP general secretariat archive.

11. In 1995, the following were accepted as members: the Hungarian Equipe of the Christian Democratic People's party (KDNP) and the Hungarian Democratic Forum (MDF); the Christian and Democratic Union (KDU), Czech Republic; the Christian Democratic Movement of Slovakia (KDH); the Slovene Christian Democrats (SKD); the Romanian Equipe of the National Peasant Party/Christian and Democratic (PNT-cd) and the Christian Democratic Party of Hungarians in Romania (RMKDP); the Fatherland Party (ISMAA), Estonia; the Christian Democratic Party of Lithuania (CDPL); the Bulgarian Equipe of the Democratic Party (DP) and the National Peasants Union (BANU); the Albanian Democratic Party; the Croatian Democratic Union (HDZ).

12. The following were granted observer status in 1995: the Christian Democratic Party (KDS), Czech Republic; the Hungarian Christian Democratic Movement, Slovakia (MKDM); the United Democratic Centre (UDC) and the Christian Democratic Union (CDU) of Bulgaria; the Croatian Christian Democratic Union (HKDU); the Democratic Federation of Hungarians in Romania (RMDZ); the Independent Small Landowners Party/Historical Section, Hungary; the Christian Democratic Union of Latvia (KDS); the Albanian Christian Democratic Party and the Albanian Democratic Alliance.

13. The following parties made applications in 1995: Albanian Christian Democratic Party of Kosovo (KPSHD); Christian Democratic People's Front of Moldavia (FPCD); Christian Democratic Party of the Ukraine; VRMO-DPMNE, former Yugoslav Republic of Macedonia. News of how these applications have been dealt with, as well as on all other developments in parties linked to the EUCD and about EUCD activities in Central and Eastern Europe, is published by the EUCD general secretariat in 'CD-New Central and Eastern Europe' (monthly since January 1995).

17 THE PROTAGONISTS

1. The 'Tindemans Report' is once again (or still) highly topical, both for its analysis and its proposals; see Europe Archive, 3/1976, pp. D55–86: Report by the Belgian prime minister, Leo Tindemans, on European Union, with accompanying notes, for the European Council.
2. On Jacques Santer and his European commitment cf. Klaus Emmerich, *Europa neu. Das Konzept des Präsidenten der EU-Kommission Jacques Santer*, Vienna 1995.
3. Jacques Santer, 'Europa ist unsere politische Zukunft', in: *An der Seite der Bürger*, vol. 8 EPP series 'Dokumentation', Melle 1989, p. 83 *et seq.*
4. Evidence of Martens's tireless involvement everywhere in Europe, and what he was saying and doing, can be found in: Wilfried Martens, *L'une et l'autre Europe, Discours européen 1990–94*, Brussels 1994.
5. In 1995, Centro Cristiano Democratico (CCD) and Cristiani Democratici Uniti (CDU), were recognised as successor parties of Democrazia Cristiana alongside the PPI. It is worth remarking that the legal and financial disputes about the inheritance between the leaderships of these parties were only resolved after the intervention of EPP leader Wilfried Martens.
6. Barbi has written about his commitment to the European idea in: Paolo Barbi, *Strasburgo e ritorno. I cinque anni al Parlamento Europeo*, Naples 1985; *L'Unione Europea. Da Fontainebleau a Lussemburgo. Storia di una grande occasione mancata*, Naples 1986.

18 RELATIONSHIPS WITH MEMBER PARTIES AND THE EPP PARLIAMENTARY GROUP

1. See Chapter 10.
2. The working group was set by the conference of heads of party and government on 19 September 1988. Its members were: Wim Van Velzen (chairman), Perre Méhaignerie, Gianni Prandini, Lutz Stavenhagen, Raf Chanterie, and Thomas Jansen. The group held a number of meetings. The chairman presented his first in summer 1989, and a revised version dated 20 January 1990, was presented shortly afterwards to the conference of heads of parties and government in Pisa, which approved the report and its recommendations.
3. Reform working group: EPP general secretariat archive.
4. In 1995. Groups are accorded staff paid for from the EP budget in proportion to their strength (the number of deputies). Independently of that, individual MEPs are able to engage a limited number of personal assistants.

Bibliography

David Alton, *Faith in Britain*, London, 1991.

Oscar Alzaga Willaamil, *Le origine della Democrazia Cristiana in Spagna*, Rome 1988.

Niels Arbol, *Kristen Demokraterne i verden*, Copenhagen, 1884.

Niels Arbol, *Et nyt Europa. Kristendemokrater viser vej*, Copenhagen, 1991.

Gianni Baget Bozzo, *Cattolici e Democristiani. Un esperienza politica italiana*, Milan, 1994.

Martin Bangemann/Egon A. Klepsch *inter alia*, *Programme für Europa. Die Programme der europäischen Parteienbünde zur Europa-Wahl 1979*, Bonn, 1978.

Martin Bangemann/Egon A. Klepsch *inter alia.*, *Die Abgeordneten Europas*, Baden-Baden, 1984.

Paolo Barbi, *Napoli–Strasburgo e ritorno. I cinque anni al Parlamento Europeo*, Naples, 1985.

Luciano Bardi, 'Transnational Party Federations in the European Community', in R. S. Katz/P. Mair (eds), *Party Organization in Western Democracies 1960–1990*, London, 1992.

Winfried Becker/Rudolf Morsey (eds), *Christliche Demokratie in Europa. Grundlagen und Entwicklungen seit dem 19. Jahrhundert, Cologne*, 1988.

Kurt Beilken (ed.), *Architekten und Baumeister des europäischen Hauses. Eine Dokumentation über das Wirken deutscher Christdemokraten für die Einheit Europas seit dem Ende des zweiten Weltkrieges*, Stiftung zur Zusammenarbeit Christlicher Demokraten Europas, Luxemburg, 1993.

Serge Berstein/Jean-Marie Mayeur/Pierre Milza (eds), *Le MRP et la construction européenne*, Brussels, 1993.

Klaus von Beyme, *Parteien in westlichen Demokratien*, 2nd rev. edition, Munich, 1984.

Robert Bichet, *La Démocratie Chrétienne en France. Le Mouvement Republicain Populaire*, Besançon, 1980.

Karl Buchheim, *Die christlichen Parteien in Deutschland*, Munich, 1953.

Rafael Caldera, *Christliche Demokratie. Ein Modell für Lateinamerika und die freie Welt.* edited and translated by Peter Molt, Mainz, 1976.

Eduard Cardona i Romeu, *La Democràcia Cristiana*, Barcelona, 1967.

Clay Clemens, *Christian Democracy. The Different Dimensions of a Modern Movement* (European People's Party, Occasional Papers, No. 1), Brussels, 1989.

Bruno Dörpinghaus, 'Die Genfer Sitzungen – Erste Zusammenkünfte führender christlich-demokratischer Politiker im Nachkriegseuropa', in: Dieter Blumenwitz *inter alia* (ed.), *Konrad Adenauer und seine Zeit. Politik und Persönlichkeit des ersten Bundeskanzlers. Beiträge von Weg-und Zeitgenossen*, Stuttgart 1976, p. 358 *et seq.*

Jean-Dominique Durand, *L'Europe de la Démocratie Chrétienne*, Brussels, 1995.

Wilfried Dzieyk, 'Programm und Satzungen der Parteienbünde in der EG', in: *Zeitschrift für Parlamentsfragen*, no. 2/1978, p. 179 *et seq.*

EVP, *Programm und Statut* (vol 1, 'Dokumentation'), 2nd edn, Brussels, 1984.

EVP, *An der Seite der Bürger. Aktionsprogramm der Europäischen Volkspartei 1989–1994 mit Berichten von Jacques Santer, Egon A. Klepsch, Lutz Stavenhagen und Thomas Jansen sowie weiteren Dokumenten vom VII. Kongress der EVP in Luxemburg*, Melle, 1989.

EVP, *Europa 2000. Einheit in Vielfalt*, Melle, 1994.

EVP, Fraktion, *Handbuch der Fraktion der Europäischen Volkspartei (Christlich-Demokratische Fraktion) des Europäischen Parlaments*, 4th ed., Brussels, 1993.

Michael P. Fogarty, *Christian Democracy in Western Europe*, 1820–1953, London 1957.

Ralph M. Goldman (ed.), *Transnational Parties. Organizing the World's Precincts*, Lanham – New York – London, 1983.

Eberhard Grabitz *inter alia, Direktwahl und Demokratisierung. Eine Funktionsanalyse des Europäischen Parlaments nach der ersten Wahlperiode*, Bonn, 1988.

Norbert Gresch, *Transnationale Parteienzusammenarbeit in der EG*, Baden-Baden 1978.

Martin Greschat/Jochen-Christoph Kaiser (eds), *Christentum und Demokratie im 20. Jahrhundert*, Stuttgart – Berlin – Cologne, 1992.

K. J. Hahn (ed.), *La Démocratie Chrétienne dans le monde. Résolutions et déclarations des organisations internationales démocrates chrétiennes de 1947 à 1973*, Rome, 1973.

David Hanley (ed.), *Christian Democracy in Europe. A comparative perspective*, London, 1994.

Thomas R. Henschel, 'Die europäischen Parteienzusammenschlüsse', in Werner Weidenfeld/Wolfgang Wessels (eds), *Jahrbuch der Europäischen Integration 1990/91*, Bonn, 1991.

Simon Hix, 'The Emerging EC Party System ? The European Party Federations in the Intergovernmental Conferences', in *Politics* 13/1993.

Simon Hix, 'The European Party Federations. From Transnational Co-operation to Nascent European Parties', in John Gaffney (ed.), *Political Parties and the European Union*, London 1995.

Simon Hix/Christopher Lord, *Political Parties in the European Union*, London, 1997.

Franz Horner, *Konservative und christ-demokratische Parteien in Europa. Geschichte, Prgrammatik, Strukturen*, Vienna – Munich, 1981.

Rudolf Hrbek, 'Parteienbünde. Unterbau der EP-Fraktionen und unverzichtbares Element einer funktionsfähigen Infrastruktur der EG. Entwicklungsstand, Probleme und Perspektiven', in *Zeitschrift für Parlamentsfragen*, no. 2/1976, pp. 179–90.

Rudolf Hrbek, 'Die europäischen Parteienzusammenschlüsse', in Werner Weidenfeld/Wolfgang Wessels (eds) *Jahrbuch der Europäischen Integration 1980*, Bonn, 1981.

Institut für Europäischen Politik, *Zusammenarbeit der Parteien in Westeuropa. Auf dem Wege zu einer neuen politischen Infrastruktur?* Bonn, 1976.

Ronald E. M. Irving, *The Christian Democratic Parties in Western Europe*, London, 1979.

Thomas Jansen (ed.), *Tradition und Aktualität der Bemühungen um eine 'Doktrin'*, Melle, 1988.

Thomas Jansen (ed.), *Zur Geschichte der christlich-demokratischen Bewegung in Europa.* Mit Beiträgen von Winfried Becker *inter alia*, Melle, 1990.

Thomas Jansen, 'Europäische Christdemokraten überprüfen ihre Doktrin', in *Politische Meinung*, no. 256/91, pp.66–72.

Thomas Jansen, 'Zur Entwicklung supranationaler Europäischer Parteien', in Oscar W. Gabriel *inter alia* (eds), *Der demokratische Verfassungsstaat. Theorie, Geschichte, Probleme. Festschrift für Hans Buchheim*, Munich, 1992, p. 241 *et seq.*

Thomas Jansen, 'Die Europäischen Parteien', in Werner Weidenfeld/Wolfgang Wessels (eds), *Jahrbuch der Europäischen Integration*, Bonn, 1995.

Philipp Jenninger (ed.), *Unverdrossen für Europa. Festschrift für Kai-Uwe von Hassel*, Baden-Baden 1988.

Karl Magnus Johansson, *Transnational Party Alliances. Analysing the hard-won Alliance between Conservatives and Christian Democrats in the European Parliament*, Lund University Press, 1997.

Alferd Jüttner/Hans-J. Liese, *Taschenbuch der Europäischen Parteien und Wahlen*, Munich, 1977.

Gerd-Klaus Kaltenbrunner (ed.), *Das Elend der Christdemokraten. Ortsbestimmung der politischen Mitte Europas*, Munich, 1977.

Eva-Rose Karnofski, *Parteienbünde vor der Europa-Wahl 1979. Integration durch gemeinsame Wahlaussagen*, Bonn, 1982.

Andreas Khol, 'Europäische Demokratische Union (EDU). Die europäische Parteiengruppe der fortschrittlichen Mitte', in *Österreichische Monatshefte. Zeitschrift für Politik*, no. 5/78, p. 4 *et seq.*

Emiel Lamberts (ed.) *Christian Democracy in the European Union (1945/1995).* Proceedings of the Leuven Colloquium 15–18 November 1995, Leuven, 1997.

Pierre Letamendia, *La Démocratie Chrétienne*, 2nd revised edition, Paris, 1993.

Hans August Lücker/Karl Josef Hahn, *Christliche Demokraten bauen Europa*, Bonn, 1987.

Siegfried Magiera, 'Organisationsformen der politischen Parteien auf Gemeinschaftsebene und ihre Funktion bei der politischen Willensbildung', in *Europa-Recht*, 46/1976, pp. 311–332.

Wilfried Martens, *L'une et l'autre Europe. Discours Européen 1990–1994*, Brussels, 1994.

Jean-Marie Mayeur, *Des partis catholiques à la démocratie chrétienne*, Paris, 1980.

Alf Mintzel und Heinrich Oberreuter (eds), *Parteien in der Bundesrepublik Deutschland*, 2nd revised edition, Bonn, 1992.

Karl-Heinz Nassmacher, *Demokratisierung der Europäischen Gemeinschaften*, Bonn, 1972.

Oscar Niedermayer, *Europäischen Parteien? Zur grenzüberschreitenden Interaktion politischer Parteien im Rahmen der Europäischen Gemeinschaft*, Frankfurt/New York, 1983.

Oscar. Niedermayer, 'Zehn Jahre Europäische Parteienbünde. Kein Integrationsschub', in *Integration 1985*, pp. 174–81.

Oscar Niedermayer, 'Die Entwicklung der europäischen Parteienbünde', in *Zeitschrift für Parlamentsfragen*, no. 3/1994.

Thomas Nipperdey, 'Christliche Parteien', in Thomas Nipperdey, *Nachdenken über die deutsche Geschichte. Essays*, Munich, 1986, p. 126 *et seq.*

Roberto Papini, *L'Internationale Démocrate-Chrétienne. La coopération entre les partis démocrates-chrétiens de 1925 à 1986*, Paris, 1988.

Roberto Papini, 'Christianity and Democracy in Europe: The Christian Democratic Movement', in John Witte, Jr (ed.), *Christianity and Democracy in Global Context*, Boulder, Col./Oxford, 1993.

Roberto Papini, *Il corragio della democrazia. Luigi Sturzo e l'Internazionale Popolare tra le due guerre*, Rome, 1995.

Melanie Piepenschneider, 'Die europäischen Partienzusammenschlüsse', in Werner Weidenfeld/Wofgang Wessels (eds), *Jahrbuch der Europäischen Integration 1991/92 et seq.*, Bonn, 1992 *et seq.*

Politische Akademie Eichholz, *Synopse der Parteiprogramme der Christlich-Demokratischen Parteien Westeuropas*, Wesseling, 1971.

Politische Akademie Eichholz, *Die europäischen Parteien der Mitte. Analysen und Dokumente zur Programmatik christlich-demokratischer und konservativer Parteien Westeuropas*, Bonn, 1978.

Hughes Portelli/Thomas Jansen (eds), *La Démocratie Chrétienne. Force Internationale*, Nanterre, 1986.

Geoffrey Pridham/Pippa Pridham, *Towards Transnational Parties in the European Community*, London, 1979.

Geoffrey Pridham, 'Christian Democrats, Conservatives and Transnational Party Cooperation in the European Community. Center-Forward or Center-Right?, in Z. Layton-Henry (ed.), *Conservative Politics in Western Europe*, London, 1982.

Daniel Louis Seiler, 'Les fédérations de partis au niveau communautaire', in: Rudolf Hrbek (ed.), *Le Parlement Européen à la Veille de la deuxième Election au suffrage universel. Bilan et Perspectives*, Bruges, 1984, pp. 449–504.

James W. Skillen, 'Toward a Contemporary Christian Democratic Politics in the United States' in: John Witte Jr. (ed.), *Christianity and Democracy in Global Context*, Boulder Col./Oxford 1993, p. 85 *et seq.*

Theo Stammen, *Parteien in Europa. Nationale Parteiensysteme. Transnationale Parteienbeziehungen. Konturen eines europäischen Parteiensystems*, Munich, 1977.

Dimitros Th. Tsatsos, 'Europäische politische Parteien? Erste Überlegungen zur Auslegung des Perteienartikels des Maastrichter Vertrages – Art. 138a EGV', in: *Europäische Grundrechte-Zeitschrift* (EuGRZ) 1994, vol. 21/no. 3–4, pp. 45–53.

Javier Tussel, *Historia de la Democracia Cristiana en Espana* (2 vols), Madrid, 1986.

Hans-Joachim Veen (ed.), *Christlich-demokratische und konservative Parteien in Westeuropa*, 4 vols, Paderborn, 1983 (1 and 2), 1991 (3), 1994 (4).

Index